MARX AND MODERN SOCIAL THEORY

Marx and Modern Social Theory

ALAN SWINGEWOOD

Lecturer in Sociology, London School of Economics

A HALSTED PRESS BOOK

JOHN WILEY & SONS
New York

First published in the United Kingdom 1975 by
The Macmillan Press Ltd

First published in the U.S.A. by
Halsted Press, a Division of
John Wiley & Sons, Inc.,
New York

Printed in Great Britain

Library of Congress Cataloging in Publication Data

Swingewood, Alan
  Marx and modern social theory.

  "A Halsted Press book."
  Bibliography: p.
  Includes index.
    1. Marx, Karl, 1810–1883. 2. Communism and
society. 3. Sociology—History. I. Title.
HX39.5.S97 1975   335.4'1   75-4554
ISBN 0 470-83998-8

CONTENTS

PREFACE

This book is an attempt to describe and analyse the basic elements of Marx's social theory and to contrast them with those of modern sociology and Marxism. No attempt has been made to cover all aspects of modern social theory but rather to focus selectively on certain significant thinkers and theories : Durkheim, Weber, Mannheim, Parsons, Schutz, Lukács, Gramsci; functionalism, phenomenology, 'voluntaristic' Marxism, radical sociology, sociology of knowledge and contemporary discussions of social stratification, authority and power. Modern in this context refers to those theories whose point of departure is industrial society as it emerges during the nineteenth century, in which the emphasis falls on division of labour, class stratification, authority and legitimation, bureaucracy, social change, and the role of ideas in social life. It is in this sense that modern social theory emerges in the work of Comte, Marx, Weber and Durkheim.

This book was first presented as lectures at the London School of Economics in the form of a course on Marxism and Sociology. I would like to thank those students who attended the lectures and made valuable criticisms and suggestions, those of my friends who read part of the revised texts and my wife, Hazel, who typed various drafts of the manuscripts and pointed out its numerous shortcomings.

June 1974   A. S.

INTRODUCTION

Marxism has been described as a synthesis of German idealist philosophy, French socialism and English political economy, a social theory combining the insights of dialectical thought, political practice and economic science. Developed by Marx in the 1840s and 1850s Marxism emerged as the first social theory to be identified with a specific social group, the industrial working class, a theory based on class struggle and conflict, and which strove to explain all past and present history through these concepts and on this basis to predict the future. In contrast to Marx's vision of irreconcilable class conflict, sociology defined and elaborated by Marx's contemporary, Auguste Comte (1798–1857), portrayed society as a potentially harmonious and ordered structure in which all social classes worked for the common good. Marx's attitude to Comte was dismissive : the founder of sociology was a poor scientist and a political charlatan. Comte never read Marx and the sociologists who followed him – de Tocqueville, Le Play, J. S. Mill, Herbert Spencer – were either ignorant of or indifferent to his theories. But after his death in 1883 sociologists such as Tonnies (1885–1936), Max Weber (1864–1920), Simmel (1858–1918), Sombart (1863–1938), Mosca (1858–1941), Pareto (1843–1923) and Mannheim (1893–1947) became increasingly aware of the importance of Marx's theories both for sociology and political practice. Some sought to reconcile Marx's thought with their own work (Sombart and Weber) while others rejected and sought to refute it (Mosca and Pareto). None the less, at the end of the nineteenth century the leading European sociologists began what has been described as a protracted debate with the 'ghost of Marx',[1] on the theories of social change, social stratification, ideology and socialism. In contrast, English and American sociology remained remarkably insular : having failed to generate a labour movement strongly influenced by Marxism, British and American society produced a sociology largely insensitive to Marxist social theory.

During the 1930s the influence of Marx's thought on sociology waned considerably in all countries : the triumph of Stalinism in the Soviet Union and the rise of Fascism in Europe seemed to challenge many of the basic ideas of Marxism : sociologists such as Mannheim and Sombart totally rejected Marx and increasingly his social theory was redefined as anti-democratic, totalitarian and irrelevant. Anglo-Saxon empiricism combining with the emerging functionalist school of sociology virtually secured Marx's eclipse. Finally, with the development of 'affluent' societies after the end of the Second World War, Marx's theories were judged to be of mere antiquarian interest.[2] True, some sociologists such as C. Wright Mills argued for the continuing validity of Marx, but it was not until the 1960s that a positive renewal finally took place. This awakened interest was partly due to the publication of some of Marx's early humanist writings and the 'discovery' of the concept of alienation, and the re-emergence within the 'affluent' societies of class and racial conflict. The concept of 'consensus' was seriously challenged and social theorists began to look for a more acceptable explanation for the emerging crisis. Liberal democracy seemed to many to have failed : the dominant social theories of the past thirty years were equally judged inadequate. 'Radical' and 'Critical' sociology thus emerges, seeking reconciliation with Marx's theories of change and conflict. Today the emphasis is on synthesis, a fusion of Marxism, extentialism, phenomenology, and rejection of functionalism, empiricism and positivism. The purpose of this book is to explore the relation of Marxism to these new ideas by contrasting the major elements of Marx's social theory with some of the key concepts of modern sociology. First, however, it may be useful to introduce the basic structure of Marx's thought.

I

Born in 1818, Marx studied at the universities of Bonn and Berlin, and completed a doctoral dissertation on 'The Difference between the Natural Philosophies of Democritus and Epicurus' in 1841.

2

Shortly afterwards he wrote an extended critique of Hegel's political philosophy. German intellectual life at this time was dominated by the idealistic philosophical system of Hegel (1770–1831), and Marx was closely identified with a group of radical philosophers known as 'The Young Hegelians' (Arnold Ruge, Bruno Bauer, Moses Hess, Ludwig Feuerbach and Max Stirner), who championed a more critical assessment of Hegel's philosophy. Hegel had been accepted as a conservative whose political philosophy had identified reason and progress with the interests of the autocratic Prussian state. In contrast, the Young Hegelians maintained that Hegel's 'true' philosophy had been distorted by his conservative interpreters and its revolutionary meaning obscured by Hegel himself.[3] In a note to his thesis Marx argued that philosophy must transcend the limitations of Hegel's idealism by becoming practical : 'The *praxis* of philosophy', he wrote, 'is itself theoretical', a statement close to his later arguments that theory and practice are indissolubly bound together.[4] As he criticised Hegel's philosophy, Marx was working as a radical journalist on the liberal *Rheinische Zeitung*, writing articles which pilloried the government and analysed the importance of economic factors in social existence. Writing on the poverty of the Moselle wine-growers, Marx argued that in studying political conditions

> one is too easily tempted to overlook the objective nature of the relationships and to explain everything from the will of the persons acting. There are relationships, however, which determine the actions of private persons . . . which are as independent as are the movements in breathing.[5]

When the government banned the newspaper Marx moved to Paris, and it was here that he met the French socialist, Proudhon, (1809–65) and involved himself more deeply in socialist organisations and socialist theory.

In Paris Marx completed his *Critique of Hegel's Philosophy of Right* (1844) and wrote the critical commentaries on eighteenth- and early nineteenth-century political economy (especially Smith, Ricardo, Say), idealist philosophy and Communism, which, published only in 1932, became known as the *Paris Manuscripts* (1843–

3

4) (or, as the Russian editor called them, *Economic and Philosophical Manuscripts*). In these short and unfinished texts Marx applied Hegel's concept of alienation to social and economic structures, arguing that capitalist society creates a condition of 'alienated labour' in which man becomes estranged from himself, society and others. Alienation was endemic in social life but under the capitalist mode of production it dominated man completely. The solution was Communism, the application of the socialist ideas of Saint-Simon (1760–1825), Charles Fourier (1772–1837) and Proudhon.

In Paris Marx met Frederick Engels and thus began a lifelong friendship. Engels (1820–95) had already written on economics but as Marx's collaborator he now moved towards socialism. In 1844 Marx and Engels produced *The Holy Family*, a polemical and critical onslaught on the Young Hegelians, whose ideas were now rejected : in place of their idealism and liberalism were substituted materialism and Communism. Marx was now a materialist attributing all man's powers to the social world, but it was not a materialism in the eighteenth-century sense. Marx was opposed to the 'mechanical materialism' which defined man in terms only of external influences and which minimised his active, conscious side. Criticising the influential materialist philosopher, Feuerbach, Marx wrote his eleven *Theses on Feuerbach* (1845) which attacked the one-sided and deterministic character of materialist philosophy. In *The German Ideology*, written in Brussels in 1846, Marx and Engels developed this criticism of the Young Hegelians in massive detail. Marx wrote later that the book settled 'accounts with our erstwhile philosophical conscience', and, unpublished in Marx's lifetime, *The German Ideology* has the distinction of being the first systematic account of what was later to be called the materialist conception of history. The orientation was critical and historical :

The premises from which we begin are not arbitrary ones, not dogmas, but real premises from which abstraction can only be made in the imagination. They are the real individuals, their activity and their material conditions under which they live, both those which they find already existing and those produced by their activity.[6]

'Consciousness', they wrote, 'does not determine life, but life determines consciousness.' The capitalist division of labour creates definite class relations and private property generates inequality and class conflict. If socialism was ever to be more than a utopian dream then it must be based not on an ethical criticism of society but on historical and empirical analysis.

These historical, materialist themes were given a more concise form in 1847, when Marx published a trenchant critique of Proudhon's economic theory, *The Poverty of Philosophy*, and a year later, with Engels, in *The Communist Manifesto*. Marx's theory of class struggle, revolution and socialism was further developed in a series of lectures delivered to workers in Brussels, *Wage Labour and Capital* (1849) in which Marx put forward the argument that under capitalism the working class must become increasingly pauperised.

In 1848 Europe was engulfed by revolution, but by the end of the year revolution had turned into counter-revolution. In June 1848 the Paris proletariat were brutally crushed by the army and National Guard. Expelled from France, Marx moved to London where, during the 1850s, he wrote his two important studies of the 1848 French revolution, *The Class Struggles in France* (1850) and *The Eighteenth Brumaire of Louis Bonaparte* (1852). The 1850s was a period of stability in the major European countries and Marx turned from writing contemporary political studies and polemics to a study of the economic foundation of modern capitalism, a task which occupied the greater part of his mature years but left unfinished at his death. In 1858 he completed a draft of a massive study of economics (*Grundrisse der Kritik der politischen Ökonomie*), 'the result of fifteen years' research, the best period of my life', a work which remained unpublished until 1939. In 1859 a section of the *Grundrisse* was published as part of Marx's *A Contribution to the Critique of Political Economy*, and years later much of the material became incorporated into *Capital*.

The *Grundrisse* is important both as a major text in its own right, and because it established a continuity of thought between the *Paris Manuscripts* and *Capital*. In the *Grundrisse* Marx not only emphasises the concept of alienation in the analysis of economic and social relations, but at times his language is positively Hegelian.

5

But there are two important differences between the two works: in the *Grundrisse* the term 'labour power' and not labour is used to describe capitalist exploitation, production is emphasised at the expense of exchange, and the groundwork is laid for the theory of surplus value and capital accumulation.[7] Similar themes are present in Marx's massive *Theories of Surplus Value* (1861–3), a detailed analysis of past and present theories of value originally intended as the fourth volume of *Capital*. But unlike many other works the *Theories of Surplus Value* was left unrevised and unfinished, to be published finally in Germany between 1905 and 1910 and become perhaps the most neglected of Marx's major writings. In 1867 the first volume of *Capital* was published, Marx's most important work but again fated to remain incomplete. The second and third volumes were finally revised and published by Engels in 1885 and 1894. A mixture of ill-health and the pressure of his political work in the First International (founded in 1864) prevented the completion of *Capital*. Marx's last major work. *The Civil War in France* (1871), was his analysis of the workers' uprising in Paris in 1871 which led to the founding of what he called the first workers' government, an experiment which was shortlived and its ending bloody.

During his lifetime Marx completed few of his mature projects. He left no 'popular' outline of his social theory, this task falling to Engels in such works as *Anti-Dühring* (1877) and *Socialism: Scientific and Utopian* (1880) as well as in numerous historical studies, introductions and prefaces to Marx's works and the many letters written at the end of his life to inquiring students of Marxism.[8] Bearing this in mind, therefore, together with the fact that many of Marx's ideas changed in the course of his development, the following represents merely a summary, an introductory sketch of the main elements of his social theory:

(1) All societies are stratified into distinct groups and classes, power and authority are linked closely with the economic organisation of society. Capitalism simplifies class relations, creating a conflict between the owners of capital (the bourgeoisie) and the working class. The relation is one of exploitation.

(2) Society is a product of class struggle and social change is more revolutionary than evolutionary. Societies pass through definite

stages of development with each stage containing contradictions and conflicts that eventuate in social transformation. But society and history are not solely external to man, for it is through man's own activity, as a member of a social class, that the social and historical world is created.

(3) Society is a totality, a structure of interrelated levels. The economic 'base' or infrastructure (mode of production) is closely bound up with the 'superstructure', the institutions which produce knowledge (mass media, church, education, etc.) and the relations of production (relations between classes).

(4) Social processes are never homogenous and uniform, but contradictory and dialectical. All phenomena are interrelated generating contradictions both within and between themselves.

(5) Society and history are characterised by certain laws, but it is man who ultimately makes the world through his *praxis*.

(6) Class society is held together as much by ideology (or 'false consciousness') as by force. Alienation tends to obscure for man the real foundation of society as one of exploitation and inequality.

II

When Marx died in 1883 the major socialist party in Europe, the German Social Democrats, founded in 1875, was pledged to Marxism. Its leaders, Eduard Bernstein (1850–1932) and Karl Kautsky (1854–1938), has been expelled from Germany, the party was illegal and Marx's prescription for revolutionary strategy accepted as realistic and inevitable. But in the 1890s the party was legalised and soon formed one of the largest parties in the German Parliament. Between 1890 and 1914 the major capitalist countries enjoyed rapid economic expansion, and one result of this was relative social stability. To many, Marxism seemed out of date, or at least in need of serious revision. The Marxism which developed during this period was mechanical and deterministic, evolutionary rather than revolutionary. The movement known as 'revisionism' emerges at this point, its leader being Eduard Bernstein who, in his book *Evolutionary Socialism* (1899), argued that capitalism was not collapsing, the class structure was not polarising around two hostile classes and the working class was not becoming impoverished. Bernstein was immediately assailed by the defenders of Marxist orthodoxy : Kautsky simply argued that Bernstein's facts were wrong and that the evidence pointed to further class antagonisms and inevitable capitalist collapse; Plekhanov (1856–1918), the leading Russian Marxist, while noticing the crudities of Bernstein's arguments, especially his misunderstanding of dialectics, equally emphasised that Marx's predictions were not falsified by new facts.[9] For Kautsky and Plekhanov Marxism had become a dogmatic, completed system, pointing to the irrevocable collapse of capitalism.

At the same time other more critical voices were raised against Bernstein : Rosa Luxemburg (1870–1919), and Leon Trotsky (1879–1940) stressed not the deterministic character of Marx's thought but the more subjective elements of consciousness, will and *praxis*. This is sometimes called 'voluntaristic' Marxism, with its emphasis on the human factor in social change although, as will be argued in subsequent chapters, such a distinction is wholly spurious. After the 1917 Russian revolution Lukács (1885–1971), notable in *History and Class Consciousness* (1923), Korsch (1886–1961) in *Marxism and Philosophy* (1924) and Gramsci (1891–1937) rejected the mechanical and evolutionary determinism of Kautsky and Plekhanov. Later, during the 1920s and 1930s, a group of German intellectuals based at Frankfurt attempted a further development of 'voluntaristic' Marxism, striving to combine philosophy with science : the Frankfurt School, as it became, included Herbert Marcuse, Theodore Adorno, Max Horkheimer, its influence still being evident in the work not merely of Marcuse but of Jürgen Habermas.[10]

But it was not this 'voluntaristic' brand of Marxism which attracted the attentions of Weber, Sombart, Simmel and Mannheim. The criticisms of these sociologists is directed less at Marx than his dogmatic interpreters. In the work of Weber and Simmel, especially, the subjective element missing in 'mechanical' Marxism as well as in nineteenth-century positivistic sociology, with its stress on invariable, external laws which dominate man, re-emerges and the social world is defined in terms of man's actions, purposes and motives. It is this 'voluntaristic' element within social theory which links Weber, Simmel, Lukács, Gramsci and the phenomenological

8

school of Alfred Schutz (1899–1959). Nineteenth-century sociology had developed the concepts of system, as for example with Comte, and it is this which modern sociologists have tended to reject : the work of Durkheim (1858–1917) has equally been interpreted as a rejection of determinism in favour of human action and subjectivity. This is indeed the theme of Talcott Parsons's *The Structure of Social Action* (1937) in which social action theory receives its most elaborate and detailed examination. Thus there is a clear link between the development of modern social theory and the work of Marx, between the 'degeneration' of Marxism at the end of the nineteenth century and the revitalisation of sociology in the work of Weber, Simmel and Schutz; and between 'voluntaristic' Marxism and 'voluntaristic' sociology. This book is an attempt to explore this relationship.

I

DIALECTICS

Marx's concept of social reality is dialectical. But neither Marx nor Marxists enjoy a monopoly over this term. During the last few years, following the publication of Marx's early writings, social scientists have rediscovered the dialectic. And, disillusioned with the deterministic implications of modern functionalism, the dialectic has emerged as a major paradigm in social theory. In sociological phenomenology it seems the dominant mode : for, building on the work of Husserl and Schutz and rejecting social theories which set society against the individual or which postulate ahistorical human nature and ahistorical social systems, phenomenologists propose 'to bring to bear a dialectical perspective upon the theoretical orientation of the social sciences'. By this is meant a concept of society as 'a dialectical process' involving both subjective human activity and an objective social structure : men produce society and are produced by it, 'the product acts back upon the producer'. Consciousness is not to be understood as a mere epiphenómenon reducible to social, political or economic structure but as a partly autonomous element capable of acting back on the objective social structure : knowledge is therefore no passive and inert property of social structure, a mere 'reflection', but is both social product and independent factor in change.[1]

Functionalism, too, has its own advocates for the dialectic. Arguing that the dialectic implies conflict, contradiction and change together with a concept of society as an integrated whole, one writer has called for a synthesis between the Marxist dialectic and the functionalist emphasis on social consensus, equilibrium and system.[2]

In these interpretations the dialectic is defined in terms of interaction, reciprocity and multiple causation and counterposed to the 'dogmatic' use of the concept in Marx's mature work where, so it is argued, a mechanical theory of base and superstructure and a single and uni-directional notion of social change replaces the 'genuine' dialectic of the early writings. Other contemporary sociologists, however, remain sceptical, dismissing the dialectic as mysticism which explains nothing, a dubious rationale for socialism and totalitarian politics, an idealist residue from Hegel's philosophy : Ralf Dahrendorf suggests, indeed, that the dialectic has exercised only a 'corrupting' influence on Marx's sociology, providing Marx with his philosophy of history at the expense of his social theory.

With these contradictory views in mind this chapter will examine what is meant by 'the dialectical point of view' and 'a dialectical theory of society'.

I

When he wrote *Capital* Marx had developed a distinct methodology for the analysis of social, economic and political structures, a method which incorporates two related concepts, dialectic and totality. Marx's contribution to social science cannot be understood apart from these two concepts which in Marx's social theory form a dynamic and interconnected union.

For Marx social relationships are mediated through labour. Classical eighteenth-century materialism had worked with a rigid dichotomy between subject and object, elaborating a passive category of perception in which mind, man's consciousness, was a blank sheet (*tabula rasa*) on which experience impressed itself mechanically. Thus consciousness, the subjective element, became necessarily suppressed as an active force by mechanical materialism and nineteenth-century positivism. Marx, having defined reality as a human reality made by men, argues for a social theory which grasps this reality not as immutable and non-historical but rather as a living process involving man in his dual role as product and producer.

Marx's social theory, then, is characterised by the precept that society is *made* not *given*, a standpoint with important ramifications for epistemology. For since society is *made* then knowledge of it cannot be regarded simply as a reflection or imitation of objective 'realities'. Epistemologically, social theory must embody within its own concepts the making not completion of social structure; social theory must grasp its human and historical nature. Thus when Marx argues that it is not man's consciousness which determines his social being but rather his social existence which determines his consciousness he is not suggesting a return to eighteenth-century materialism, for the term social existence implies both man's objective material environment as well as his actions, i.e. the notion of purposive activity. This is surely the meaning of Marx's well-known criticism of Enlightenment philosophy and utopian socialism :

> The materialistic doctrine that men are the products of circumstances and education, and that changed men are therefore the products of other circumstances and a changed education forgets that circumstances are changed by men, and that therefore the educator must himself be educated. Consequently, materialism necessarily divides society into two parts one of which is superior to society (in Robert Owen for example). The coincidence of the transformation of circumstances and of human activity can be conceived and rationally understood only as revolutionary practice.[3]

For when man constructs an objective picture of the world through reflection, then the act of cognition itself changes the external reality, for the thought becomes part of that reality and removes what Hegel called its 'external determinateness' allowing man to act and thus change it. A social theory which lacks adequate mediation, that is, one which dissolves man and his activity into a mere reflex of external conditions and objective historical and social laws, failing to grasp the complex relationships between man's material and cultural environments, will tend to be contradictory and inconsistent. For if man is no more than the mere product of his surrounding environment then the same must be true of those who call for his education and moral transformation. In the utopian socialism of Owen and Saint-Simon the leaders are elevated to a privileged status outside society, are beyond the laws which they have argued necessarily affect all others, enjoying mystical communion with 'truth'. In the work of Comte, Mill and Durkheim an élitist conception of change and progress flows directly from a social theory which divides society into those who are the passive recipients of a determinate externality and those who stand aloof from the mundane involvement of practical life. Nineteenth-century social theory was dominated by this contradiction : man is made by an environment which he is powerless to change except through the reforming zeal of bourgeois intellectuals. There was therefore no grasp of the dialectical relation between the social theories proposed by bourgeois intellectuals and their social position and practice. The achievements of nineteenth-century positivism consist precisely in this : unmediated, undialectical, it failed to advance significantly beyond the mechanical materialism of the eighteenth century.

Undialectical social theory, however, was equally elaborated in Marxist theorists such as Plekhanov, Kautsky, Bernstein and Bukharin. In his book *Evolutionary Socialism* (1899) Bernstein consciously repudiate the dialectic as sheer pedantry; socialism was validated not by reference to historical necessity and the inevitable dialectical movements of conflict and change, but rather through an *a priori* ethical imperative derived from Kant which taught that in socialist society men would treat others not as means to ends but as ends in themselves. Bernstein's contemporary, Trotsky, held a different view : Marxism without dialectics, he wrote, is like a clock without a spring,[4] while Lenin, after rereading Hegel, could write that 'It is completely impossible to grasp Marx's *Capital* . . . if you have not studied through and understood the whole of Hegel's *Logic*. Consequently, none of the Marxists for the past half century have understood Marx.'[5] Marx never wrote a systematic treatment of dialectics, and this most important work was left to Engels and it is from his writings that most of the controversy over the dialectic has sprung. In his *Anti-Dühring* and the posthumously published fragmentary *Dialectics of Nature*, Engels attempted to systematise, popularise and apply the concept of dialectics to society, history, knowledge and nature : 'Dialectics . . . is nothing more than the science of the general laws of motion and development of nature, human society and thought.'[6]

In his notes to the *Dialectics of Nature* Engels made the distinction between 'objective' dialectics, which prevailed through nature, and 'subjective' dialectics, that is, dialectical thought, describing it as 'the reflex of the movement in opposites which asserts itself everywhere in nature and which by the continual conflict of opposites and their final merging into one another, or into higher forms, determines the life of nature.'[7] For Engels dialectics was a process which characterised all natural and social phenomena, of the laws which underpinned development and change and the interconnections of these elements; the dialectical method was a form of cognition in which facts were not isolated but grasped in their subtle and manifold interconnections, their movement and transformation into other *things*.

The essence of the dialectic is process and change through contradictions and development to higher, more complex stages through the struggle of opposites. The concept of the dialectic is frequently subsumed under the famous triad, thesis, anti-thesis, and synthesis, or, in more Hegelian language, affirmation, negation, and negation of the negation, and the law of the transformation of quantity into quality. It should be noted that in Marx's many analyses of society and history he never made use of these terms, while Engels appears to define the dialectic in strictly formal terms. Thus he argues that each phenomenon develops its own negation with which it necessarily struggles until a synthesis is reached when a new, higher phenomenon emerges; in turn this generates its opposite and the process is repeated *ad infinitum*. The synthesis, Engels emphasises, is not something wholly different from the negated phenomenon but contains the essence of both at a qualitatively higher level. In his treatment of dialectics Engels provides a number of examples, mainly drawn from Hegel, to illustrate the argument. Much of this work, however, is frankly misleading, muddled and confusing and while it is true that Marx read and approved the text of *Anti-Dühring* it does not follow that Engels actually developed Marx's own ideas : in the realm of natural science, for example, Marx, in the absence of his own research, tended to accept Engels's knowledge of developments in chemistry and electricity. Engels was a systematic but facile thinker; it is not an accident that the mechanical and positivist interpretations of Marxism tend to flow from his work rather than from Marx. This is amply documented by Engels's concrete discussion of dialectics.

A grain of barley, falling on suitable ground and under the influence of heat and water changes dramatically into a plant and this, says Engels, is 'the negation of the grain'. The plant now grows and flowers, producing more barley grains which cause the stalk to die : 'As a result of this negation of the negation we have once more the original grain of barley, but not as a single unit, but ten, twenty or thirty fold.' As with botany so with mathematics : to negate a we get $-a$ which, when it itself is negated by multiplying by $-a$ gives us a^2, 'the original positive quantity, but a higher degree, raised to its second power'.[8] Of course, to negate something does not mean to destroy it and Engels stresses that the first negation must be constructed in such a way that a second negation takes place naturally and spontaneously. The transformation of an object or entity into something higher occurs only because the negation of the negation implies that a continuous accumulation of contradictions and tensions have been allowed to develop to a critical nodal point when a sudden explosive change is inevitable, a leap from one attribute to one qualitatively different. There occurs, to use Hegel's phrase, an interruption in gradualness. Movement is thus always a unity of contradictory elements and not an homogeneous evolution.

Dialectical laws apply to practical life. It should be unnecessary to draw attention to the negation of the negation involved in sexual orgasm, the transformation of quantity into quality, the fusing of opposites, the sudden explosive leap, all this is well known. And Engels once wrote that 'the dialectical conception of life' is that the negation of life is contained within life itself 'so that life is always thought of in relation to its necessary result death'.[9]

For Engels, the dialectic was both a method of analysis and an objective process equally applicable to the natural and social world. But his formulations seem mechanical and deterministic and his presentation differs quite sharply *in some respects* from Marx's own work. For while Marx accepts the major laws of the dialectic as enunciated by Engels, his actual analyses of social and historical structures are more subtle and complex. But before discussing this it may be useful to consider more precisely the meaning and implications of the dialectic for social theory.

Dialectics is as old as Western philosophy. The concept derives from the Greek words '*dia*' and '*logos*' which quite simply refer to a form of reasoning which seeks to reconcile two conflicting and contradictory positions. The Greeks were the first major school of dialecticians, their philosophy dominated by the concepts of change, motion and process. Heraclitus, for example, whom Lenin regarded as one of the founders of dialectics, wrote of the world as an eternal living fire regularly becoming ignited and extinguished, constantly changing, perpetually in unrest.[10] In other philosophies dialectic has often found its expression in what Hegel called lifeless and logical forms. Pascal and Kant were great dialectical thinkers, and it is obvious that dialectical thought did not originate with Hegel, Marx and Engels. But from the point of view of social theory the application of dialectics to society and history is of quite recent origins. Within the field of social theory, as distinct from philosophy, dialectics is given its first *sociological* form in the work of the eighteenth-century bourgeois historians and political economists. In Adam Smith's *Wealth of Nations* (1776) and Adam Ferguson's *Essay on the History of Civil Society* (1767), for example, society is analysed as an historical process involving conflictive economic and social elements. However, it is not the emphasis on conflict as such which constitutes the dialectic but rather, as Smith and Ferguson show, the ways in which one set of actions and purposes become transformed into their opposites within the fabric of social life.

In his description of the rise of capitalism Smith analysed the development of the social division of labour, the growth of technology and the social co-operation of individuals necessitated by the production, exchange and consumption of wealth. For Adam Smith the growth of an economic system was proof of social progress; yet he was clearly aware that economic progress implied social deprivation. The individual worker becomes transformed from a skilled craftsman into a mere appendage of a machine. Economic progress turns men into objects in a society geared solely for private profit; production itself is threatened by the logic of a system which necessarily creates great wealth at one pole and immense suffering and squalor at the other. There is here an awareness, as in the early writings of Hegel, that at the very moment when social theory grasps the bourgeois class's economic ascendenacy it portrays, however partially, its actual historical negation – the alienated proletariat.[11]

On one level Smith's *Wealth of Nations* is a complex apologia for the historic emergence of the bourgeois class and is written within the epistemological framework which bourgeois thinkers from Locke onwards had developed as a method for understanding external phenomena. Smith's materialism is broadly speaking mechanical, that is, it radically denies the importance of man's own activity in shaping the social world. In the *Wealth of Nations* Smith is describing the evolution of commercial capitalism and with it the rise of the bourgeois class. If he had adhered strictly to the mechanical premises of eighteenth-century materialism Smith must surely have concluded that in the transition from the feudal to the capitalist mode of production the bourgeois class played no positive role, its emergence and success being simply the result of external, economic necessity. In fact Smith is forced to subvert his mechanical model precisely because, as an intellectual representative of the rising bourgeoisie, his work theoretically expresses the social aspirations of that class. The dilemma is solved by invoking the concept of the unintended consequence of human action. In his *Essay on the History of Civil Society* Ferguson had written that 'Every step and every movement of the multitude . . . are made with equal blindness to the future . . . and nations stumble upon establishments, which are indeed the results of human action, but not the execution of any human design.'[12] Smith argues that capitalist development was partly caused by the desire of the landed aristocracy for the new consumer goods produced by the urban bourgeoisie, and the bourgeoisie's ambition to achieve the rank of gentlemen : as agriculture declined under spendthrift and inefficient management the industrious bourgeoisie bought out the agricultural holdings of the barons and, employing their virtues of rationality and calculability, created the strong agricultural sector essential for feeding the expanding urban centres. Social change was unintended, unconsciously effected by two social classes whose selfish actions, as they worked through the complex, collective life of society, were transformed into their opposites:

> To gratify the most childish vanity was the sole motive of the great proprietors. The merchants and artificers, much less ridiculous, acted merely from a view to their own interests, and in pursuit of their own pedlar principle of turning a penny wherever a penny was to be got. Neither of them had knowledge or foresight of that great revolution which the folly of the one, and the industry of the other, was gradually bringing about.

Smith's formulation is important because it demonstrates the way in which a dialectical element existed within his largely mechanical model of society, expressing the contradiction between conscious intentions and eventual concrete ends:

> As every individual . . . endeavours as much as he can to employ his capital . . . that his produce may be of the greatest value; every individual necessarily labours to render the annual revenue of society as great as he can . . . he intends only his own gain, and he is in this, as in many other cases, led by an invisible hand to promote an end which was no part of his intention.[13]

It is thus the dialectical interplay between the individual's personal actions and the social, collective ends which ultimately promotes social change.

Equally significant is the concept of negativity. As capitalism promotes affluence, knowledge, happiness, it unintentionally creates a social stratum dominated by poverty, ignorance and misery. Of course, this negative element within bourgeois social theory could not be tolerated as such, since it could so easily turn into a threat to the existing society. It became essential, therefore, to show how, through the beneficent influence of education and religious instruction, the workers became adjusted to the harsh but necessary realities of capitalism. In this way the worker would know his duties and draw little sustenance from dangerous radical politics.

Bourgeois social theory, then, had disclosed a negative factor; but as a bourgeois theory it could not develop this insight. The negative must be rendered positive; it must be assimilated and its contradictory aspects eliminated. The moralising tone of eighteenth-century materialism flows from its inability to understand its own discovery : the social world was dialectical.

In Hegel's philosophy these achievements of eighteenth-century materialism are acknowledged, assimilated, and *developed*; but developed in an idealist philosophical framework which enthrones negativity as the basis of all things. In the *Science of Logic* Hegel argues that 'everything is inherently contradictory', that 'contradiction is the root of all movement and vitality; it is only in so far as something has a contradiction within it that it moves, has an urge and activity'.[14] Unlike Smith and Ferguson, whose materialism was basically mechanical although shot through with dialectical elements, Hegel's philosophy is a completely dialectical structure. Negativity and contradiction are therefore disclosed not as by-products but as essential structures; they are not to be assimilated and emasculated but rather grasped as constituting the essential basis of thought, life, movement. The negative element, Hegel tirelessly repeats, is not a static, immutable and frozen thing but an essential component of any process, a 'becoming'.

All that is necessary to achieve scientific progress is the recognition of the logical principle that the negative is just as much positive, or that what is self-contradictory does not resolve itself into a nullity, into abstract nothingness, but essentially only into the negation of its *particular* content, in other words, that such a negation is not all and every negation but the negation of a specific subject matter which resolves itself, and consequently is a specific negation, and therefore the result essentially contains that from which it results. . . . Because the result, the negation, is a *specific* negation it has a *content*. It is a fresh notion but higher and richer than its predecessor; for it is richer by the negation or opposite of the latter, therefore contains it, but also something more, and is the unity of itself and its opposite.[15]

An object without contradictions, Hegel wrote, is a pure abstraction serving only to hide the negative elements subsisting in all phenomena. For without negativity there can be no change or motion, simply stasis, for in the negative 'lies the ground of becoming, or the unrest of self-movement'.[16] Everything has its positive and negative sides, and the dialectical method lies in grasping 'opposites in their unity or of the positive in the negative', a unity which is not 'abstract, dead and inert, but concrete'.[17] Contradiction is thus the 'root of all movement', but Hegel stresses that this movement is not forced upon an object externally but flows from *within*. This is the *core* of Hegel's dialectic : 'Dialectic is commonly regarded as an external, negative activity which does not pertain to the subject matter itself', – the standpoint of Smith and Ferguson – rather its essence lies in spontaneous, internal self movement, the fact 'that something is therefore alive only in so far as it contains contradiction within it, and moreover is this power to hold and endure the contradiction within it'.[18]

It is in these senses that Marx's class conflict model of society can be understood. Social change, social movement occurs because of the conflict and contradictions within society, between the divisive interests generated through the capitalist division of labour, between the social aspects of production and its private control, between the requirements of profit maximisation and human social needs. The capitalist division of work, based on the private ownership of property, creates the exploitive relation between the buyers and sellers of labour power; it necessarily divides society into a propertyless proletariat and a small but powerful ruling class based on industrial and commercial capital. Class conflict is thus a necessary element of capitalist civilisation, for as the working classes are brought together within large-scale factory organisation they find it impossible to live without developing a sense of solidarity, collectivism and mutuality. At the same time as the capitalist division of labour brings great wealth, improved productivity and technological innovation, it fails to solve the problems of inequality, poverty and exploitation. Yet as it divides it unifies : the industrial proletariat, through its experiences in large-scale production, comes increasingly to identify with other, similarly placed workers and through this common class situation a consciousness emerges fundamentally hostile to private property and the inequalities of wealth and status based upon it.

It is important to emphasise that dialectical analysis does not work with false, moral and arbitrary abstractions such as the 'good' and 'bad' effects of the division of labour. Marx's criticism of Proudhon in *The Poverty of Philosophy* can be read both as a criticism of utopian socialism and of Comte's and Durkheim's theories of the division of labour. For Proudhon, wrote Marx, 'every economic category has two sides – one good the other bad. He looks upon these categories as the petty bourgeois looks upon the great men of history : Napoleon was a great man; he did a lot of good; he also did a lot of harm. . . . The problem to be solved : to keep the good side while eliminating the bad.' Dialectical thought rejects these false anti-theses and grasps '. . . the co-existence of two contradictory sides, their conflict and their fusion into a new category. The very setting of the problem of eliminating the bad side cuts short the dialectical movement. It is not the category which is posed and opposed to itself, but its contradictory nature. . . .'[19]

Marx's dialectical approach is nowhere better brought out than in the chapter on money in the *Grundrisse*. Capitalism, he argues, is built around commodity production and the social division of labour : the product, the commodity has therefore a 'double' nature as something practically useful and as exchangeable for money, a contradiction between its natural and its social qualities. Originally money was identical with the commodity as its exchange value; but as the division of labour grows so too does the power of money, establishing itself 'as a power external to and independent of the producers'. Money now appears as an object distinct from the commodity, as a commodity itself :

What originally appeared as a means to promote production becomes a relation alien to the producers. As the producers become more dependent on exchange, exchange appears to become more independent of them, and the gap between the product as product and the product as exchange value appears to widen. Money does not create these antitheses and contradictions; it is, rather, the development of these contradictions and antitheses which creates the seemingly transcendental power of money.[20]

This passage makes clear that Marx's concept of contradiction involves both internal and external relations and properties of a particular phenomenon : money is contained with the commodity yet differentiated from and external to it.

As with money so with the division of labour : production demands a complex division of work which, as social relations – the class structure – generate conflict and contradictions. It is these negative characteristics of the division of labour which lie at the heart of Marx's dialectical theory of society. But already with Adam Smith the potentially disruptive features had been noted and analysed. In the nineteenth century positivistic sociologists studied the problem from a rather different, non-dialectical standpoint.

III

Like Smith and Ferguson, Comte was fully aware of the contradictory social effects of the division of labour which promote on the one hand co-operation, on the other ignorance, squalor and class conflict. The functions of what he called 'wise government' were to eliminate these contradictions and inculcate a system of 'shared moral beliefs' And since the workers were 'privileged in that freedom from care, and that thoughtlessness which would be a serious fault in the higher classes', society must be organised by enlightened capitalists and sociologists. Fortunately the workers realise that the capitalists are their intellectual superiors and thus relegate 'burdensome responsibilities' to their 'wise and trustworthy guidance'. But how is this possible given Comte's basic conception of the division of labour as largely disruptive of social harmony? His answer is the creation of 'artificial' social institutions to make men realise that subordination is both necessary (the diffusion of skills for example) and natural.[21]

In contrast, Durkheim shows how the division of labour *normally* engenders co-operation, sociability and social solidarity; where it does create conflict and a dispersion of interests its form is 'abnormal' and 'pathological'. Unlike Smith and Marx, Durkheim's analysis is designed to prove that moral and social unity lie inherently within the function of the division of labour and not that it generates alienation and conflict.

Durkheim begins his inquiry by defining the division of labour in terms of its functions. In the 'Preface' to the second edition of *The Division of Labour* he wrote that the division of work does not necessarily lead to 'dispersion and incoherence' rather, when its functions are 'sufficiently in contact with one another [they] tend to stabilise and regulate themselves'. Thus normally a system of co-ordinated functions in harmony with each other results. But these functions can be co-ordinated only by an external authority such as occupational groups. The functions of the division of labour, then, are not spontaneously co-ordinated and unless there is this external regulation conflict and abnormality may result.[22]

Durkheim's model, unlike those used by Smith and Marx, is un-historical. He compares the functions of the division of labour with the functions of the living body, deriving from this organismic analogy his concept of social health. Normal comes to mean those conditions most generally distributed while abnormal is defined by the negative features. By 'generally distributed' Durkheim means those elements which complement each other rather than those which oppose and exclude. At this point he invokes the concept of human nature : man likes diversity for 'as richly endowed as we may be, we always lack something, and the best of us realise our insufficiency'. Man therefore seeks friends with qualities he lacks and joins organisations where 'a *true* exchange of services' takes place (my emphasis). The division of labour determines relations of friendship, and Durkheim concludes that the 'true function' of the division of labour is 'to create in two or more persons a feeling of solidarity'. Thus 'normally' the division of labour promotes social harmony (exchange of services, reciprocity of obligations, interdependence, etc.), an essentially co-operative institution facilitating the growth of the individual (through developing his special talents) and the whole (society).

During the course of the nineteenth century, however, the division of labour seemed to be deviating from the 'normal' mode. Durkheim argued that these 'pathological' forms, exemplified in wide-spread strike action, were no more than momentary aberrations. For Smith and Marx the division of work within the capitalist mode of production creates conflict and its negative effects are built into its very structure. With Marx, social theory *begins* with an awareness of this negative factor implying for him a revolutionary potential (the working class), but Durkheim comes to the negative features only after a lengthy discussion of its ideational 'normal' forms which are never concretely related to class and power but only to the moral effects they supposedly generate. When Durkheim discusses the 'pathological' mode of the division of labour he notes that with in-dustrial development the conflict between labour and capital inten-sifies and the worker becomes increasingly separated from the em-ployer. As we have said, Smith, Ferguson and Marx had emphasised these features, so that by the 1890s surely they must be regarded as 'normal'? But Durkheim – working from an abstract definition of the division of labour in terms of interpersonal needs, 'differentiated but not wholly opposed interests' – has simply read back from the ap-parently harmonising function of the feudal guilds and nineteenth-century middle-class professional associations, to a *general*, all-embracing ahistorical model. Thus during the nineteenth century the 'pathological' form emerges to produce 'disastrous conse-quences' and a 'debasement of human nature' in which man becomes an 'inert piece of machinery'. And why? Because the division of labour is not functioning 'for it to be itself'. But what does Durkheim mean by for itself? To be itself, writes Durkheim, nothing must intrude 'from without to denature it'. For the division of labour normally means that the individual does not 'close himself in' (as a result of greater work specialisation) but keeps in contact with 'neighbouring functions' for: 'the division of labour presumes that the worker, far from being hemmed in by his task, does not lose sight of his collaborators, that he acts upon them, and reacts to them'.[23]

.The negative element has been explained away: the functions of the division of labour have been defined *external to its specific historical setting* and grasped as something which *stands outside* real, empirical history. In *The German Ideology* Marx wrote that his method started from 'real premises', 'real men' living not in isolation 'but in their actual empirical perceptible process of development under definite conditions'. Any social institution, therefore, had to be grasped firstly in terms of the conditions of its actual existence, its mode of life, its activity – in short, its specific historical setting. For Durkheim, the division of labour becomes a timeless abstraction, *a thing for itself*, which, under the definite historical conditions of nineteenth-century capitalism, is 'denatured'.

> The essence of a fish is its existence, water . . . the essence of a fresh water fish is the water of a river. But the latter ceases to be the 'essence' of a fish and is no longer a suitable medium of existence as soon as the river is made to serve industry . . . polluted by dyes and other waste products.[24]

Marx's criticism of Feuerbach can be read as a criticism of Durkheim's non-dialectical theory. The 'abnormal' form of the division of labour is but one aspect of the 'normal' development of capitalist society, a complex structure of opposing elements. It may justly be said that sociological positivism failed to grasp contradiction and negativity as indispensable elements of social theory.

I V

In both his early and later writings Marx affirmed the principle of negativity. Hegel had argued for the self-movement of matter and in Engels's discussion of nature the dialectic is presented as all-pervasive. This extension of the dialectic to nature has been frequently criticised : Sartre and Lukács have denied that dialectical processes operate independently of men and society. In *History and Class Consciousness* Lukács criticised Engels's extension of the dialectic to nature and science and argued that the dialectical method was 'inseparable from the "practical" and "critical" activity of the proletariat'. The dialectic was historical and social, mediated by human *praxis*. It is true that Engels's discussion of dialectics is somewhat confusing and in his hands historical processes, by their nature infinitely complex, become simplified. His ready-made application of the dialectic to history is well known :

All civilised peoples begin with the common ownership of the land. With all peoples who have passed a certain primitive stage, this common ownership becomes in the course of the development of agriculture a fetter on production. It is abolished, negated, and after a longer or shorter series of intermediate stages is transformed into private property. But at a higher stage of agricultural development, brought about by private property in land itself, private property conversely becomes a fetter on production, as is the case today both with small and large landownership.[25]

Thus Communism is restored but at a higher level of material and mental culture. And it is one step from this to the argument that history has a meaningful pattern independent of men, a movement in the direction of a unified humanity. The famous sequence, primitive communism, slavery, feudalism, capitalism, socialism and communism can easily degenerate into a dogmatic philosophy of history, a teleological order, historicism, in which man is necessarily caught up in an inevitable, because dialectical, forward movement. It is in this sense that dialectics has been attacked as 'fatalism', a secular prophecy drawn not from facts but from the 'insidious' influence of Hegel's dialectic.[26] For Hegel, the 'cunning of reason' consisted in history's own secret purposes in making events, which to the individual seemed arbitrary and meaningless, cohere into one unified universal goal, while for Engels the meaning of history lay in its immanent and necessary progression towards freedom and communism. But dialectics does not imply a necessary and inevitable historical development. Indeed, as Marx and Engels pointed out in *The Communist Manifesto*, historical regression is as possible as progression, citing the case of the decline of Rome whose advanced economy and technology were destroyed through warfare and where no higher social form resulted from this 'negation of the negation';[27] and in the *Grundrisse* Marx analysed those modes of production – Asiatic and Slavonic for example – which remained static and where little economic and social development had occurred.[28]

Engels's discussion of the dialectic and in particular the examples drawn from nature – water turning into steam or ice at a certain temperature – pose the critical problem of the relationship between *matter* and *praxis* and the question of meditations. An important distinction must be made, however, between an existing, external world and a real objective world as understood through common sense. If man did not exist then matter and the movement within and between it *would* exist although not historically. But the co-existence of nature, man and society implies a subject/object relation in which the 'external' world is mediated to become 'objective and real'. It is in this latter sense that the dialectic is historical, living in and through historical practice. As Gramsci says, 'It might seem that there can exist an extra-historical and extra-human objectivity. But who is the judge of such objectivity? . . . objectivity always means "humanly objective" . . .'[29] To affirm a reality independent of men, as Engels does, is to invoke a metaphysical concept of matter as external and absolute. The weak side of Engels's analysis of dialectics lies here, in his failure to grasp mediations and to forget that 'history does nothing', it neither fights battles nor wins wars and it is only man, living within a definite historical epoch who through his actions *makes* change.

Consciousness and practice are crucial for Marx. 'Positivistic' interpretations of Marxism are largely based on a non-dialectical understanding of the unity of what critics refer to as the 'activist' and the sociological sides of his work, a separation which is itself profoundly non-dialectical. Again and again Marx argues that it is man living and working within a specific historical situation who determines historical change : 'It is by no means "History" which uses man as a means to carry out its ends as if it were a person apart; rather History is nothing but the activity of man in pursuit of his ends.'[30] Man here is not the isolated individual of eighteenth-century bourgeois social theory, for while history is made by man it is made within a context he has not freely chosen and as part of a social collectivity, the group or class. The individual who exists independently of a group or class is simply a fiction : by himself the individual can achieve nothing and history thus becomes the history of definite groups and classes of men engaged in the pursuit of ends which brings them increasingly into conflict with other groups. The collective pursuit of ends in a society characterised by inequalities of property can mean only periodic crises and conflict. Social theory

28

therefore discloses both this *fact* and through this becomes itself part of the struggle to change the world. In 1880 Marx could write :

> Man stands in a relation with the objects of the external world as the means to satisfy his needs. But men do not begin by standing 'in this theoretical relation with the objects of the external world'. Like all animals they begin by eating, drinking etc., i.e. they do not stand in any relation, but are engaged in activity, appropriate certain objects of the external world by means of their actions, and in this way satisfy their needs (i.e. they begin with production). As a result of the repetition of this process it is imprinted in their minds that objects are capable of 'satisfying' the 'needs' of men.

To repeat that the social world is made by man is doubtless a platitude yet it is a platitude with important ramifications for social theory. Marx is not arguing for a deterministic, teleological social nexus. For him 'purposive' action is class action oriented to certain defined goals and refracted through ideology. In *Capital* he wrote that :

> At the end of every labour process, we get a result that already existed in the imagination of the labourer at its commencement. He not only effects a change in the form of the material on which he works, but he also realises a purpose of his own that gives the law to his own modus operandi, and to which he must subordinate his will. And this subordination is no mere momentary act. Besides the exertion of the bodily organs, the process demands that, during the whole operation, the workman's will be steadily in consonance with his purpose.[31]

Man intervenes directly in the historical process but only as part of that process. Social development does not of itself create ends; only men can will ends, and only men can bring *their* purposes to fruition. But, of course, what men can will is conditioned by the prevailing state of material and cultural forces. The negative element in pre-Marxist bourgeois social theory – the unintended consequences of action, Hegel's 'cunning of reason' – is transformed into conscious willed action directed against capitalist society and its institutions. Thus when Marx talks of the iron laws of capitalist development he does so only in terms of a social theory whose function is to *unmask* the ways in which capitalism works so that conscious planned change can take place; it is not a blueprint for pre-ordained, pre-given ends, but to show how the negative element, the proletariat, through its *praxis* can transform capitalism into socialism. The category of practice, so crucial for Marx, can only be based on real, historically immanent tendencies within capitalism ('self-movement') which create an objective conflict of interest between capitalist and workers. But this does not mean that class conflict on its own is a sufficient condition for revolutionary *praxis*, that the laws of capitalism alone necessarily lead to total economic breakdown. Purposive activity implies that for the proletariat socialism must be willed and fought for; it is not granted by history, its laws or its tendencies.

The argument, therefore, that situates Marx as an historicist employing spurious generalisations on the basis of a dogmatic understanding of historical trends is clearly misleading. Karl Popper, for example, has suggested that Marx makes unconditional prophecies on the nature of capitalist development, that the lot of the working class must progressively deteriorate to the point of violent revolution, and that nothing can reverse this. He quotes the passage in the first volume of *Capital* where Marx appears to argue in this mechanical way.

. . . the greater the social wealth, the amount of capital at work, the extent and energy of its growth . . . the larger is the surplus population. . . . The size of the industrial reserve army grows as the power of wealth grows. But . . . the larger the industrial reserve army, the larger are the masses of the workers whose misery is relieved only by an increase in the agony of toil; and . . . the larger is the number of those who are sufficiently recognised as paupers. This is the absolute and general law of capitalist accumulation.[32]

On the basis of this quote Marx is indeed an historicist : but the next sentence in his text reads : 'Like all other laws it is modified by a number of circumstances the analysis of which does not concern us here.'[33] Clearly, then, Marx does not make unconditional statements about the future. He was much more aware than his predecessors, the utopian socialists, of the complexity of historical change, of the contradictory, uneven development of human society. For among the other factors affecting the operation of his law was the element of human action, of class consciousness, of political practice.

If historical regression or historical development occurs then it does so by virtue of *action* taken by men in definite classes *against* other men. It is only necessary to add that this is not a theory of 'speeding up' history to its 'inevitable end', for the progress of humanity is never wholly upward but is racked by the most appalling defeats. For the dialectic is not motion external to man's actions but involves man both objectively and subjectively for it is only through men that social change occurs at all. The 'correct' *praxis* cannot be guaranteed in all circumstances, as the history of Stalinism and the army of left-wing intellectuals who supported both its theory and *practice* in the 1930s illustrates : such a fragile concept lying at the heart of Marx's social theory is evidence enough against the naïve and mechanical view which ascribes to dialectics definite, historically upward necessity.

v

What, then, is dialectics? Sociological phenomenologists define dialectics as reciprocity and multiple causation but in so doing they divest it of its contradictory nature, for a dialectical relation is not one of even, reciprocal interaction. To say that men produce society and are produced by it and that consciousness is an active not passive factor in social change and then call this dialectical is to eliminate precisely those properties which for Hegel and Marx provided life and movement, negation, contradiction, and to set up not a dialectical theory of society but a theory of factors – x influences y; y influences x. From the point of view of dialectics this is pre-Hegelian !

Yet the theory of factors, or multiple causation, has frequently been defended as dialectical and Marxist. Engels, for example, replying to the criticism that Marxism reduced all phenomena to the economic structure of society argued that 'the whole vast process proceeds in the form of interaction – though of very unequal forces, the economic movement being by far the strongest, most primordial and most decisive – . . . .'[34] Dialectic here has been reduced to an interplay between external objects, whereas the essence of the concept for Hegel and Marx lay in the *intrinsic* contradictions as well as those between phenomena, for it was only in this way that the specific connections and relations between the economic and other elements could be analysed.

Dialectical thought reflects the real movement of phenomena, their internal contradictions and the conflict this engenders, their inter-connectedness and unity. For Engels, scientific socialism was possible because dialectical laws dominated both nature and history and social development was both historically necessary and progressive since it worked through the law of the negation of the negation. Such a formulation, however, succeeds only in reifying the historical process itself, turning men into objects of an external necessity and making them mere instruments of the dialectical laws themselves. Of course, Engels popularised Marxism through such works as *Anti-Dühring* but this fact should not inhibit criticism of the ways in which he applied dialectics, for the dialectical method does not consist of applying a set formula to an existing content. In his commentary on Hegel's *Science of Logic* Lenin wrote that the dialectic 'cannot be applied in its given form, it cannot be taken as given. One must separate out from it the logical (epistemological) nuances . . . and not apply a concept *ready made*, externally.'[35] Engels's simple inversion of Hegel's dialectic is non-dialectical, and in applying dialectics to society his paraphrasing and wholly external demonstrations had the effect of minimising the complex dialectical relationship between social consciousness and social structure.

THE PROBLEM OF METHOD: TOTALITY

In Marx's early writings Hegel's dialectical philosophy is summarily rejected. In particular the *Science of Logic* is vehemently attacked for its metaphysical abstractions. But by 1858 Marx had reached a different conclusion, and in a letter to Engels he wrote of the great value for scientific methodology of Hegel's *Logic* and the importance for rendering in an accessible form 'what is rational in the method which Hegel discovered but at the same time enveloped in mysticism'.[1] This is the distinction which Engels made later between Hegel's *method* and his *system*, the necessity to extract 'the rational kernel within the mystical shell',[2] and develop a materialist dialectic. To do so Marx took over from Hegel the category of totality, not as a philosophical, speculative principle, but rather as methodological precept which grasps the relationship of the simple to the complex. Thus Marx begins *Capital* with the simple form of value, the exchange of one commodity for another, arguing that within the commodity are found the basic contradictions of capitalism. But the commodity is also a *part* which must be related to a *whole*, a totality, capitalism as an economic, social and political system.[3]

I

The dialectical approach in Hegel and Marx is pre-eminently a method for analysing the interconnections of phenomena, of grasping *facts* not as isolated, rigid and external data but as part of an all-embracing process. 'The relations of production of every society', Marx wrote, 'form a whole' and can be understood only in this sense.[4] Methodologically, of course, it is necessary to isolate and separate the different social elements from one another but these elements can have meaning only within their specific total context. Pre-Marxist social theory had, in general, worked with an atomistic conception of society in which the individual was depicted as standing apart from, although a member of, the collectivity. In the philosophies of rationalism and utilitarianism the individual is both historically and logically prior to the whole, to society; the contract theory of society, for example, assumes a pre-social individual who, through a miraculous alchemy, is capable of calculating the benefits of joining society; utilitarianism begins from the individual and postulates both a knowledge of ends and the means available in every situation to help maximise happiness. The starting-point being the individual, bourgeois social theory had the effect of turning man into a purely egoistic, non-social being whose appetites could be restrained only through some form of external regulation. In his early writings Marx had criticised this one-sided interpretation which, starting from the fiction of the *individual*, failed completely to reconstruct the whole, for having analysed society from the standpoint of the individual, bourgeois social theory found great difficulty in finding its way to the concept of totality.

For the individual is part of a pre-existing whole; he acquires significance only in terms of his relations with other parts and with the whole. It is in this spirit that Lukács has argued for totality as the crucial element in social science :

> It is not the primacy of economic motives in historical explanation that constitutes the decisive difference between Marxism and bourgeois thought, but the point of view of the totality . . . the all-pervasive supremacy of the whole over the parts. . . . Proletarian science is revolutionary not just by virtue of its revolutionary ideas which is opposed to bourgeois society, but above all because of its method. *The primacy of the category of totality is the bearer of the principle of revolution in science.*[5]

For Lukács the method of social science which merely reproduced the surface of social life without probing more deeply to the inner movement determining social structure and history, must always

34

end with *abstract* universal laws applicable to all men in all societies (eighteenth-century theories of progress, and the sociology of Comte, Spencer and Durkheim fall into this category). The growth of the division of labour within intellectual activity has further facilitated the development of theories which assert the supremacy of the part over the whole, and the monographic method in sociology has been aptly described as the most effective way of blurring connections, denying history and process and obscuring the real problem. 'Exact' description of the parts takes over from totality.[6]

The category of totality, however, has more than methodological significance : it carries with it clear political implications, for as the individual is meaningfully related to others only in terms of the whole, and since change must always be change of wholes, then a total social transformation is called for. The young Marx, indeed, writes in precisely these terms arguing that only a revolution which transforms both civil and political structures can succeed in liberating humanity from capitalist alienation.

Such a standpoint has met with severe criticism, especially from those whose ideal of social science, like Marx, lies in analysing wholes (i.e. an organised structure such as capitalism) but unlike Marx 'in descriptive or nominalist terms, viz., *in terms of individuals*, their attitudes, expectations, relations etc.' Thus conservative social theorists such as Hayek and Popper have criticised Marxism for asserting the theory of totality at the expense of the individual, and linked it with political totalitarianism. For Popper and Hayek, Marxism and Fascism are identical in their assertions of the priority of the whole over the part, the state over the individual. They argue for 'methodological individualism', that is, building wholes directly from the experiences of those individuals who comprise them. Social studies, they suggest, are pre-eminently subjective in their content, concerned exclusively with men's actions, and in order to understand social action we must grasp 'what the acting people mean by their actions', for :

Not only man's action towards external objects but also all the relations between men and all the social institutions can be understood only in terms of what men think about them. Society as we

35

know it is . . . built up from the concepts and ideas held by the people; and social phenomena can be recognised by us and have meaning to us only as they are reflected in the minds of men.[7]

Such an extreme formulation of social atomism is one which few modern sociologists would accept. Yet there is a sense in which Hayek actually expresses the methodological subjectivism of the mono-graphic and 'public opinion' approach. In studies of voting behaviour which originate to throw some light on social stratification, it seems a methodological axiom that people's 'opinions' are more 'real' than objective historical analysis, that in order to understand the class structure it is essential to take account of the 'definitions of the situation' which people have of their environment and experiences and *begin* from these. Of course, this is not to argue in favour of positivism, the elimination of the subjective element, but only to point out that in explaining society it is not possible to begin from the individual's consciousness of it. The methodology of the social sciences begins from unanalysed wholes (i.e. capitalism, the state, etc.) and then breaks them down into their constituent parts and levels. Society is not simply a discrete heap of individuals but a com-plex, structural whole in which the subjective element, conscious-ness, is an *objective* element also, in the sense that it exists for others. Societies are complex structured unities in which the units of analysis are not the individual but the group, the community, the class. Engels is in serious error, therefore, when he writes of history in terms of the 'conflict between many individual wills' and society as the 'aggre-gate' of such wills, for he has slipped into the camp of the methodo-logical individualists. Engels has forgotten *structure* and thus totality.[8]

The sociology of Max Weber is somewhat ambivalent on the con-cept of totality, and his theory of social action strives to define society, not in atomised terms, but rather as a complex of individuals and institutions governed by definite norms. Modern sociological pheno-menology and ethnomethodology spring from Weber's central tenet of 'social relationship' and the subjective meaning of individual action. In his critique of Weber, Alfred Schutz draws attention to the influence of Georg Simmel on social-action theory for his 'notion that all concrete social phenomena should be traced back to the modes of individual behaviour and that the particular social form of such modes should be understood through detailed description'. Schutz goes on to argue that it is only through understanding individual action that the meaning of social relationships and structures can be elaborated by interpreting the subjective meaning 'as found in the intentions of individuals'. The social world, therefore, is a complex of 'meaning-endowing intentional acts' which alone constitute reality. Schutz writes :

> What we call the world of objective meaning, is, therefore, abstracted in the social sphere from the constituting processes of a meaning-endowing consciousness, be this one's own or another's. . . . when we speak of subjective meaning in the social world, we are referring to the constituting processes in the consciousness of the person who produced that which is objectively meaningful.[9]

It has already been pointed out that Marx's social theory incorporates the concept of 'purposive action', subjective states, consciousness, but that this is not his starting-point, rather that society is a complex structural unity involving human action and ideas. The stress is on society as a definite structure within which human intentions and actions occur. In essence, therefore, Marx's approach is the opposite of methodological individualism and sociological phenomenology : he rejects the theory of interactions, dialectical or not, which the phenomenologists see as constituting social relationships. However, before discussing these theories in more detail it is necessary to define more precisely what is meant by totality.

II

For Lukács the point of view of totality is the major distinction between Marxist and bourgeois thought, but in this he is simply wrong. Both functionalism and structuralism employ a similar category, that the parts can have meaning only in terms of the whole. For Marxism, totality is an important but by no means dominant element in its methodology and social theory. In Hegel's idealist philosophy the concept is contrasted with the social atomism implied in rationalism and empiricism, and he argues strongly against any attempt to base philosophy on the individual – a standpoint which necessarily leads to fragmentation and loss of unity. The relation of whole to part is at the core of Hegel's philosophy, embodying the 'essential relation' in which wholes and parts *condition* each other'. For Hegel, 'the whole is not abstract unity, but unity as of a diverse manifoldness', and he emphasises the contradictory, dialectical relationship which characterises parts and wholes.[10] For everything has its positive and negative aspects, its positive and negative determinations : totality is the unity of such contradictions.

Of course, the concept of totality was not invented by Hegel. In Smith's *Wealth of Nations* there is a profound grasp of society in terms of a whole which dominates its constituent parts, of the interrelationships between the different branches of production, division of labour, social stratification, family, religion.[11] This emphasis was something new in social theory for pre-1750 social thought had no grasp of totality, of society as a whole. Contrasting Montesquieu with Smith it is clear that Montesquieu had only a partial and limited approach to analysing society : beginning from a *political* perspective, and thus classifying society in political terms by the ways in which political power was exercised, he failed to analyse real historical societies with their systems of production, consumption, division of work, stratification. Writing in the 1740s his work marks the summit of pre-bourgeois social theory : after Montesquieu the concept of civil society – that is, the sphere of property relationships, social classes, production – comes to dominate social theory in the political economy and history of the late eighteenth century. Thus although Montesquieu can write, in a manner close to the materialism of Smith and Marx, that 'Mankind are influenced by various causes : by the climate . . . religion . . . laws, by the maxims of government, by precedents, morals and customs; from this is formed the general spirit of the nations', he could not extend this mechanical causal analysis to social institutions, the social role of the division of labour and social stratification. He shows little awareness of the problem of social change and has no theory of the transition from one society to another. The mode of production is not pivotal to Montesquieu's analysis and his theory remains one-sided and partial.[12]

In the work of Smith this partial approach is replaced by an awareness that bourgeois society is a complex whole which is not reducible simply to politics; Smith's emphasis lies with its civil elements, private property, division of labour and social class. The main focus is no longer on the strictly empirical, on establishing causal connections, but rather grasping society as an historical process in which the constituent elements are analysed in terms of the whole; and for the first time in social theory history is seen at work within and through society, for the different elements are analysed from the standpoint of change, of transition. But although Smith grasped society as an *historical* totality it yet remains a 'mechanical totality' in that the whole is dominated by one factor, property, thus leaving no room for the dialectical interplay between 'base' and 'superstructure'. Thus Smith concludes that social change occurs only through the unintended consequences of individual actions and not as a result of the inherent contradictions within the system itself. Social change becomes individualised as well as unseen and unplanned : the individual's own selfish interests turn into the general interest. Smith therefore retains the standpoint of the individual within his concept of totality.[13]

Smith's work may have influenced Hegel, but it was Marx, writing in the wake of the massive class struggles in England and France during the 1820s and 1830s – at a time when a definite socialist ideology had developed (Robert Owen, Charles Fourier, William Thompson) – who grasped and went beyond the contradictions implicit in bourgeois social theory. Like Hegel he repudiated social atomism arguing that the isolated individual is a mere fiction : 'The egoistic individual of bourgeois society may in his silly imagination and petrified abstraction puff himself up into a self-sufficient atom . . . into an absolute and blessed creature, independent and free from any need',[14] but the actual, historical development of bourgeois society contradicts its own ideology :

> But the epoch which produces this standpoint, namely that of the solitary individual, is precisely the epoch of the (as yet) most highly

39

developed social (according to this standpoint, general) relations.
Man is . . . an animal that can be individualised only within
society. Production by a solitary individual outside society . . . is
just as preposterous as the development of speech without individuals who live together and talk to one another.[15]

Social atomism is rejected and the standpoint of Marx's social
theory becomes that of the socialised individual of capitalist society
whose private existence is wholly dependent on his group and class
relations. The individual exists only as part of a whole – family,
occupational group, class. Both society and the individual are to be
understood and analysed from this point of view.

Marx's method is summed up concisely in his 1859 'Preface' to
the *Contribution to the Critique of Political Economy*. Human
society, he argues, originates in the material conditions of existence,
the 'totality' of which Hegel and the eighteenth-century philosophers
and historians embraced 'within the terms civil society'. The 'guiding
thread', Marx went on, to the vast studies he had carried out during
the 1850s into economic, social and political history was that in the
course of social production men

. . . inevitably enter into definite relations, which are independent
of their will, namely relations of production appropriate to a given
stage in the development of their material forces of production.
The totality of these relations of production constitutes the economic structure of society, the real foundations, on which arises a
legal and political structure and to which correspond definite
forms of social consciousness.

Thus man's consciousness is determined by his material existence and
at a definite historical point a conflict is generated between the
forces of production and the relations of production, between capital
and labour. Writing in somewhat mechanical terms Marx suggests
that the forms of development turn into 'fetters' and social revolution
becomes necessary to transform a now stagnant society.[16] He goes on
to link the 'superstructure' – legal, political, religious institutions –
with the economic 'base' in an apparent causal nexus. It is this

totality which dominates Marx's social theory: production, distribution, exchange and consumption are 'links of a single whole' and in the scientific analysis of each it becomes absolutely essential to relate them to one another and to the whole: 'There is an interaction between the various aspects. Such interaction takes place in any organic entity.'[17]

But in what sense is this analysis different from the mechanical materialist analyses of eighteenth-century political economy and history? One of the most remarkable texts in the development of materialist social theory is John Millar's 'Introduction' to his study of social stratification written some eighty years before Marx's 'Preface'. Millar's formulations are strikingly similar to those of Marx as he attempts to explain the material foundations of governments, constitutions and legal systems. Social research, Millar argued, must point to

> ... differences of situation ... fertility and barrenness of the soil, the nature of its productions, the species of labour requisite for procuring subsistence, population, mutual transactions. . . . The variety that frequently occurs in these and other such other particulars, must have a prodigious influence upon the great body of the people; as by giving a peculiar direction to their inclinations and pursuits, it must be productive of corresponding habits, dispositions and ways of thinking.[18]

Here, in this astonishingly precise text, Millar outlines his *totality*, which, like that of his contemporary Smith, is essentially static: everything is related to a determinate causal nexus and the 'superstructure' exercises no autonomy. Social action is ruled out (apart from the unintended of course) and the subjective element, consciousness, is entirely eliminated.

Critics have argued that Marx commits the same mistakes in his 1859 statement. But in what way does Marx's approach differ significantly from Millar's? Is Marx's totality a mechanical totality too? Of course Marx had a profound grasp of dialectics, of the contradictory relationship between man, the world, social consciousness, and from what has been argued in the previous chapter it should be

41

clear that the subjective element sharply differentiates him from Millar and Smith. Marx's text quoted above does seem mechanical, but other texts, both from his early and later writings show how, in the interests of *precision*, Marx had seemingly subverted his essentially dialectical totality into its opposite. For the dialectical thinker society is never static, but constantly expanding through contradictions and disturbances which have become resolved in new syntheses. A totality is thus never immobile but in a constant state of tension between parts and whole. For Marx, the concept of totality embraces social, economic and political institutions as well as all forms of social action, and a tense balance always exists between consciousness and social structure. Marx's totality is one which stresses the role of human *praxis*, of social consciousness, of men transforming the social world and it is these actions, when they take revolutionary form, which conflict with economic and political institutions. To use the language of modern functionalism, Marx's totality is a 'moving equilibrium'.

But totality has another meaning as a methodological precept lying at the heart of the dialectical method. Marx's method is in essence a constant movement from the part to the whole and from the whole to the part. For a fact is something which is not *given*, a thing which is simply there as Durkheim's sociology assumes for example. The isolated *fact* has meaning only within the context of the whole of which it forms an inseparable part :

. . . a dress becomes really a dress only by being worn, a house which is uninhabited is indeed not really a house; in other words a product as distinct from a simple natural object manifests itself as a product, *becomes* a product, only in consumption. It is only consumption which, by destroying the product, gives it the finishing touch, for the product is a product, not because it is materialised activity, but only in so far as it is an object for the active subject.[19]

What Marx expresses here is that analysis of facts is meaningful only in terms of *mediation* and their relationship with wholes. There is no such thing as an external fact which researchers can approach objectively simply because, to quote Voltaire's Doctor Pangloss, 'everything is as it is and cannot be otherwise'. Facts are not immediately given, concrete things, but exist within the specific totality of human, social relationships and institutions and are mediated by human consciousness and *praxis*.

In what way does this help us to understand Marx's sociology? Much of the confusion which surrounds Marx's work is related to a misunderstanding of his methodological procedure, and critics read *Capital*, for example, unaware of the problems presented in interpretation by Marx's distinct approach. In the 'Preface' he wrote that 'in the analysis of economic forms neither microscopes nor chemical reagents are of use. The force of abstraction must replace both.'[20] In a formal sense Marx's method is close to that of his economic predecessors, Smith and Ricardo. Indeed the American Marxist, Paul Sweezy, has suggested that Marx was 'a strong adherent of the abstract-deductive method . . . characteristic of the Ricardian school',[21] but this formulation tends to be misleading for the whole point is the way in which Marx developed beyond the methods of classical political economy. The decisive text for understanding Marx's method is the 1857 'Introduction' to the *Contribution to the Critique of Political Economy* (never published during his lifetime and intended as part of the unfinished *Grundrisse*), in some twenty pages of which Marx outlines, in a remarkably precise way, his methodological approach to social and economic analysis. It is a text of great importance and yet in the numerous analyses of Marx's sociology it has largely been ignored. In order to appreciate Marx's method and the critical way it diverges from nineteenth-century sociological methodology some discussion of the 1857 text is necessary.

III

Marx begins by arguing that superficially the correct scientific approach in social and economic analysis is that which starts from 'real and concrete elements' as the classical economists did by beginning with population. Such a procedure, however, is wrong for the apparently concrete is in reality abstract :

43

Population is an abstraction if, for instance, one disregards the classes of which it is composed. These classes in turn remain empty terms if one does not know the factors on which they depend, e.g. wage, labour, capital and so on. These presuppose exchange, division of labour, prices, etc. For example, capital is nothing without wage labour, without value, money, price, etc. If one were to take population as the point of departure, it would be a very vague notion of a complex whole and through closer definition one would arrive analytically at increasingly simple concepts; from imaginary concrete terms one would move to more and more tenuous abstractions until one reached the most simple definitions. From here it would be necessary to make the journey again in the opposite direction until one arrived once more at the concept of population which is this time not a vague notion of a whole, but a totality comprising many determinations and relations.[22]

Here is the essence of dialectical methodology : social analysis consists of a constant shuttling between the parts and the whole, not simply in one direction but in both. It is not sufficient to begin social analysis with concrete facts as such but rather with abstract wholes. Classical political economy was correct to begin with population but wrong to see it as a concrete fact and not as an abstract whole which required filling with specific social, economic and political content. This method, writes Marx, 'of advancing from the abstract to the concrete is simply the way in which thinking assimilates the concrete and reproduces it as a concrete mental category'. For the simplest concrete economic category, exchange value for example, is always part of a complex totality comprising population which in turn, under specific historical conditions, produces definite communities, families, states : 'The concrete concept is concrete because it is a synthesis of many definitions, thus representing the unity of diverse aspects. . . . Exchange value cannot exist except as an abstract, *unilateral*, relation of an already existing concrete organic whole.'[23]

The part, then, cannot be abstracted from the whole and sociologically examined apart from it and then mechanically inserted again after analysis. When Marx writes that 'the subject, society, must always be envisaged . . . as the pre-condition of comprehension' he means simply that no category on its own is sufficient as the starting-point for adequate sociological analysis. Marx provides an example drawn from Hegel : in Jurisprudence, ownership, 'the simplest legal definition of the subject', seems the correct point of departure, but 'no ownership exists . . . before the family, or the relations of master and servant are evolved, and these are much more concrete relations'. But they are only concrete within the context of a whole, a totality.[24] For the fundamental principle of dialectical theory is that empirical facts must be integrated into a whole or they remain abstract, superficial, and theoretically misleading.

The abstract knowledge of the part, particular facts, can be made concrete, then, through studying its relation with other parts and the whole. Methodologically, this means that it is wrong to begin social analysis from immediately recognisable and isolated facts (particular families, 'deviant' groups, occupational groups) because these pre-suppose a specific society, economic structure, etc., of which the groups form a necessary part. To study the working class in isolation from the class structure as a whole, and the wider economic, social and political structure is to commit the methodological errors which Marx's 'Introduction' criticised : a study of the working class in terms of specific occupational categories (car workers and craft workers in a particular locality, for example) which generalises to the working class as a whole on the basis of factual data gathered, is both to ignore the historical dimension involved in any analysis of social class, but equally important, to isolate a part from its whole and to remain with an abstract, one-sided relation. The many 'determinations and relations' of class are missed entirely; the isolated segment is then inserted into a 'totality' at the conclusion of the study and general laws and tendencies applying to the whole working class postulated.

Marx's method in *Capital* is wholly different. Discussing production Marx argued that usually it is thought of in terms of specific persons or historical periods. But all stages of production have certain landmarks in common – common purposes. '*Production in general* is an abstraction, but a sensible abstraction in so far as it actually emphasises and defines the common aspects and thus avoids repetition.' Marx goes on to say that certain of these features can be found in the 'most modern as well as the most ancient epochs'. The relation between production and distribution, exchange and consumption can be established only by isolating the specific determinations common to all periods of production. The point lies in grasping the ways in which these features depart from the general and common since in this lies the secret of their development. For while all stages of production share similar categories which through analysis become the 'general categories', the 'so-called *general conditions* of all and any production . . . are nothing but the abstract conceptions which do not define any of the actual historical stages of production'.[25]

Marx's method, then, is to begin from a pre-given whole which will be necessarily abstract (population, state, family, etc.) and to abstract further the elements which comprise this whole, and then through a process of successive approximations relate them organically to the whole. Thus in the first volumes of *Capital*, Marx abstracts and simplifies capitalist society to one basic relation, capital and labour, its 'pure essence', arguing that should this prove to be the dominant relation then certain laws, trends and thus predictions can be made. It is only in this way that many of Marx's predictions on the development of capitalism can be properly understood.

It may be useful at this point to indicate how an inadequate grasp of Marx's method can lead to a complete misunderstanding of Marx's social theory. The example chosen is the famous 'Marxist' law of immiserisation.

In his *Philosophy of History* Hegel had argued that the scientific understanding of history rested on the ability of science to distinguish the essential from the inessential. As we have seen, the 'leading thread' of Marx's studies in the 1850s had led him to the view that to understand history and society it was essential to analyse the modes of production of different societies, since it was largely from the economic structure that class relations, class conflict and ideology necessarily flowed. Thus for Marx, grasping society as an historical product made by man in determinate situations and relationships, the essential elements were those which underpinned and expressed themselves in class conflict, and those factors which tended to negate the existing social order, especially the conflict generated by wage labour and private capital, socialised work and private ownership of property. In *The Communist Manifesto* this basic contradiction is expressed in purely dichotomic terms as a conflict between proletariat and bourgeoisie; and society is characterised as splitting into 'two hostile camps' with wholly irreconcilable interests, a situation which must eventuate in civil war and the transition to socialism. Yet while Marx abstracts and isolates the labour/capital relation, he rarely discusses social classes and it is not until the third volume of *Capital* that the sociology of class is attempted and only then in fragmentary form. The reasons for this omission, in a work which ideologically celebrates the collapse of capitalism through class conflict, will appear strange only if Marx's methodological approach is misunderstood. In *Capital* Marx, through 'the power of abstraction', has isolated the 'essential' relation of labour and capital reducing it to its 'purest forms' free from all other determinate relations which might influence its specific historical character. 'For there are here only two classes : the working class, disposing only of its labour-power, and the capitalist class, which has a monopoly of the social means of production and money.'[26] Marx's model thus assumes that the 'laws of capitalist production operate in their pure form'[27] and therefore :

(1) With the labour/capital relation assumed as the dominant element underpinning the development and structure of capitalist society Marx's analysis eliminates the 'superstructure' from exercising any determinate influence.

(2) The capital/labour relation is reduced to its most simple form. Capitalists and workers are seen as standard types, 'the personifications of economic categories, embodiments of particular class relations and class interests'.

In the first volume of *Capital* Marx analyses the labour/capital relation as an exchange relation in which money is transformed into capital through the buying and selling of one commodity – labour power. The first volume operates at this high level of abstraction – the simple abstraction – and the material collected

47

illustrates the dominance of surplus value and exploitation for society as a whole. Volume II deepens the analysis as Marx discusses the reproduction of capital, the processes of production and circulation, all of which form the theory of the accumulation of capital. In volume III capitalist production *as a whole* is analysed embracing the theories of surplus value and capital accumulation. It is absolutely crucial to grasp Marx's method : he has provided civil society (the state is not analysed at all) with the most favourable conditions for the exchange of commodities and expunged all complicating circumstances and elements ('determinations'). Thus the abstractions which underlie the first volume – that commodities exchange according to the cost of producing them in standard man hours, the complete absence of monopoly, the fact that the entire economic surplus is appropriated by the capitalist class, society as a simple two-class model, the exclusion of external trade – all these simplify the analysis. It is not until the subsequent volumes that Marx removes them, introducing more complex elements as he approximates to a less 'pure' model of reality. All parts are dialectically related to the whole, the abstract is made concrete.

It follows from this that the tendencies and laws which Marx enunciates in *Capital* are not to be taken as concrete predictions about the future for, as was pointed out in the previous chapter, they may be 'modified' by 'other circumstances'. For Marx, capitalism constituted a differentiated totality, the parts of which, including those elements comprising the 'superstructure' are bound together as a contradictory unity. The importance of social and political institutions for 'modifying' Marx's generalisations cannot be exaggerated. Thus Marx's theory of 'capitalist crisis' has frequently been misinterpreted as a theory of inevitable class conflict and economic and social breakdown. There are passages in the first volume of *Capital* which lend support to this view, but when the concept of crisis is analysed within the context of totality a different interpretation is called for :

> From time to time the conflict of antagonistic tendencies finds vent in crises . . . momentary and forcible solutions of the existing contradictions . . . violent eruptions which for a time restore the

disturbed equilibrium. The contradiction . . . consists in that the capitalist mode of production involves a tendency towards absolute development of the productive forces, regardless of the value and surplus-value it contains, and regardless of the social conditions under which capitalist production takes place; while on the other hand, its aim is to preserve the value of the existing capital and promote its self-expansion to the highest limit. . . .[28]

Clearly Marx does not hold a straightforward breakdown theory. Indeed, his emphasis on consciousness and the conservative role of ideology in society point emphatically towards *praxis* if the capitalist equilibrium is to be shattered. Marx never tires of repeating that social change is not a mechanical process which casts man as mere onlooker but involves him, through his values and social consciousness, in action. Marx's concept of totality is not a passive aggregate of interrelated institutions, therefore, but an active living reality. It is the organic relationship between man's conscious class activity and the institutions within which he lives that constitute the 'other circumstances'. Perhaps the most important are the following :

(1) The social democratic political parties which developed in the latter half of the nineteenth century and directly influenced the growth of a revolutionary consciousness within the European working class – these parties constitute one of the most significant mediations of consciousness more especially as they command the loyalty of a vast section of the working class;

(2) the complex modes of ideological legitimation in which the dominant values are ratified by appeal to the classless universals of the state, nation and national interest;

(3) the trade unions which seek reforms within the existing structure, fostering a pragmatic, conservative and piecemeal adaptation to the *status quo*;

(4) the presence or absence of a revolutionary socialist party with organic links with the working class.

The totality of relations, then, is always historically concrete and specific, lived not fixed : in some circumstances the specific historical situation generates opportunities for political reformism and, experiencing this through generations as an integral part of the labour movement, the working class may indeed become 'respectable' and bear no similarity whatever to 'the revolutionary proletariat'. Society, its institutions, norms, values, practices is not a vast 'totalising' structure bound to some 'possible' future but a densely structured whole in constant change through men's actions.

I V

The concept of totality found in Smith, Hegel and Marx finds no echo in the subsequent bourgeois social theory of the nineteenth century. In sociology the tendency became one of substituting abstract laws and processes, as in the conflict sociology of Ludwig Gumplowicz (1838–1909), where the concept of conflict is so generalised that social development is no longer analysed in terms of concrete historical forms but as a series of vague ahistorical abstractions.[29] Sociological positivism, with its emphasis on precise, useful, factual knowledge had the further effect of turning sociology into purely statistical inquiries on such issues as 'The condition of the working class' (Le Play in France, Charles Booth in England). The result was either a fragmented and partial point of view or a specious philosophical cum historical theory of 'progress' and change.

Twentieth-century thought has largely recovered the concept. The problems raised by the category of totality find expression in the work of such diverse thinkers as Weber, Lukács, Mannheim and Sartre. Weber is the key figure here : there can be no doubt that he exercised a significant influence on both Lukács and Mannheim and the subsequent development of the sociology of knowledge. In particular Weber's critique of positivism leads directly to the question of relativism within social theory : Lukács and Mannheim will be discussed in more detail in the following chapter and this chapter will conclude with a brief analysis of Weber's position.

Weber rejects the positivistic maxim that the methodologies of the natural and the social sciences are identical; social science is more concerned with subjective elements, 'ideal' or 'spiritual' phenomena which are unique and unrepeatable. Weber emphasises that subjectivity does not imply subjectivist sociology, for the 'ideal' elements of culture (values, beliefs etc.) have to be analysed as objectively as purely economic factors. The method he proposed for this task was that of the 'ideal type', an approach which many sociologists have argued brings him close to Marx's own methodology. Indeed, Weber himself suggests that 'all specifically Marxian "laws" and development constructs' are ideal types.[30]

Weber defines an ideal type as '. . . the one-sided *accentuation* of one or more points of view . . . the synthesis of a great many diffuse, discrete, more or less present and occasionally absent *concrete* individual phenomena, which are arranged according to those one-sidedly emphasised viewpoints into a unified *analytical* construct.'[31] The ideal type, therefore, is not a description of a specific phenomenon but a construction by the sociologist of its essential properties combined into one model. The elements used to build up this ideal model are abstracted from many diverse sources – different historical periods and specific phenomena (the ideal type bureaucracy is built up from essential elements found in the bureaucracies of feudal, capitalist and socialist society). The ideal type, therefore, embodies 'the one-sided accentuation of one or more points of view', a perspective of 'total reality'. But how is the ideal type constructed? How does the researcher decide what is essential or non-essential, significant or insignificant? The answer to these questions raises the problem of epistemology, for part of Weber's argument is that the concepts used in social science hinge on *a priori* value judgements outside the sphere of science itself.

Weber argues that only a tiny fragment of reality is knowable and that the whole remains hidden, a methodological agnosticism which leads him to write, pessimistically, 'that the path of human destiny cannot but appal him who surveys a section of it [and] he will do well to keep his small personal commentaries to himself . . . unless he knows himself to be called and gifted to give them expression in artistic or prophetic form'.[32]

There is here a critical difference between the work of Marx and Weber: Marx's social theory is built around a dialectical and materialist epistemology; Weber's methodology springs from a theory of knowledge based on the idealist tradition of Kant, in particular the neo-Kantianism which dominated German intellectual life at the turn of the century. Philosophically neo-Kantianism was anti-materialist. The basic argument against the materialist standpoint was that human reality, or experience (Kant's 'phenomenal world'), was mere appearance, fluid, shifting, constantly changing and thus by definition incapable of providing the guide to the truth. Reality was thus equivalent to this ambiguous realm of experience, of facts. But lying behind the facts, hidden from the ordinary observer and consciousness, was the real essence, what Kant called the unknowable 'thing in itself', reflected in the facts themselves as they are presented to human consciousness and experience. The task of science, then, lay in grasping the essence, Kant's 'noumena', through divesting its phenomenal forms of all its empirical content, thus leaving only its true essence, its 'form'.

Neo-Kantianism raises other problems: the dualism of facts and values and the relation between concept and the reality it describes. Weber argued that social science could never evaluate ends but only render explicit those ideas which underpinned the ends themselves: 'It is self-evident that one of the most important tasks of every science of cultural life is to arrive at a rational understanding of these "ideas" for which men either really or allegedly struggle.'[33] It is not the task of social science to judge ends, that is the work of philosophy. In contrast, Marx argues that values and facts are not separated into two mutually exclusive domains, but are bound together in an indissoluble dialectical union. It was not a question of grasping the 'good' or the 'bad' sides of things but of their movement, interconnectedness, the dialectical transformations, of analysing values as an essential part of the struggle within bourgeois society between capital and labour: socialism and socialist values co-exist with capitalist values and are in conflict with them. For Marx, values were social products relating to man's activity in shaping the world and bound to particular economic or political interests. A human value is both a reflection of man's attempts to master the natural and social world and an active force in *praxis*, a mediation of the 'facts'.

Weber, however, argues that the method of the 'cultural sciences' lies in analysing life in terms of its cultural significance, but not all parts are worth investigating because of what Weber calls their 'value relevance'. Culture is defined as a 'finite segment of the meaningless infinity of the world process, a segment on which human beings confer meaning and significance'. But what of the choice? Who decides the question of 'value relevance?' Weber continually reiterates that significance is universal, things are significant for all of 'us', as if there existed a commonly accepted structure of values both for individuals and society. Thus he writes that knowledge of cultural reality is only knowledge from 'particular points of view' and that 'only a small portion of existing concrete reality is coloured by our value-conditioned interest and it alone is significant to us', an individualistic point of view modified by the fact that the investigator is 'determined by the evaluative ideas' of his 'age'.[34]

For Marx, of course, the 'evaluative ideas' of any epoch would simply mean the dominant ideas of the ruling class and therefore significance would mean only significance from the perspective of capitalist society and its dominant class. Weber's methodology is shot through with problems : he accepts the existence of 'values' and thus of 'significance' without disclosing their social basis; the values simply exist and as such are irreducible to particular interests.

Weber's individualistic approach is thus clear. For him the existence of values determines the way the researcher will construct his object of study, 'the concrete *individual* viewpoint which directs our interest at any given time'.[35] But this raises the question of perspective. The fact that many, presumably contradictory, values exist implies no one scientifically valid perspective and in distinguishing the essential from the inessential in the construction of ideal types wholly subjective criteria are unavoidable. In fact the problem of the multiplicity of standpoints which follows from Weber's agnostic method is never raised (although it is taken up by Lukács and Mannheim) and his 'perspectivism' means that there can never be a theory of theory, only that there are different points of view, different values both individual and collective ('of the age'). Thus when Weber writes that in order to make sense out of the flux which is reality a concept must be 'highly selective' and valid only 'within the scope of its own postulates' he implies a thoroughgoing relativism and subjectivism :

Life with its irrational reality and its store of possible meanings is inexhaustible. The *concrete* form in which value relevance occurs remains perpetually in flux, ever subject to change in the dimly seen future of human culture. The light which emanates from these highest evaluative ideas always falls on an ever changing finite segment of the vast chaotic stream of events, which flows away through time.[36]

Weber's method has effectively eliminated the concept of totality from social theory. We are left with scepticism and a mere 'slice' of reality; the whole, including the social foundation of values, remains unknowable. Indeed, there are passages in Weber's work which come close to the highly subjective postulates of methodological individualism. Writing of socialist society, he argues that sociological investigation begins from those motives disposing 'the individual members and participants in this socialistic community to behave in such a way that the community came into being in the first place and that it continues to exist'. Significantly, he adds that analysis 'which proceeds from the whole to the parts can accomplish only a preliminary preparation for this investigation', and therefore its concepts will be abstract and lack 'fullness of concrete content', a disadvantage Weber sees remedied by 'a greater precision' of sociological concepts.[37] The concepts are the 'pure' types, ghostly abstractions empty of the rich, historical material which remains at the centre of Marx's category of totality. For Marx's 'pure model' of capitalism is in fact *historically specific*, relating concretely to a particular form of commodity production and the extraction of surplus value and not to production in general. In his discussion of method Marx is categorical: the 'general conditions' of production (the equivalent of Weber's ideal type) is an abstract conception without any determinations, and therefore *empty* and useless for social science : 'The conclusion which follows from this is . . . that production, exchange and consumption . . . are links of a single whole, different aspects of one unit.'[38]

Weber's ideal types remain ahistorical abstractions; his method is to compare one with another, the ideal type of bureaucracy with a real historically specific form. Thus the essence of Marx's dialectical methodology – that the abstract is made concrete only when integrated into a concrete whole from which the initial abstraction was originally made, a process involving a constant shuttling between parts and whole – forms no part of Weber's sociological method. Marx's 'pure capitalism' is never an 'ideal type' precisely because capitalist contradictions are historically specific. The fundamental contradiction, the conflict between private and socialised production, is set within a complex totality built up through the elimination of simplifying assumptions (the 'pure' model) so that its many determinations are concretely specified. To put the matter more precisely : the contradiction exists through the complex determinations of economic, social and political structures so much so that only 'vulgar Marxism' attributes solely to the economic factor the power of change through contradiction. It is the movement of many factors within the totality which characterises Marx's method from Weber's, a balance of contradictory forces (determinations) subsisting in equilibrium and broken only by conscious class action.

v

But paradoxically Weber is right in his basic argument that one cannot know the whole, that totality is an illusion. Indeed, Engels once suggested that the analysis of any contemporary social formation must always be in the nature of rough approximations to 'the truth' not the least because the gathering and compilation of the complex statistical data essential for scientific study lags behind the practical historical events.[39] This limitation suggests that Marxism, far from constituting an exact science is imprecise and provisional in its powers of prediction, more so as the subjective element of consciousness must always be taken into account. None the less, totality remains a valuable category and methodological guide to the relation of parts to wholes, to living, historically concrete forces.

A more subjective sense of totality, however, has emerged in recent years in sociological phenomenology and in the existentialised form of Marxism propounded by Sartre. For both, totality is defined in terms of consciousness :

To act means to modify the figure of the given in such a way that a field is structured which, to the actor, constitutes a meaningful *totality*. This totality is the presupposition for any particular meaningful action within it. In other words, the totality is broken up into finite provinces of meaning, each of which is the scene of particular types of action. While man, as an acting being, is constantly engaged in structuring the world as a meaningful totality (since otherwise he could not meaningfully act within it), this process is never completed. Totality, then, is never a *fait accompli*, but is always in process of being constructed.[40]

This theme of man as an active, creative agent is one which informs Marx's social theory in both the early and later writings; but it is a concept securely anchored within a structured and historical definition of society. Of course, consciousness is not passive and in this the phenomenologists have badly misunderstood Marx. Their commitment to his explicitly *humanist* writings and denigration of the later work is built around the false view that in *Capital* a mechanical theory of consciousness replaces the former emphasis on dialectics. To be sure, Marx argues that consciousness is formed on a material basis comprising external social and economic conditions which it both reflects, comprehends and strives to go beyond through *praxis* : but such comprehension is possible only through class-conscious action guided by Marxist theory. When Sartre writes, therefore, that 'Marxism ought to study real men in depth, not dissolve them in a bath of sulphuric acid' and avoid the 'totalizing' of living human realities into impersonal collectivities such as the bourgeoisie, imperialism and class struggle, he is criticising 'vulgar', positivist Marxism rather than Marx.[41] He argues that a reductionist conception of totality eliminates the real, lived relations and the corresponding concrete mediations : the complex levels of economy and culture disappear if subsumed under collective terms and the 'fundamental determinations' are lost.

Sartre opposes the reduction of individuals to the status of group or class representative. Like the phenomenologists he criticises the mechanical, ahistorical conceptions of totality found in functionalist sociology and some branches of social psychology (Kurt Lewin's

56

Gestalt theory for example). Totality is a dynamic and expanding concept reflecting man's historical activity in constantly changing the social world and himself. In this sense totality is never an absolute (as with Hegel) but what Sartre calls 'detotalized'. Totality is never complete : man's *praxis* is never ending and therefore totality 'exists at best only in the form of a detotalized totality'.[42]

As we have seen, Marx's method employs a dialectical movement from abstractions (collectivities) to their historically specific concrete content and the method seeks to integrate these enriched concepts within a total structure (society as a whole). Thus the bourgeoisie as an abstraction is also a totality; the various social strata within it are parts of this whole; but within these exist other sub-divisions, groups and communities. The point is that totality is always a part of something larger and the part is simultaneously a totality. But because Sartre defines totality in subjective terms, made by man through *praxis*, his stated ideal of locating man specifically and historically in modern society must remain a pure chimera. For what Sartre does is to resurrect the ghost of historicism, that history, working through the individual consciousness, is engaged on a vast 'totalizing movement which gathers together my neighbour, myself, and the environment in the synthetic unity of an objectification in process'. And this movement is 'progressive', linked organically to the future : 'The dialectical movement . . . enables us to understand that the ends of human activity are not mysterious entities (but) . . . represent simply the surpassing and the maintaining of the given in an act which goes from the present toward the future.'[43] A transcendent philosophy, however, forms no part of Marx's methodology and social theory : men make history historically, which means under specific social, economic and political conditions. History is not a force outside these specific structures and man is not an instrument of a 'totalizing' movement even if he supposedly makes it himself. Sartre's historicism and fundamentally idealist concept of totality is ultimately derived from Lukács and not from Marx. The following chapter will explore in more detail the category of totality as it relates to the problem of ideology and knowledge.

3

IDEOLOGY AND THE
SOCIOLOGY OF KNOWLEDGE

Marx's social theory has been described so far in terms of *praxis*, dialectics and totality. The broad argument is that contrary to many critics (both friendly and hostile) Marxism is not a species of mechanical materialism or positivism. Those who interpret Marxism in this mechanical sense tend either to exaggerate Engels's influence or misread the mature writings of Marx. Such critics usually seize upon the well-known distinction made by Marx and Engels of 'base' and 'superstructure' (economy and culture), and the related concept of ideology, to show how this necessarily produces a mechanical, 'copy', 'transcript' theory of knowledge : in short, that the economic structure of society creates knowledge as a social product which, in the context of class relations, means illusions and errors − ideology. One writer has suggested, somewhat extravagantly, that 'Marx debunks as ideological the entire history of philosophy from Plato to Hegel', and that with the exception of the physical sciences 'all existing knowledge has been debunked as ideological'.[1] It is true that in *The German Ideology* Marx and Engels argued that ideas enjoy no history outside the specific societies in which they first develop and that they embody practical interests, especially the economic, thus producing the distortions of reality termed ideology. The concept of ideology here clearly describes the social and historical world; ideological thinking turns real empirical processes into illusions and fantasies. This suggests that all knowledge is interest bound, a 'false consciousness' and clearly a threat to the ideas of scientific objectivity and impartiality. The sociology of knowledge largely springs out of this problem : how to reconcile knowledge as social *praxis* with knowledge as objective and scientifically attainable.

Marxism is often credited with discovering the modern concept of ideology by relating specific types of thought to determinate social, political and economic conditions,[2] and showing how the material 'base' of society necessarily generates a 'superstructure' of ideas and values. Some critics have gone further and argued that in situating knowledge within the economic infrastructure Marx and Engels succeeded in turning all thought into a mechanical reflection of class interests; knowledge thus becomes epiphenomenal, with no active role to play and ideology a mere passive mirror reflection of external economic phenomena. Max Weber's sociology of religion may be read as an attempt to 'round out' what he took to be a mechanical reflection theory so that ideas, ideology as religious consciousness, exercise an important motivational and thus active factor in social change. Defining the capitalist spirit as 'that attitude which seeks profit rationally and systematically', Weber argued that capitalist development was not explicable solely in terms of economic factors since such an explanation minimises the most crucial factor in social change – the actions of men. Why did the capitalist entrepreneurs act as they did? What factors motivated them to a lifetime of profit-seeking?

> Concerning the doctrine of the more naive historical materialism, that such ideas originate as a reflection or superstructure of economic situations . . . it will suffice for our purpose to call attention to the fact that without doubt in the country of Benjamin Franklin's birth (Massachusetts) the spirit of capitalism . . . was present before the capitalist order.[3]

Thus the origins of capitalism must be sought for not only in economics but, equally important, in the ideas which men form of the social world and their duties within it. The Protestant religion, especially its ascetic varieties such as Calvinism, through its concept of the 'calling' and the requirements of a worldly programme of 'good works' as a guarantee of election, provided the ethical and thus the psychological motive for economic activity. It is in these senses that Calvinism is not a passive reflection of economic conditions but an active ideological orientation to social action and therefore a crucial factor in social change. This is Weber's definition of ideology, but it must be noted that he was mistaken in ascribing a purely mechanical conception to Marx, for in both Marx's and Engels's writings ideology does not function simply as a distorted, passive reflection of reality but is itself a highly potent source of political legitimacy and social change.

In *The German Ideology* Marx and Engels argued that with the development of capitalism specialised division of work becomes the general condition throughout the entire social structure. The division of society into social classes, as opposed to the rigid estate structure of feudal society, produces a further separation into sub-groups based on industry, commerce and land; and within the ruling class a further differentiation takes place, in which a special intellectual stratum emerges whose social function lies in producing the ideas which underpin social order and consensus. When Marx writes that the ruling ideas of each historical period are those of the ruling class, he implies not a conspiracy of the rich over the poor, but that the ruling class genuinely believes in the rightness of its ideas for *the whole of society*. When the bourgeoisie has supplanted the semi-feudal traditional and landed social strata as the ruling class, then it must justify its domination not through the claims of traditionalism, as did previous rulers, but by appeals to a secular and pragmatic ideology. With the development of capitalism, ideology becomes an increasingly important element in achieving social cohesion and political legitimacy, especially as capitalism itself generates anti-capitalist social theories, socialism and Marxism, which, based on the proletariat, continually challenge bourgeois authority.

Ideology is defined by Marx and Engels as reflecting social, political and economic life in such a way that distortion, illusions and a 'false consciousness' of the social world are produced. For Marx ideology was closely bound up with alienation, mystification and reification, for an alienated social consciousness is one which has become dominated by the world of things, in which reality is no longer seen as a human reality but one divested of human attributes. To the ideological thinker the world appears 'upside down', as for those who believe that religion offers an adequate guide to an understanding of the social world. The genuinely religious consciousness is one which defines human life as the extension of God rather than the materialist doctrine which sees religion as a social product. In this definition of ideology Marx and Engels come close to a mechanical theory in their emphasis that the ideas which men carry in their minds are mere 'reflexes and echoes' of the 'life-process' :

The phantoms formed in the human brain are . . . sublimates of . . . material life-processes, which is [sic] empirically verifiable and bound to material premises. Morality, religion, metaphysics, all the rest of ideology and their corresponding forms of consciousness, thus no longer retain their semblance of independence. They have no history, no development; but men, developing their material production and their material intercourse, alter, along with this real existence, their thinking and the products of their thinking. Life is not determined by consciousness but consciousness by life.[4]

In the frequently quoted 'Preface' to the *Contribution to the Critique of Political Economy*, a similar thesis of strict causal interaction between the economic base and the ideological 'superstructure' is put forward : the forces of production 'constitutes the economic structure of society, the real foundation, on which arises a legal and political superstructure and to which correspond definite forms of social consciousness. The mode of production of material life conditions the general process of social, political and intellectual life'.[5] It is in this apparently deterministic sense that Engels frequently uses the concept of ideology : 'Ideology is a process accomplished by the so-called thinker consciously indeed, but with a false consciousness. The real motives impelling him remain unknown to him, otherwise it would not be an ideological process at all.'[6] On this basis it seems that all thought would qualify as ideology. And if that is so how is it possible for Marx and Engels to maintain that *their* standpoint is non-ideological? Engels's argument seems to suggest a thorough-going relativism, a position which he himself never sustained for he clearly believed in the *non-ideological advances* made in ninteenth-century natural science. Critics, of course, are quick to point out the imprecise nature of the whole formula and the ambiguity of criteria for the true and the false : is ideology to include logic and mathematics for example? But Engels is quite clear that although ideology can have no independent life apart from society, no history as autonomous reality, none the less, there is a *partial* autonomy and, although an inversion of the real world and therefore a 'false consciousness', ideology is *not* a passive reflection of the economic structure of society. Weber's argument that Marx and Engels defined ideology as mere epiphenomena is clearly untenable. Engels is quite specific :

> The economic situation is the basis, but the various elements of the superstructure : political forms of the class struggle . . . juristic, philosophical theories, religious views . . . also exercise their influence upon the course of the historical struggles and in many cases preponderate their form.

There is, writes Engels, mutual interaction of all elements, but in the last resort 'the economic movement finally asserts itself as necessary'.[7]

Like other of Engels's formulations his analysis of ideology is sometimes couched in mechanical terms and is full of ambiguity. After all, to say that the economic factor is the ultimate arbiter of *everything* is to say precisely nothing and to eliminate dialectics completely. When, for example, he argues that the ways in which an ideology is accepted hinge on the *receptivity* of the social strata to whom it is directed, the state of their economic as well as their political and social situations,[8] and that the false conceptions of nature held by certain social groups – belief in spirits and magic etc. – are partly explained by the backward economic structure of society which itself is 'partially conditioned and even caused by the false conceptions of nature', he is reverting to pre-Marxist theories of multiple causation which fail to specify the precise relationship. Writing of philosophy, for example, he argues that it develops

. . . through the operation of economic influences . . . upon the existing philosophic material handed down by predecessors. Here economy creates nothing new, but it determines the way in which the thought material found in existence is altered and further developed, and that too for the most part indirectly, for it is the political, legal, and moral reflexes which exercise the greatest influence upon philosophy.[9]

This is the standpoint of eighteenth-century materialism – mutual interaction between the different factors within a given situation : there is nothing dialectical in this (nor for that matter in Weber's arguments which can be accommodated easily to Engels's formulations). To suggest that the 'superstructure' can exercise a 'partial autonomy', while true, merely repeats that two-way interactions take place. The precise nature of the relationship must be specified.

A more dialectical approach to ideology by Engels, however, is suggested in his distinction between 'higher' and 'lower' ideologies (although there is ambiguity here also) and he argues that the more removed from practical life the less obvious are the connections between thought and economic factors – 'The interconnection between concepts and their mutual conditions of existence becomes more and more complicated, more and more obscured by intermediate links. But the interconnection exists.'[10] And : 'The farther the domain we are examining gets from economy and the closer it comes to pure abstract ideology, the more we will discover accidental elements in its evolution and the more its curve will trace a zig-zag.'[11] Engels expresses here, however crudely, one of the key concepts of Marxist sociology : *the dialectical relationship of society and ideas.* The history of thought is a dialectical history; the analysis of it equally must be dialectical. In 1857 Marx had posed the question : what is the relationship between culture and economy, between art and social structure? His tentative answer emphasised an *unequal relationship* : 'It is well known that certain periods of the highest development of art stand in no direct connection with the general development of society, nor with the material basis and the skeleton structure of its organisation.' Greek art, he argued, and thus its ideology, was far in advance of its material basis in social production.

Equally, the brilliance of French and German philosophy in the eighteenth century cannot be accommodated easily to the 'progressiveness' of these countries' economic structures, which remained semi-feudal, semi-capitalist.[12]

But Marx's most important contributions to the analysis of ideology are his extensive critiques of previous economic theory (seventeenth-, eighteenth- and early nineteenth-century political economy especially). His analysis of the social theories of production and exchange in the *Theories of Surplus Value* shows how the work of certain writers was partially scientific and partially ideological, while for others, working in the same areas, almost completely ideological. The extensive discussions of Smith, Ricardo and Malthus exemplify Marx's subtle dialectical grasp of the relations between thought and society.

In the 'Afterword' to the second edition of *Capital* Marx wrote that classical political economy, especially that of Adam Smith and Ricardo, 'belongs to the period in which the class struggle was as yet undeveloped', and that the absence of sharp class conflict helped to create a partially scientific political economy. But with the sharpening of class conflict in the early years of the nineteenth century a dramatic change occurs : with the conquest of power by the French and English bourgeoisie

the class struggle, practically as well as theoretically, took on a more and more outspoken and threatening form. It sounded the knell of scientific bourgeois economy. . . . In place of disinterested inquiries, there were hired prize-fighters; in place of genuine scientific research, the bad conscience and the evil intent of apologetic.[13]

From the moment when the bourgeoisie became the ruling class, that is, from the time of its ascendency in the political sphere (it had been economically dominant during the eighteenth century) then the class struggle ceased to be one of bourgeoisie against aristocracy, but bourgeoisie against proletariat. It is now that political economy and the science of sociology (in France with Comte) are directly involved in promoting integration within an exploitative society. In the

Theories of Surplus Value, Marx established two crucial elements of ideology :

(1) All thinkers who discuss society and develop theories adopt a position towards their object of study – society – which is directly related to their own activity in the world. That is, all social thought is written from a practical standpoint : in the case of Smith and Ricardo from the perspective of a 'revolutionary bourgeoisie' in conflict with the landowners.

(2) Ideological elements will subvert the genuinely scientific elements of social theory only if the standpoint is that of an economically declining social group or class as with Malthus, whose perspective was that of landowners against the bourgeoisie and proletariat.

To illustrate Marx's concept of ideology it will be necessary to compare his critiques of Smith, Ricardo and Malthus.

It is striking that in discussing Smith and Ricardo, both bourgeois economists, Marx frequently uses the term 'honest inquiries' and points to their rigorous scientific temper. Adam Smith, writes Marx, in his discussion of productive labour from the standpoint of capitalist production has 'got to the very heart of the matter, hit the nail on the head', his distinction between unproductive and productive labour 'is one of his greatest scientific merits'. Smith had penetrated to the essence of capitalism, had defined 'productive labour as labour which is directly exchanged with capital'. Smith's scientific merit, Marx argues, lies in his grasp that only labour which creates capital can be regarded as productive; unproductive labour exchanges for revenue (wages, profits etc.) and does not make capital (hotel cooks are productive as their labour is transformed into capital by the hotel owner; in so far as they work as servants for the wealthy their labour is unproductive).[14]

For Smith, then, productive and non-productive labour is always conceived from 'the standpoint of the possessor of money, from the standpoint of the capitalist', never from the point of view of the worker. In contrast, Ricardo shows the conflict necessarily engendered between capitalist and labourer based on the unequal economic relation of one to the other. Marx writes that Ricardo 'wants production for the sake of production' irrespective of its social consequences, 'a ruthlessness . . . not only scientifically honest but also

. . . a scientific necessity from his point of view'. Ricardo expresses through his economic theory the historic triumph of the bourgeois class over society as a whole : and in this sense his work expresses a genuinely scientific spirit. Of course, Ricardo's theories have their ideological elements : 'Ricardo's conception is . . . in the interests of the industrial bourgeoisie, only because, and in so far as, their interests co-incide with that of production or the productive development of human labour.'[15]

Marx has made an important distinction here between ideology and scientific knowledge : 'The rough cynical character of classical economy', – its honesty – is in effect 'a critique of existing conditions'. Thus when Smith discussed the 'unproductive labourers' employed by the state, especially the religious functionaries whose ideological function lay in legitimising aristocratic political rule, they are analysed from the point of view of private property. Marx cites the section of the *Wealth of Nations* where Smith 'gives vent to his hatred . . . of the clergy' whom he uncharitably but scientifically describes as 'unproductive labourers . . . maintained by a part of the annual produce of the industry of other people' and Smith brackets them with 'lawyers, physicians, men of letters'. Marx comments :

This is the language of the still revolutionary bourgeoisie which has not yet subjected to itself the whole of society, the State, etc. All these illustrious and time honoured occupations . . . are from an economic standpoint put on the same level as the swarm of their own lackeys and jesters maintained by the bourgeoisie and by idle wealth. . . .[16]

As the intellectual expression of a rising class, then, classical political economy had penetrated more deeply into the social and economic order than previous theory : its concepts and criticism are organically related to its social practice as an historically 'progressive' class whose worldly activity, in business and industry, linked them, not with past societies, but with the future. Adam Smith and Ricardo thus reflect the dynamic, capitalist-oriented *praxis* of a class which had yet to establish its authority within a society not wholly capitalistic. These points are brought out quite sharply in Marx's discussion

66

of Thomas Malthus, a contemporary of Ricardo, but whose economic theories are totally ideological.

Marx's high regard for Ricardo passes into contempt for Malthus, whom he chillingly describes as a 'plagiarist by profession' (he 'stole' his economic ideas from the eighteenth-century Scottish economist Adam Anderson and failed to acknowledge his debts), 'a professional sycophant of the landed aristocracy, whose rents, sinecures, squandering, heartlessness etc., he justifies economically'. Marx argues that Malthus reflects not the interests of the bourgeoisie but the aristocracy whom he defends against the workers. Malthus admires and lavishes praise on the 'productive workers' employed by the aristocratic state, the very people Smith had attacked as 'unproductive', lauds the Established Church and, unlike Ricardo, seeks to maintain the economic domination of the landed classes over the industrial bourgeoisie. Marx writes :

> But when a man seeks to accommodate science to a viewpoint which is derived not from science itself (however erroneous it may be) but from outside, from alien, external interests, then I call him 'base'.
>
> It is not a base action when Ricardo puts the proletariat on the same level as machinery or beasts of burden or commodities because (from his point of view) their being purely machinery or beasts of burden is conducive to 'production'. *This is stoic, objective, scientific.*[17]

From these texts, then, it is clear that Marx's theory of ideology is not reductionist. Eighteenth-century political economy had exposed as scientifically as was possible from within a bourgeois perspective, the class roots of capitalist society and its basic structure of inequality and exploitation. From this standpoint it levelled positive criticism on the inhuman consequences of the division of labour and attacked the 'unproductive' state functionaries. But when the bourgeois class finally acquired political power, when society *as a whole* was subjugated to this class's domination then it ceased progressively to defend itself scientifically against its critics but sought refuge increasingly in the world of ideology. And it must do this because its activity as a class is to exploit the labour of the working class, to build a society based on exploitation and inequality, and yet justify all this in terms of its own slogans – liberty, freedom, equality. Nineteenth-century bourgeois political economy thus champions bourgeois society against the rising critics of socialism. Like Malthus, therefore, the bourgeoisie accept the 'ideologist' as a productive worker for he now works for the bourgeoisie against the proletariat. The political economists who followed Ricardo, however, because they analysed society from the point of view of a victorious bourgeoisie, could not understand the contradiction which the political and social power of the bourgeois class had engendered. Social and economic theory, therefore tended to eliminate contradictions in favour of evolution and progress, and beginning with the Chartist movement in the 1830s bourgeois social theory is forced to see the 'social problem' increasingly in ideological terms.

II

We are now in a position to define more clearly the concepts of knowledge, science and ideology in Marx's social theory. Firstly, the relation of knowledge to society is dialectical, contradictory, uneven in its development. Knowledge, therefore, will not reproduce passively the economic structure. This leads to the second point : knowledge can be partially autonomous and constitute criticism of the existing society. And finally, knowledge is scientific or ideological to the degree it corresponds with the practical interests of a 'progressive', 'rising' class. Of course, these formulations remain anchored in Marx's dictum that social existence determines consciousness and it might seem, therefore, that all Marx has demonstrated is that between 1780 and 1830 the British bourgeoisie 'needed' a specific kind of knowledge consonant with its social role, and that political economy emerged as an intellectual response to the burgeoning bourgeois economy. In other words a *functional* rather than dialectical relationship subsists between knowledge and society.

There is some truth in this argument : Smith and Ricardo were linked socially to the bourgeois class as a whole through their membership of specific groups within the class, and their theories reflect the aspirations of that class. But to suggest that such theories were merely 'appropriate' to the broad social interests of the bourgeoisie is to eliminate the dialectical element – knowledge as partially autonomous – for while it remained highly critical of the aristocracy, bourgeois theory was also critical of the very forces (i.e. the division of labour, class structure) which were bringing modern bourgeois society into being. It seems to follow, therefore, that when knowledge corresponds completely with economic interests it will tend more to ideology than science; and conversely, when the relationship of thinker to class is complex and elusive, when he belongs to specific groups within the class whose social position enables them to criticise society, then the chances are higher for science.

At the heart of this analysis is Marx's concept of knowledge as *praxis*. In the *Theses on Feuerbach* the dialectical relation between purposive social activity (*praxis*) and knowledge of the world had been posed. Social theory is indissolubly bound to the living practice of men, their understanding of the social world mediated through the social groups to which they belong as social animals. Marx's injunction that man sets himself only those problems which can be solved *at the time* applies forcibly to the history of social theory; for problems in social theory are precisely to do with practical questions, the distribution of power, class inequality, the development of social consciousness. While ideology, like science, aims to analyse reality it has the tendency to subvert *praxis*. Adam Smith's work, for example, exemplifies the striving of the bourgeois class towards political and social domination and the totality expressed in his writings embodies a complete grasp of the essential features of social life both in terms of the present and the past. Smith's 'false consciousness', his ideology, may be said to lie in his belief that bourgeois society was the culmination of history, that the world was a completed whole at that point, and therefore there was no need for man to change it. History had ended; so had man's *praxis*.

Ideology within social theory, then, minimises the function of *praxis*, of men changing the social world. Theory and practice cannot be separated : modern political ideology – Stalinism, Democratic pluralism, Fascism – emphasises the essential passivity of the individual, that society can be run only by those with 'expert knowledge', a standpoint which justifies élitism as the only viable foundation for social progress. A genuinely scientific theory of society will grasp social reality as an organic whole, one involving both values and human action. The philosophies of utilitarianism and rationalism and the political credos of Stalinism and Conservatism are characterised by one essential feature : they deny the need for human *praxis* in order that the social world be created. This is the importance of consciousness for Marx and why his social theory diverges sharply from classical sociology and from 'vulgar' Marxism :

> The question whether objective truth can be attributed to human thinking is not a question of theory but is a practical question. Man must prove the truth, i.e. the reality and power, the this-sideness of his thinking in practice. The dispute over the reality or non-reality of thinking that is isolated from practice is a purely scholastic question.[18]

The point here is that consciousness has a practical intent in that it is necessarily oriented towards activity. Consciousness is not created in isolation but in terms of dialectical reciprocity and social action within the objective structure of social groups, classes and society. This is why Smith, Hegel and Marx embody in their writings a totality embracing past and present, a structure of thought which grasps the whole as dominant over its parts, in which action is dialectically related to change and consciousness, oblique or direct. But although Smith's political economy contains an awareness of concrete historical change (society developing through different economic stages) woven with the pristine dialectic of unintended consequences of action, and Hegel's dialectical idealist philosophy conceives change as the progressive self-consciousness of the 'Spirit' (i.e. Man), it is only in the work of Marx that the fundamentally *contemplative* stance of these thinkers is finally surmounted and the concept of *praxis* placed at the heart of social theory.

Marx, in short, presents the first social theory which is capable of grasping other theories in terms of their social context, of evaluating their historical, ideological and scientific structures. For a social theory is more than an explanation of the social world as totality : it must seek to explain why other opposed theories co-exist, theories of society which fundamentally aim to analyse the same problems. It is in this sense that Marx develops a theory of theory by proposing criteria for assessing their scientific merits and situating the theorist historically and specifically within a group, class, society. It bears repeating that Marx does not reduce social theory simply to the level of reflecting economic interests, but postulates, in his discussions of Ricardo and Malthus, the *dialectical* development of social thought, the contradictory, uneven relation between the social theorist, his group and class, society and history. 'Vulgar' Marxism, however, by turning Marxism into a purely scientific study of objective economic laws removed this dialectical relation between objective conditions and social consciousness, transforming consciousness into a mere epiphenomenon of economic necessity. Having thus diminished the subjective element, knowledge and ideology were conflated as reflections of external forces : Marxist knowledge was thus defined in terms of the working class, bourgeois knowledge in terms of the bourgeois class. It became impossible to judge other social theories : 'vulgar Marxism' conceived ideology as empty fantasy, illusion, the simple reflection of material interests. It is in this important sense that 'vulgar' Marxism and sociological positivism meet, not as opposing but complementary theories : for both defined ideology in terms of a crude theory of interest, a reflection of external material elements, thus leaving no way open for *evaluating* the truth or falsity of competing theories. Knowledge and ideology were granted an existential basis : that was all.

It was in this situation that the notion of relativism in social theory was raised. For Weber, Mannheim and Lukács the question left unanswered by nineteenth-century sociological positivism and 'vulgar' Marxism was simply how to validate the truth of one's own theories over others. If knowledge flowed directly from economic interests and had an existential basis in social life then surely all knowledge is relative to its material determinants including Marxism itself? Was Marxism the ideological expression of 'a rising class' or rather an objective, scientific analysis of society? How was it to be validated? At the close of the nineteenth century the concept of ideology became a dominant element in sociological thought :

Vilfredo Pareto and Georges Sorel reflected the growing anti-rationalist, anti-positivistic and anti-Marxist trend within social theory in advocating unreason, intuition, will, myths, and non-logical behaviour as crucial elements of social life. For these thinkers social theory must take its departure from the 'ideological' (irrational) understanding that man has of society and thus abandon both the search for the objective conditions of consciousness and of ideology itself : it must accept ideology as given. For Weber, Marxism was simply ideology and sociology, only scientific in so far as it eliminated values from its structure. His methodology, built around the concept of perspective, implicitly accepted that the slice of the social world analysed is dependent on the subjective values and thus ideology of the individual researcher. The work of Mannheim and Lukács can be seen as two related attempts within sociology and Marxism to go beyond the scepticism induced by 'perspectivism' and 'positivist' Marxism.

III

It was Max Scheler who coined the term 'sociology of knowledge' during the 1920s acknowledging Marx's work as an important although not decisive influence. But it was Karl Mannheim who produced the first systematic theoretical and empirical studies in the field of the sociology of knowledge (analyses of 'Historicism' and 'Conservative Thought' for example) and the first serious critique within academic sociology of Marx's concept of ideology.[19] Mannheim was also influenced by Weber's agnostic solution to the problem of objectivity and knowledge : if reality is merely the sum of divergent standpoints then who is to say if one is more valid than another. In opposition to Weber's relativism and scepticism Mannheim proposed 'a dynamic conception of the truth', an absolute standard by which to judge the validity of different theories. His answer to sociological relativism is historicism. Hegel had argued that the truth 'is the whole', a philosophical standpoint adopted by Mannheim in his argument that history itself has an immanent tendency to totality, that knowledge of the whole is made increasingly accessible through the social accumulation of knowledge by groups, institutions and individuals. It is this historicist element which makes the claim that Mannheim was 'a bourgeois Marx' difficult to sustain. Rather, his sociology of knowledge aims to replace Marxism by a more exact and historically valid science.

In *Ideology and Utopia* Mannheim argued that with the exception of mathematics and natural science all thought was socially determined and that the task of the sociology of knowledge lay in establishing the precise links between different types of thought and social structure. At once this raises the problem of mediations and the question of the partial autonomy of thought. Mannheim emphasises that knowledge must be related to its social origins and he rejects the individualistic interpretation arguing, in the spirit of Marx, that it is neither the individual nor men in general who produce knowledge but men in groups engaged in collective social activity. It is collective man who creates what Mannheim calls particular 'styles of thought', broad complexes of knowledge held together by an inner unity and coherence. The mediation, therefore, between knowledge and society is the group and, using the concept of 'collective subject' taken from Heidegger, Mannheim suggests that the individual thinker does not express his individual point of view but rather that his work constitutes a collective expression of external, social tendencies.[20]

Mannheim argues that the first theorist who grasped these complex relations was Marx, who, through the concept of ideology, disclosed the ways in which knowledge is socially distorted. However, ideology must be rendered 'useful' for research purposes and methodology must show 'the interrelationships between the intellectual point of view held and the social position occupied' and demonstrate 'that every point of view is particular to a social situation'. And although praising Marx for his insights which 'went to the heart of the matter' Mannheim makes the important distinction between 'particular' and 'total' ideologies, between the 'simple' theory of ideology and its general formulation in the sociology of knowledge. Particular ideologies are defined as individual disguises or illusions, rationalisations of situations threatening the individual's interests and which operate on a psychological level : total ideology refers to the thought of a social class or epoch, a style of thought such as 'bourgeois', 'proletarian', 'conservative', a *Weltanschauung* in which the individual 'participates only in certain fragments . . . the totality of which is not in the least a mere sum of . . . fragmentary individual experiences'.[21] Marxism, by fusing these two different meanings of ideology, transformed it into a weapon for political practice, 'the exclusive privilege of socialist thinkers to trace bourgeois thought to ideological foundations and thereby to discredit it'.[22] The task of the sociology of knowledge was to purge ideology of its political connotations, by focusing on knowledge, the group and the style of thought.

But to define a style of thought in terms of the intellectual expression of a particular group is to pose directly the problem of relativism. For to state that all historical knowledge is 'relational knowledge and can only be formulated with reference to the position of the observer' seems on the face of it deterministic and non-dialectical. Mannheim's distinction between *relationism* – the relation of the thinker, his social position and the knowledge produced – and *relativism* – the belief that objective truth is impossible – is no solution : he argues that not all standpoints are equally valid, but this begs the question of criteria for judging them. Lukács, whose theoretical position on these issues is similar to Mannheim's, proposed the more radical historicist answer that the optimum of truth is consistent only from the standpoint of the proletariat. Mannheim, too, relies on historicism, arguing that truth emerges through a synthesis of the different perspectives into a unified whole. And the means whereby this task is accomplished is a 'free-floating intelligentsia', a social stratum unattached to concrete interests and thus capable both intellectually and socially of fusing the different points of view into a coherent whole. Mannheim is quite clear : Marx's concept of ideology is bound to the interests of a particular group, the proletariat. The concept is thus relativistic and partial. Only knowledge which is free from interests can hope for a genuine scientific status :

> . . . it was not possible for the socialist idea of ideology to have developed of itself into the sociology of knowledge. It seems inherent in the historical process itself that the narrowness and the limitations which restrict one point of view tend to be corrected

by clashing with the opposite points of view. The task of the study of ideology . . . is to understand the narrowness of each individual point of view and the interplay between these distinctive attitudes in the total social process.[23]

Totality is thus rendered through the synthesising function of the intelligentsia, a social stratum apparently unaffected by Mannheim's basic dictum that all knowledge of the social world is related to the particular situation of the individual thinker and his group interests. The eclectic gathering together of widely separated strands of thought – the *good* parts being sifted from the *bad* – is precisely the method which Marx had criticised in his polemic against Proudhon. In his concrete analysis of Smith, Ricardo and Malthus, Marx emphasised the practical function of their theories and attempted to show how the social interests which they defended constituted a major element in their scientific value. But Mannheim's main thrust is against *interests as a whole* which he sees as impediments to the triumph of reason and science in society. Like Liberalism and Conservatism, Marxism is too enmeshed in an interest nexus to generate a valid sociology.

This is the meaning of Mannheim's distinction between ideology and utopia : ideology is defined as the process whereby 'ruling groups can in their thinking become so intensively interest-bound to a situation that they are simply no longer able to see certain facts which would undermine their sense of domination'. Ideology implies 'that in certain situations the collective unconscious of certain groups obscures the real condition of society both to itself and to others and thereby stabilises it'. In contrast, utopian thought reflects the struggle of oppressed groups to change society, so much so that they see only 'those elements in the situation which tend to negate it'. Utopian thinking is therefore incapable of a correct analysis of the existing social situation. Utopian thought – Mannheim's examples include the orgiastic chiliasm of the Anabaptists, Liberal humanitarianism, Conservatism and Communist socialism – grasping only the negative elements in situations seeks change which is impossible since its concepts are 'incongruous with the state of reality within which it occurs'. At this point Mannheim introduces a pragmatic

75

criterion for truth : a theory is wrong, he says, when 'it uses concepts and categories which, if taken seriously, would prevent man from adjusting himself at that historical stage'. If the theory generates norms inconsistent with the particular situation, such as lending money without interest during the rise of capitalism, then it quickly degenerates into ideology and thus conceals rather than reveals the real meaning of the historical moment.[24]

The arbitrary *ex post facto* character of these 'proofs', combined with the appeal to pragmatism – man adjusting to a *pre-existing* situation – indicates the degree to which Mannheim has rejected Marx. For Mannheim is suggesting a *mechanical* not dialectical relationship between man, society and knowledge. Society is given : man adjusts. Such dualism is entirely foreign to Marx's concept of *praxis*, through which man changes both himself and the social world and his injunction that social theory must grasp this union of subject and object at both the epistemological as well as practical level. Mannheim has seriously misinterpreted Marx's dialectical conception of 'base' and 'superstructure'; for him, Marx's theory is mechanical. When Mannheim criticises 'vulgar' Marxism for reducing 'the most esoteric and spiritual products of the mind [to] the economic and political power interests of a certain class' instead of 'elucidating the total configuration of intellectual life' he comes close to Marx's method.[25] But when he analyses one style of thought – 'Proletarian thought' – he simply eliminates the specific mediations : his analysis remains abstract and speculative, and he never attempts to show how the complex differences *within* Marxism are bound up with specific groups : Lenin, Trotsky and Rosa Luxemburg, for example, emphasised the 'voluntaristic' components of Marxism and interpreted it in internationalist and revolutionary terms; Plekhanov, Kautsky and Bernstein defined Marxism in broadly evolutionary and somewhat dogmatic terms. All were contemporaries and associated with the international Marxist movement. Why the differences therefore? Mannheim's sociology of knowledge does not provide an answer, as Marxism as a whole is identified with the ahistorical abstraction 'proletarian thought'.

These mechanical elements in Mannheim's thought are brought out particularly in his argument that Marxism exemplifies a 'chiliastic' striving to utopia 'assimilated and incorporated' specifically into Bolshevism. Lenin's Marxism was simply utopianism : the situation in Russia during 1917 demanded a completely different 'adjustment' to that proposed and carried through by the Bolsheviks. But in fact the Bolsheviks came to power precisely because their theory grasped the crucial fact that the Russian bourgeoisie was too weak and vacillating as a class to defend basic democratic rights. In 1917 two revolutions, the February Bourgeois Democratic and the October Proletarian were telescoped into one revolution; and this was the only way in which democracy in Russia could have been saved let alone extended. Mannheim's analysis of Marxism as chiliastic striving to utopia, and thus incapable of 'adjusting' man adequately to the existing situation, is manifestly absurd : the Marxism of the Second International ended by supporting the nationalist, capitalist governments' war aims, while that of the Bolsheviks called for international proletarian revolution and defined the First World War as imperialist slaughter. Which was the more realistic adjustment : for capitalism or against it?

It is the absence of specific mediations in Mannheim's analysis of 'proletarian thought' and his failure to grasp Marx's dialectical theory of ideology which leads him to adopt a methodological standpoint that cannot account for contradictory although contemporary theories (Ricardo and Malthus, Lenin and Kautsky). Mannheim's sociology of knowledge simply does not contain a fully worked out *theory of theory*, only the somewhat mundane observation, already present in Enlightenment philosophy, that 'truth' and 'knowledge' is truth and knowledge from the point of view of a particular social and political situation. There is no critical awareness of the profound dialectical relationship of social class, group and interests to knowledge and ideology.

Lukács's study of ideology, *History and Class Consciousness*, is equally concerned with the problem of mediations and relativism, but unlike Mannheim, Lukács adopts a concept of *interest* as the basic factor in the determination of 'truth' or 'falsity'. He argues that the proletariat simultaneously constitutes the subject and the object of history – the proletariat is the knowing subject which approaches truth through its awareness that history's mission for it

77

is none other than the liberation of all men from capitalist alienation. In Lukács's interpretation Marxism becomes the intellectual
expression of the revolutionary movement itself, the 'self-consciousness' of capitalism embodied in the class consciousness of the proletariat. Revolutionary *praxis* – socialism – therefore transcends the
problem of relativism and raises the truth of Marxism beyond the
reach of bourgeois thought through its central precept of the proletariat's historical task :

> . . . the essence of the method of historical materialism is insepar-
> able from the 'practical' and 'critical' activity of the proletariat :
> both are aspects of the same process of social evolution. So, too,
> the knowledge of reality provided by the dialectical method is
> likewise inseparable from the class standpoint of the proletariat.[26]

Lukács argues that the subjective and objective 'self-knowledge'
of the proletariat 'at a given point in its evolution is at the same
time knowledge of the stage of development achieved by the whole
society'.[27] It is important to note that Lukács, like Weber and
Mannheim, has accepted perspectivism : Marxism becomes as much
a perspective as bourgeois thought itself and thus an ideology, but
an ideology more advanced sociologically and philosophically than
any other 'style of thought'. In this way Marxism is applied to itself,
defined not as a complete system (as in Kautsky, Plekhanov) but as
both a *praxis* and a constantly developing theory.

Both proletariat and bourgeoisie (Lukács follows Weber in defining them as ideal types) share a similar social reality – capitalism.
Their experience is identical in that each class comprehends the
world as an external, fixed datum, but the ways in which this sense
of irreducibility and immediacy is raised in consciousness is wholly
different. Bourgeois thought and consciousness, Lukács argues, is
imprisoned in 'the mire of immediacy' and unable to distance itself
through mediating concepts from the objects of reality it seeks to
describe and analyse. Bourgeois thought, therefore, accepts the self-
evident and immediately given social forms, grasping society as an
unmediated structure. The result of such 'unmediated contemplation'
is that the bourgeoisie cannot comprehend historical development

and genesis for, accepting the *given*, immediate forms, any change 'must then appear to be a catastrophe, a sudden, unexpected turn of events that comes from outside and eliminates all mediations'. Bourgeois thought is non-historical precisely because in order to create the object in thought it must possess mediating concepts which embody 'the structural principles and the real tendencies of the objects themselves', that is, 'real' historical development, and this it cannot do.[28]

In contrast, proletarian thought is self-knowledge of its concrete historical situation and the necessary historical changes which this consciousness implies. Proletarian knowledge is in essence a rejection of the immediately given social structure in favour of 'real' and 'true' historical change. This rejection of immediacy is not a moral or subjective evaluation of the faults within capitalism, it is not, as it is with Mannheim, an ought or a 'utopia'. If it were, the problem of ideology and relativism would remain, for to transcend reality (the given)

> . . . can only mean that the objects of the empirical world are to be understood as aspects of a totality, . . . as the aspects of a total social situation caught up in the process of historical change. Thus the category of mediation is a lever with which to overcome the mere immediacy of the empirical world and as such it is not something [subjective] foisted on to the objects from the outside. . . . It is rather the manifestation of their authentic objective structure.[29]

Lukács's argument is thus perfectly clear : Marxism does not imply relativism because the standpoint of the proletariat necessitates a mediated understanding of the 'immanent meanings' implicit in the historical process which now become 'objectively effective and . . . enter the consciousness of the proletariat'. The social theories of the bourgeoisie and proletariat are directly opposed : both are ideologies, but proletarian ideology is 'on a higher scientific plane objectively' for, unlike bourgeois theory, it transcends the barrier of empirical immediacy through corresponding to the real dialectical development of history. On the other hand, the class interest of the bourgeoisie necessitates a social theory which makes objective truth within a one-sided, false immediacy :

> For the social existence of the proletariat is far more powerfully affected by the dialectical character of the historical process in which the mediated character of every factor receives the imprint of truth and authentic objectivity only in the mediated totality. For the proletariat to become aware of the dialectical nature of its existence is a matter of life and death.[30]

Bourgeois thought, therefore, is ideological precisely because by considering objects in isolation from the total process and structure of society, from the standpoint of the individual, the whole must forever remain hidden; the *part* thus becomes 'fetishised' at the expense of totality. Proletarian thought, however, because it is based on a totality, the proletariat (Marx's 'universal class'), aspires, either consciously or unconsciously through its knowledge and practice to grasp society as a totality, to comprehend it as 'a coherent whole', and unlike the bourgeoisie 'the proletariat always aspires towards the truth even in its false consciousness and . . . substantive errors'. Ontologically privileged the worker is none the less turned into a commodity, an object; his condition thus corresponds to the capitalist transformation of social relations into relations between objects and things. Thus the fact that his labour power is appropriated as a thing means that the proletariat can achieve a consciousness of its real position, a self-knowledge about society. In the act of knowing subject and object coincide : the cognitive and practical components of knowledge are fused within proletarian thought. This self-consciousness of the proletariat is identical with the revolutionary transformation of capitalism. The movement towards socialism and the consciousness of this movement are one and the same thing. Knowledge is no epiphenomenon, no simple reflection of external objects but is bound indissolubly with the revolutionary practice of the proletariat.[31]

Lukács's *History and Class Consciousness* represents one of the most challenging works in the history of social theory; it has exercised a seductive power over Marxist and non-Marxist scholars

(Marcuse, Adorno, Sartre, Goldmann) as well as proving a decisive influence over the development of Mannheim's sociology of knowledge. But like Mannheim, its fundamental theses have very little connection with Marx's social theory. To argue against relativism by attributing to history a purpose outside the concrete class struggles which constitute its structure and momentum is merely to define Marxism in historicist terms. But the validity of Marx's thought does not hinge on a *philosophical* relationship with the proletariat or as the ideology of a 'progressive' class. Of course, Marxism is bound up with the working class historically and sociologically. But as classical political economy was more than the ideological expression of the bourgeoisie, so Marxism, assimilating the innovations and discoveries of previous thinkers strives to a scientific analysis of capitalist society and thus produces the necessary knowledge for achieving social change. Marx always emphasised the scientific character of his method : hypotheses relating to class structure, economic formations, social change are *testable* by concrete historical facts and processes. Totality is part of this method whereby the many complex determinations of social phenomena are analysed separately and then integrated into the social whole. But this is not to be confused with the ahistorical abstractions of Lukács – proletarian against bourgeois thought as undifferentiated wholes – or with an immanent tendency towards totality on the part of the working class. To quote Marx against Lukács : when a thinker accommodates science 'to a viewpoint which is derived not from science itself' but from outside 'alien, external interests' – that is, the messianic historicism which underpins Lukács's argument – then his theory is false and the thought 'base'. For the proletariat is no homogeneous revolutionary mass counterposed to a similarly homogeneous bourgeoisie : both classes are differentiated into distinct layers and within these levels exist the most complex and contradictory ideologies (for example, the stratum within the working class which consistently votes for Conservative political parties). Like Mannheim, Lukács has eliminated the concrete determinations of class structure and consciousness in favour of a purely abstract model. Marx's social theory (as we shall see in Chapter 5) relates class specifically to particular historical situations and cultures. It does not postulate any supra-historical mission for the proletariat, no purpose outside concrete living history, history which is made by men guided by knowledge of the social world. It is this dialectical grasp of fundamentally contradictory processes, of knowledge as a *praxis* bound to specific groups yet partially autonomous, which distinguishes Marx's thought from that of Mannheim and Lukács.

For Marx, then, knowledge was not equivalent to ideology, for although closely bound up with material forces (class interests for example) it is more than epiphenomena. The concept of *praxis* is important in that social knowledge represents man's attempt to assimilate the raw experiences of the world and help him master both nature and society. Mannheim, too, argues that knowledge is related to practice, mediated through social groups struggling and competing for political domination.[32]

Ideology, however, has another meaning apart from intellectual knowledge : it is a 'material force', a kind of cement which binds together the social structure of class societies. Ideology exercises a stabilising role in society : as Marx wrote, the dominant ideas of each epoch are those of the ruling class – a theorem, which, translated into sociological terms, suggests that society is legitimised through 'everyday knowledge' or rather, the dominant ideology is transmuted into ordinary, mundane ideas.

If this interpretation is correct then it becomes possible to see the Marxist theory of the sociology of knowledge working on two different but interrelated levels :

(1) society as a structured whole, a totality, its form and momentum dependent on the workings of objective economic laws and tendencies;

(2) society as human purposes, will, initiative, *praxis*.

.The point at issue here is the distinction drawn between the methods of the natural and the social sciences as wholly different. On the basis of this, Weber, Simmel and Alfred Schutz developed a distinctive social theory which has exercised considerable influence in modern sociology. But the separation is essentially artificial : it is not a simple question of one or the other. The fact that the social sciences are characterised by human subjectivity separates them from the natural sciences, but it does not follow that this constitutes sufficient grounds for rejecting the scientific method which analyses society in terms of objective laws and tendencies and defines society as a structured, dynamic whole.

It is this challenge to positivism in the work of Weber, Simmel and Mannheim which leads to the destructured anti-historical concept of society which informs modern sociological phenomenology. An exaggerated emphasis is given to human subjectivity and the 'human' situation which leads to the argument that 'everyday life' should form the subject matter of a sociology 'grounded in the pulsating inter-subjectivity of the real world of men'.[33] The result is that the sociology of knowledge equally must concern itself with 'everything that passes for knowledge in society'. Ordinary knowledge rather than intellectual ideas must form the basis of a science which is to focus on what is 'real' for the individual members of society. Mannheim's concern with intellectual knowledge is thus replaced by a 'common-sense' oriented sociology of knowledge which maintains that ordinary knowledge 'constitutes the fabric of meaning without which no society could exist'.[34] Alfred Schutz makes it quite clear that 'the starting point of social science is to be found in ordinary social life', in men's everyday knowledge of society, a knowledge which, like scientific knowledge, involves mental constructs, syntheses, generalisations and formalisations 'specific to the respective level of thought organisation'.[35] The concepts of social science, therefore, must agree with the common-sense experience of the social world.

Superficially there seems a close kinship between Marx's criteria of validity through practice and the phenomenologist's identity of concepts and ordinary consciousness. Gramsci, for example, raised the question : can Marxism be in opposition to the non-theoretical common sense of the masses? His answer was unequivocal : 'Between the two there is a "quantitive" difference of degree, not one of quality.' This is the basis of Gramsci's assertion that everyone is a philosopher in that it is not a question of introducing science into people's lives from the outside but rather of 'renovating and making "critical" an already existing activity'. It is here, in this conception of theory and practice, that a critical difference between Gramsci and Schutz emerges. For Grasmci, common sense is incapable of generating an intellectual order, since it cannot be reduced to unity and coherence either within an individual or a collective consciousness : common sense is essentially fragmentary, a disparate collection of ideas and opinions part of which – Gramsci calls it 'good sense' – humanises man's anti-social instincts and provides direction and purpose to his daily activities. Gramsci suggests that philosophy as an intellectual activity developed from common sense – it is indeed the 'common sense of the intellectuals' – and therefore must always remain in contact with it, since it is only through this relationship that philosophy discovers the source and the practical remedies of the problems it strives to solve. Thus Marxism does not ignore the simple elements in common sense but attempts to develop them to a higher conception of life.[36]

Gramsci makes it clear that common sense – consciousness – can only be understood if it is analysed both in terms of a totality of social relations as well as the dominant ideology. Sociological phenomenology, by accepting everyday knowledge as given, in effect eliminates the problem of ideology from the sociology of knowledge. Schutz, for example, defines everyday knowledge almost exclusively in terms of Weber's 'traditional' category of social action, that is, action which is custom bound, has become so habitual and ingrained that it is no longer meaningfully oriented to goals and ends. This 'taken for granted' knowledge forms 'the great bulk of everyday action'. The individual is born into this world and accepts it as legitimate : he is socialised through specific social relationships of which he has both direct knowledge (his family) and indirect knowledge (teachers) and in order to relate to this inter-subjective world he forms what Schutz calls 'typical common-sense constructs' attributing to others 'typical functions' and 'typical relations'. It is through these typical constructs of expected behavioural patterns that the social world is rendered intelligible and maintained in the routines of everyday discourse (habits, etc.). The result is that the individual translates these routines into 'cookery-book knowledge', formulae that provide immediate unreflective knowledge of how to begin and end certain actions – and Schutz suggests that most of daily life is based on such recipes.[37]

The emphasis here is clearly on the maintenance of social structures : through the routines of everyday life man invests his existence and society with meaning, a concept of *praxis* very different from Marx for whom practice was not only the ultimate arbiter of truth but the only way in which man could free himself from the alienation and reification endemic in capitalist ideology. To be sure, the stability of society hinges on the acceptance by the subordinate strata of the prevailing ideology, a process which can take place only through the dominant institutions such as the educational, political and religious. But as we have said this knowledge is not a coherent expression of a particular group, but rather a contradictory structure of opinions, values, sentiments. Berger and Luckmann, for example, argue that social life is made up of shared meanings and shared common-sense knowledge expressed 'in the normal, self-evident routines of everyday life', and that although knowledge is transmitted through social institutions there emerges a common consensus, 'a shared core universe' of meanings and knowledge. But it is most unlikely that the specific labour traditions found in working-class organisations and groups would find any sympathetic echo within either the middle or upper class, or that these traditions would be seen in terms of common sense : militant trade unionism may be 'good sense' for the working class but decidedly bad sense for the employers and the vast majority of non-unionised and conservative middle class. These groups would neither understand nor wish to tolerate them.[38] But this example raises an important point : sociological phenomenology quite rightly emphasises that only a fraction of human experience and knowledge can be retained in consciousness, the rest becoming 'sedimented', 'congealing as recognisable and memorable entities' within certain institutions.[39] Gramsci refers to this process as 'the stratified deposits in popular philosophy',[40] the good part of common sense which is neither universal nor epiphenomenal, but lies dormant waiting for the moment when it will once again rise into consciousness – for example, the slogans associated with working-class revolution and the specific working-class institutions such as Soviets and Workers' Councils which have duplicated themselves in Russia, Hungary,

Italy and France, at different times and in different circumstances. These institutions and the revolutionary rhetoric which goes with them are in no sense universal.

But the phenomenologists do not define everyday knowledge in terms of this *praxis*. Their concern is with society *as it is* and the means whereby its structures are legitimised and stabilised, the whole held together through the routines associated with the 'prosaic' mind. This association of social order with common-sense knowledge has the effect of removing the contradictions within popular consciousness and treating it as a coherent structure. The point, however, is the dialectical structure of consciousness in which certain elements are oriented to stability while others to criticism and change. (This aspect of consciousness will be discussed in more detail in the analysis of the 'affluent worker' in Chapters 4 and 5.)

Ideology, therefore, can be seen as the cement which binds society together and thus necessarily as striving to emasculate any awareness within common-sense thought of social contradictions and conflicts. It is in this sense that Marx's concept of ideology is essential for understanding the role of everyday, common-sense knowledge in society, as a contradictory structure which can resonate both the values of the dominant class *and* oppositional ideas.

4

ALIENATION, REIFICATION AND HUMAN NATURE

The concept 'alienation' is now one of the key words of modern sociology widely used in empirical and theoretical work. Originating with Hegel, it was first used by Marx in his early writings to describe and criticise a social condition in which man, far from being the active initiator of the social world seemed more a passive object of determinate, external processes. The social world in which man moved seemed hostile and dehumanised, a world in which man was a stranger to himself and to others. For the young Marx, man's alienation from the world his own labour had created was bound up with the growth of private property and capital and the development of a market economy in which man and his human activity became a saleable object, a commodity to be bought and sold to the highest bidder. The world of man thus became increasingly thing-like with the products of human activity – labour – confronting the individual as objective, alien forms.

This theme of alienation is found in the work of other sociologists apart from Marx, especially Simmel for whom the social world was a world totally dominated by reification. An interesting point for the history of ideas is the eclipse of the concept of alienation after Marx. It was only at the turn of the century that sociologists such as Simmel and Weber rediscovered alienation, although using it differently from Marx, while in Marxism the term had played no role in the work of Engels, Plekhanov, Lenin, Trotsky and Kautsky and it was only with the publication of Lukács's *History and Class Consciousness* that alienation and the related concept of reification were defined as important categories in Marxist social science. Lukács suggested, indeed, that Marx's mature writings, *Capital* especially, revolved around these apparently philosophical ideas. Orthodox Marxists, however, were shocked by these suggestions, more so as Marx's early writings were as yet unpublished, and Lukács came under attack for 'revisionism' and philosophical idealism. In fact it was not until 1932, with the publication of the *Economic and Philosophical Manuscripts*, that the concept of alienation became more widely known. During the 1930s Erich Fromm and Herbert Marcuse wrote sympathetically on the significance of the young Marx's concepts and his relation with Hegel, while in a different sense alienation found its expression in the existentialist philosophy of Martin Heidegger and Sartre. Today, alienation is used extensively in sociology, psychology and literature and has become a blanket term to describe every conceivable aspect of cultural fragmentation, social isolation and philosophical *angst*.

I

In the *Paris Manuscripts* Marx developed his first analysis of capitalism through the categories of Hegel's idealistic dialectical philosophy and those of classical political economy. From the latter he took the concept of labour as 'man's self-confirming essence', the activity through which man defines himself in nature and society and the ultimate source of all wealth. But political economy, Marx argued, had grasped man's activity, his labour, as an object, 'one-sided, mechanical', as a thing. In the writings of the eighteenth-century economists the worker becomes 'an abstract activity and a belly . . . increasingly dependent upon all the fluctuations in market price, in the employment of capital, and in the caprices of the rich'.[1] The worker's human activity thus becomes progressively non-human.

The concept of alienation, however, was not part of political economy's conceptual structure or language and it was from Hegel's philosophy that Marx derived the concept, transforming it from an essentially idealist to a materialist and critical concept. In *The Phenomenology of Spirit* Hegel had argued that the history of man was the history of what he called the 'Absolute Spirit', a consciousness which progressively unfolds through a series of dialectical contradictions in the direction of increasing self-knowledge; 'unlimited consciousness' is the ultimate state when 'Spirit' is at one with the 'ethical world'. For Hegel, 'History' possessed an immanent meaning in the sense of embodying this ceaseless activity and drive towards total consciousness. 'Spirit', of course, was man, and the actual concrete historical situations which characterise historical development are analysed by Hegel as the historically specific 'moments' which, in their material form, embody the dialectical development of 'Spirit' from unreflective unity with society and culture to an organic and conscious unity (the Renaissance, the Enlightenment, the French Revolution). But as 'Spirit' unfolds itself through history it is confronted by each concrete historical moment as a part of itself, as something its own activity has created; it therefore experiences this activity as something external and alien. 'Spirit' therefore seeks to recover these alienated moments and it is this movement which partially drives it onwards towards 'absolute' and thus non-alienated consciousness.[2]

In his early writings Marx inverts Hegel's idealist historical explanation arguing that such speculative history totally ignored 'real men and real conditions'. Following the keenly felt empirical structure of political economy, Marx made man's labour the basis of history and human society and not the manifestation of a suprahistorical force. 'Spirit's' ceaseless activity in Marx's inversion becomes man's activity through his real, concrete labour, situated in specific historical periods and closely bound up with the prevailing mode of production. For Marx alienation is described as a process by which man is progressively turned into a stranger in the world his labour has created, a theme central to Hegel's *Phenomenology*. It is also the theme of Feuerbach's *Essence of Christianity* (1838), which exercised a profound impact on Marx's early work, helping him to translate Hegel's idealist structures into materialist ones. Feuerbach, for example, had argued that religion was simply man's essential nature refracted through idealism : 'My doctrine in belief is as follows : Theology is anthropology, i.e., that which reveals itself in the object of religion . . . – is nothing other than the essence of man. In other words, the God of man is nothing other than the divinised essence of man.'[3] Feuerbach's point was simply that religion as well as philosophy required 'materialising', that is, inverting. When Marx writes that philosophy is religion 'brought into thought and developed by thought' he is thinking of the Hegelian philosophy; the task he sets in the *Paris Manuscripts* is the reduction of philosophy and religion to *something else*, although not simply to Feuerbach's anthropology, man's nature, but rather to political economy. Hegel's standpoint, he wrote, must be understood not as abstract, speculative history 'but that of modern political economy'. Hegel's concept of alienation, while shrouded in obscure language and ambiguous concepts, is none the less a reflection of alienation in 'real life', in the economic structure of society. The metaphysical concepts can thus be transformed into material categories.

Marx argues that the social division of labour creates vast accumulations of capital and personal wealth at one pole of society, an increase in the value of things achieved only at the cost of progressive devaluing of human life. The capitalist organisation of labour has the effect of directly transforming man's labour into a saleable commodity: 'This fact implies that the object produced by labour, its product, now stands opposed to it as an *alien being*, as a *power independent* of the producer. The product of labour is labour which has been embodied in an object and turned into a physical thing; this product is an *objectification* of labour.'[4]

It is important to grasp the distinction Marx draws between objectification and alienation. He criticises Hegel for confusing and rendering them synonymous terms. Objectification is the process through which man externalises himself in nature and society, for example, by producing things such as tools, a process whereby he becomes *necessarily* an object for others, within the structure of social relations built upon the simplest form of economy. Alienation occurs only when man, having externalised himself in nature and society, finds his activity, his 'essence', operating on him as an external, alien and oppressive power. For Marx, objectification was unavoidable if man was to humanise and transform nature into an expression of himself, a necessary evil for the growth of a truly humane and social man. As such, objectification is not identical with alienation, for in capitalist society Marx argued 'this process of objectification appears . . . as a process of alienation from the standpoint of labour, and as appropriation of alien labour from the standpoint of capital'.[5] The point is clear : objectification within capitalist society implies alienation, since capitalism constitutes the total alienation of human labour, for capital dominates it completely. Hegel, in making objectification and alienation identical terms, concluded that man ('Spirit') must remain forever trapped in alienation as his essential and ultimately tragic condition. Marx, however, by linking alienation with economic and social structure grasped its historical character, and argued that the abolition of its cause, private property within capitalism, will finally liberate man in Communism. For in Communist society the act of objectification does not imply alienation, since labour would be seen from the standpoint of socialised, that is, fully humanised production.

Marx identified four main characteristics of alienation : man's alienation from nature, from himself, from his 'species being' (a term taken from Feuerbach) and from other men. Capitalism alienates man essentially from his own activity, from the product of his labour ('alienation of things'), thus turning labour's product into an alien object; the more he works the more the worker finds himself dominated by the world of objects his own labour has created : 'The worker puts his life into the object, and his life then belongs no longer to himself but to the object. The greater his activity . . . the less he possesses. What is embodied in the product of his labour is no longer his own. The greater this product is . . . the more he is diminished.'[6]

Man's 'self-confirming essence', his labour, turns increasingly against him under the capitalist direction of industry and alienates him from productive activity; his work becomes a 'forced activity', an 'external thing' denying rather than fulfilling him, serving to stunt his faculties, inducing misery, exhaustion and mental despair. Work is wholly instrumental : '. . . the more refined his product the more crude and misshapen the worker; the more civilised the product the more barbarous the worker; the more the work manifests intelligence the more the worker declines in intelligence and becomes a slave of nature.'[7]

Thus under capitalism work is an oppressive necessity; man feels free only outside work in his leisure time or with his family. Man feels free only as an *individual* and is thus alienated as a 'species being', for unlike the animals, man, through his activity, produces not merely for himself but for the whole of nature. He has, too, an awareness of this activity and continually reproduces himself in both consciousness and real life. But alienated labour turns the product of labour from an activity of the species into the activity of the individual. Capitalism defines the worker as an individual possessing a saleable commodity, labour, which is then purchased by 'another' and his activity is no longer *his* activity. Now, like the animals, man produces only for himself; he is isolated, his life fragmented, living no more as a species man but as a mere individual, living for *himself*.[8]

Marx's early writings thus propound two basic themes : firstly, that while man creates the social world through his own activity he experiences it as alien and hostile; and secondly, that both idealist philosophy and political economy, the theories which first disclosed this alienation, depict human relationships not as relations between persons but as relations between things. Political economy is thus the ultimate expression of this process of reification :

It is self-evident that political economy treats the proletarian . . . [as] a *worker*. It can, therefore, propound the thesis that he, like a horse, must receive just as much as will enable him to work. Political economy does not deal with him in his free time, as a human being, . . . but . . . conceives the worker only as a draught animal, as a beast whose needs are strictly limited to bodily needs.[9]

The most alienated social class by virtue of its economic function is the proletariat. But the proletariat can exist as a class only through the private ownership of the means of production, the very basis of alienated labour. Therefore Marx argues that the emancipation of the worker from his alienated condition includes the emancipation of all humanity : 'For all human servitude is involved in the relation of the worker to production and all types of servitude are only modifications or consequences of this relation.'[10] It follows that in capitalist society everyone is alienated, from the capitalist whose life is dominated by the compulsive laws of capital accumulation and the necessity for seeking more and more profit, to the writers

92

and artists who sell their creative talents to the highest commercial bidder. A total revolution is thus called for and the spearhead is the working class, a class which constitutes the 'effective dissolution' of the capitalist order, for when it demands the abolition of private property 'it only lays down as a *principle for society* what society has already made a principle *for the proletariat*, and what the latter already involuntarily embodies as the negative result of society'. The alienation of the working class is the alienation of the whole society : the exploitative relation between capital and labour seeps through the entire social structure and '*an inhuman power*' rules everything.[11]

Political economy could probe no further into its descriptions of the social world and its contradictions. It could not explain why capitalist society produces such obvious antagonisms as an alienated social world and increasing material affluence, for, beginning from the fact of private property and assuming its universal quality, it never sought to explain the laws of development or economic relations : 'When . . . the relation of wages to profits is defined, this is explained in terms of the interests of the capitalists; in other words, what should be explained is assumed.'[12] Political economy ended with the celebration of bourgeois activity as universal activity and the capitalist mode of production as the close of history. The contradictions, the negative elements were eliminated.

Alienation is thus a denial of man's potentiality for creative intelligence and the building of a truly humane society. Capitalism, writes Marx, is built around this denial, a society compounded from contradictions and thus conflict. Freedom from alienation thus becomes indissolubly bound to total revolution.

II

In recent years a number of critics have argued that the 'essential' Marx, the genuine fighter for human freedom and dignity, is here in these early writings, and that the 'theory' of alienation constitutes the cornerstone of his social theory. In short, alienation becomes a normative concept relating to a philosophical anthropology which asserts the primacy of an all-sided non-alienated man whose essence is subverted by capitalist organisation. In contrast to this is the argument that Marx's ideas developed beyond his early *philosophical phase* through an 'epistemological break' to the mature, scientific theories of *Capital*; there is thus a minimum of continuity between his early and late writings. The decisive text in this transition is *The German Ideology* where Marx, so it is argued, rejects his 'humanist' past, abandons 'species man' and embarks on the more scientific study of 'real men and real conditions', a process finally consummated in the *Contribution to the Critique of Political Economy* (1859).

These extreme interpretations must be rejected. It is a common fallacy, for example, to ascribe a wholly *idealist* notion of human nature to Marx's early writings and then suggest an idealist *continuity* to his thought : on this view *Capital* becomes an ethical treatise declaiming against capitalist exploitation. But at no point in the *Paris Manuscripts* does Marx write of an ahistorical man ; indeed, the emphasis is directed against the idealist arguments of previous philosophers which had been built largely on an abstract and non-historical conception of man, on a *fixed* human nature. In his discussion of Hegel's concept of 'estrangement' Marx makes it perfectly clear that he is rescuing the 'rational kernel' within it from its idealist distortions. His discussion of classical political economy emphasises the empirical and *historical* : man, he writes again and again, is a social being, he is no abstraction 'squatting outside the world' but is himself 'the human world, the state, society'. Of German philosophy he observed that its great speculative structure had omitted 'the *real* man', that is, a social and historical being.[13] The whole purpose of these early writings lay in their criticism of theories which, starting out from human nature, had failed to grasp human nature as the historical activity of men and not as a timeless essence. In *The Holy Family*, Marx was more specific : human nature was no more than 'the totality of social relations'.

The claim, then, that in Marx's theory of social development 'man's nature remains the same underneath and that when the capitalist death knell has sounded human beings will step forth, once again able to lead the kind of whole, unfragmented lives they had known before the rises of private property' is patently absurd,[14] for even in the early writings Marx is fully aware of the complex relation between human nature and society. For the whole point of human nature was its contradictoriness : Adam Smith, for example, had argued in the *Wealth of Nations* that man was in essence an egoistic and selfish being seeking his own interests before that of the community; but in his *Theory of Moral Sentiments* (1757) Smith postulated a sociable, altruistic individual whose moral conduct flowed from his awareness of social obligation and interaction, a contradiction within Smith's work he was unable to solve. But Marx, setting out from the *fact* of these contradictions implicit in bourgeois philosophy and political economy, was able to develop his argument that man is both the product and the producer of his environment, is both egoistical *and* altruistic. Thus the essence of human nature lay in its many-sidedness, in its contradictory not homogeneous structure. Marx's point, of course, was that human nature is not a property which simply inhabits man, such as the egoism of 'economic man', but is rather a relation between men.

All this, however, is not to suggest that the Marx of the *Paris Manuscripts* is the 'mature' Marx. On the contrary, at this stage of his development, alienation was largely understood in *abstract* rather than concrete historical terms cohering around the political economists' and philosophers' argument of the 'fragmentation' of man. Marx does have a view here of the *whole* man whose human stature is lessened by the power of capital; man must be returned to a non-alienated state, reunited with nature, other men and society. As late as 1846 he could write in this 'utopian' strain that in Communism the division of labour would no longer allocate men to specific occupational roles but allow man, if he so wishes, 'to hunt in the morning, fish in the afternoon, rear cattle in the evening, criticise after dinner . . . without ever becoming a hunter, fisherman, shepherd or critic'.[15]

After 1846 a more scientific and rigorous approach emerges and it is in this very general sense of Marx's *development* that the concept of alienation has to be understood. The argument that the concept of alienation in *Capital* is substantially identical with that employed in the *Paris Manuscripts* suggests the untenable view that although Marx's method and his theory of surplus value and exploitation underwent extensive revision in the 1850s, especially in the *Grundrisse*, the analysis of alienation remained at the same conceptual and empirical level. Alienation in the *Paris Manuscripts* was organically related to Marx's understanding of economics and philosophy at that time; by the 1850s his economic theory had changed considerably. Thus from a purely logical standpoint it would seem that those concepts which are retained in the mature writings – alienation, reification etc. – will imply something radically different from their earlier usage. The appeal of the early writings undoubtedly lies in their portrayal of man as the ultimate arbiter of the social world; sociological phenomenology places great emphasis on Marx's depiction of man as an active agent, duplicating himself and his powers through continuous acts of reciprocity. Yet the picture which emerges from the *Paris Manuscripts* is not as voluntaristic as this suggests, for if alienation dominates the social world to the extent of debilitating man's creative and natural powers, transforming him into an object, then how can man *act* to change the world, how is *praxis* possible? It is this contradiction which leads Marx to posit Communism as the ideal state which men *ought* to strive for, and the proletariat as the negation of capitalist alienation. What is missing from Marx's account is dialectics, a sense that the relation of man to the social world his labour has created is contradictory and uneven : Marx's humanist concept of alienation is one-directional and deterministic, more philosophical and speculative than sociological and concretely historical.

Between the writing of the *Paris Manuscripts* and *Capital* Marx had decisively rejected Feuerbach's humanistic philosophy as the starting-point for social theory. His main criticism related to Feuerbach's concept of *man* as the index of the social world; Marx argues that the human essence is the totality of social relations, a view more precise and *empirical* than Feuerbach's own more general philosophic humanism. But it does not follow from this that Marx abandoned some of his early concepts. In *Capital*, it is true, the term alienation does not often occur, but the related concepts of 'fetishism of commodities' and reification are frequently discussed and these form an important part of Marx's analysis of modern capitalism; these concepts cannot be understood except in terms of alienation. In both the *Grundrisse* and the 'mature' *Theories of Surplus Value* the term alienation is frequently used : thus discussing the growth of manufacturing industry and the necessity for an extended division of labour, Marx argues that the workers 'assembled together as wage-workers . . . as workers who must sell their labour power because their conditions of labour confront them as alien property, as an independent alien force'.[16] A particular form of social labour becomes increasingly seen in terms of the commodity, money and capital :

> The effects of things as materialised aspects of the labour process are attributed to them in capital, in their personification, their independence in respect of labour. They would cease to have these effects if they were to cease to confront labour in this *alienated form*. The *capitalist*, as capitalist, is simply the personification of capital, that creation of labour endowed with its own will and personality which stands in opposition to labour.[17]

Marx's social theory then, had moved beyond the essentially humanistic writings of 1843–5 to a grasp of the 'inner movement' of the capitalist social system as opposed to its apparent alienated forms. The *Paris Manuscripts* had not developed a theory of social change, of social dynamics, of what Marx called the 'inner nature' of capital itself : '. . . a scientific analysis of competition is not possible before we have a conception of the inner nature of capital just as the apparent motions of the heavenly bodies are not intelligible to any but him, who is acquainted with their real motions, motions which are not directly perceptible by the senses.'[18] In the *Paris Manuscripts* there is no sociological link between commodity production and the concepts of alienation and reification. The theories of surplus value and exploitation had not yet emerged as scientific discoveries; alienation thus functions in the early work as a 'critical' concept attacking the dehumanisation of man within the capitalist system.

III

Alienated labour, Marx had written in the *Paris Manuscripts*, was the chief characteristic of the social world of modern capitalism. The worker is converted into a mindless appendage of machinery, his faculties crippled by the division of labour. As we have seen earlier, this was a theme common to political economists (Smith), historians (Millar) and philosophers (Hegel). In the nineteenth century bourgeois voices continued to be raised declaiming against the crippling and inhuman social consequences of the division of labour. Tocqueville, for example, wrote that as the worker became more skilled in his one operation 'he loses the general faculty of applying his mind to the direction of work', and in proportion as 'the workman improves, the man is degraded. . . . In proportion as the principle of the division of labour is more extensively applied, the workman becomes more weak, more narrow-minded, and more dependent. The art advances, the artisan recedes.'[19] Comte, too, criticised the division of labour for its potentially dangerous social effects, but only Marx grasped that the alienation which they described but failed to understand or *name* was not simply the product of work specialisation but rather of the organisation of labour within a definite historical mode of production. For both Comte and Tocqueville alienation was an inescapable part of the *human condition*, an identification the young Marx had criticised from an abstract historical standpoint. All this had changed by the time Marx wrote his *Grundrisse*. Whereas in the *Paris Manuscripts* for example, he had not fully understood the notion of an economic surplus, in the *Grundrisse* the emphasis shifts away from competition to production; there is, too, a significant change in terminology, labour becoming labour power, indicating Marx's awareness that man's labour power was a unique commodity within the capitalist system. In the early writings Marx had followed Smith and Ricardo in defining labour as 'abstract, general and social labour' – an approach which actually hid the precise relation between the creation of value (expressed in money, for example) and human activity (expressed in labour). Labour power is a commodity; labour *in general* is not. The creation of wealth is possible only through the exploitation of labour power, the transformation of man's labour into a commodity. It is in this sense that Marx divided the working day into two sections : necessary labour (that expended on replenishing the labourer in the form of wages) and surplus labour (that which accrues to the capitalist in the form of surplus value). This is the heart of Marx's theory of exploitation, for it is only within capitalism that 'exchange values' come to dominate 'use values'. In slave and feudal societies the exchange of products took place to a great extent on the basis of legal rights and exchange value was not the dominant principle it is within capitalism. Every commodity, Marx argued, has both a use and exchange value, with use value expressing a definite relation between the consumer and the object being consumed, while exchange values appear as quantifiable indices of relations between things, between commodities.[20]

But Marx argues that such distinctions are false, for although exchange value expresses a relation between commodities it is in fact a social relation : 'In the exchange value the social relations of persons are transformed into the social conduct of objects.' The individual within a society dominated by exchange values feels that he is no longer influenced by personal, human processes but rather by impersonal, external and *alien* forces. The transformation of all activities and products into commodities creates a social world characterised by the movement of *things*.[21] Capitalist production aims at the expansion of value : the capitalist's subjective purpose is merely the corollary of the objective dictates of commodity production. 'Use-values must therefore never be looked upon as the real aim of the capitalist; neither must the profit on any single transaction. The restless never-ending process of profit-making alone is what he aims at.'[22]

In a society dominated by exchange value, the real social foundation of the unequal exchange between capital and labour are hidden and 'mystified'. In a famous passage Marx writes of the commodity as 'a mysterious thing' which hides the social character of man's labour and presents the relations between the producers and the totality of their labour 'as a social relation, existing not between themselves, but between the products of their labour'.[23] Social relations become wholly inverted : within capitalism 'every element, even the simplest, the commodity for example, is already an inversion and causes relations between people to appear as attributes of things and as relations of people to the social attributes of things'.[24] The social world of modern capitalism, Marx is arguing, is a perverted world of the 'fetishism of commodities' in which the products of labour generate an apparent *independence*, in which objects begin indeed 'to rule the producers instead of being ruled by them',[25] and where those engaged in capitalist production 'live in a bewitched world' in which their own relationships 'appear to them as properties of things, as properties of the material elements of production'.[26] Man becomes *dominated* by the world of things, by processes which his own activity has created but which, through the capitalist mode of production, turn against him, as objective independent processes. In the *Grundrisse* he writes that 'social wealth confronts labour in more powerful portions as an alien and dominant power . . . a monstrous objective power' which, created through social labour 'belongs not to the worker, but . . . to capital'. The emphasis, Marx notes, is 'not on the state of being *objectified*, but . . . of being *alienated*, dispossessed, sold'.[27] And, in almost identical language he writes in *Capital* :

> We have seen that the growing accumulation of capital implies its growing concentration. Thus grows the power of capital, the alienation of the conditions of social production personified in the capitalist from the real producers. Capital comes more and more to the fore as a social power, whose agent is the capitalist. This social power no longer stands in any possible relation to that which the labour of a single individual can create. It becomes an alienated, independent social power, which stands opposed to society as an object, and as an object that is the capitalist's source of power.[26]

The extraction of surplus value, the control over labour power invested in the individual capitalist and capital, results in the development of a social world in which human life is progressively devalued as the world of objects is exalted. Marx had commented on this tendency in the *Paris Manuscripts* : 'The worker becomes an ever cheaper commodity the more goods he creates. The devaluation of the human world increases in direct relation with the increase in value of the world of things.'[29] Here, then, is the connecting link between Marx's early and later writings : capitalist production creates great wealth but it does so only at the cost of diminishing man's potentiality. Life becomes increasingly dominated by quantitative judgements. There are two clear aspects to this process both of which have been substantiated by contemporary sociological research:

(1) An emphasis on the ownership of *things* as an index of a successful life;

(2) The grasp of time in thing-like terms, as something external to the individual, which must be suffered in order to acquire something else through wages etc.

Thus it is a commonplace of modern industrial sociology that the worker engaged in highy routinised work tasks develops 'a heightened time consciousness' and many surveys report that workers, asked if their job was boring, replied that 'the time passes'.[30] In a world dominated by commodities and surplus value the worker's labour power is quantified, measured as precisely as possible, treated as an external thing. The social world of commodity production is a world of external things which are not understood by those who act upon and create them. Reification has taken over: men comprehend the products of their labour (embodied in social relations and institutions) as autonomous, objective forces unconnected with human activity.

This reification manifests itself most sharply in a social consciousness which grasps the social world in natural terms as something fixed and immutable. Those who see society in reified categories will stress the world's externality, its deadness; it will be a world in which the individual is a passive object of determinate external processes, ruled by blind, inexorable laws seemingly beyond the control of the individual, a world in which 'dead things are the only really active elements'.[31] In pre-industrial society, on the other hand, in societies where use value was not dominated by exchange value, social relations were clear and unequivocal. Within the feudal mode of production, for example, social relations were largely based on personal ties and obligations, an unequal relationship grounded in custom and tradition and understood as such. The social structure of capitalism, however, is based on the impersonal relationships which flow from the supremacy of exchange value over use value. Thus in societies where exchange value has replaced direct use value (although, of course, all commodities still retain a use value) a formal equality pervades and masks class relations; the world of capitalist commodity production appears as a world of equals bound by free contractual agreements.

But this is a world which conceals its essential feature, exploitation and the division of the working day into necessary and surplus labour. The exchange between capital and labour bears the illusion of a free exchange of equivalents (labour for wages) and it is at this point that the mystification of social relations occurs : the worker acts as if his labour power is not exploited, that in return for a 'fair day's work' he will be justly rewarded. He acts as if capitalist social inequality is something natural and therefore essential, possibly inevitable; as if differential rewards are necessary if society is to function adequately. The worker fails to understand that with others engaged in commodity production he has become part of capital itself and is but a special mode of its existence :

> Hence, the productive power developed by the labourer when working in co-operation, is the productive power of capital. This power is developed gratuitously, whenever the workmen are placed under given conditions, and it is capital that places them under such conditions. Because this power cost capital nothing, and because, on the other hand, the labourer himself does not develop it before his labour belongs to capital, it appears as a power with which capital is endowed by Nature – a productive power that is immanent in capital.[32]

Sociological research into the structure of the modern working class and especially the attitudes and consciousness of the modern 'affluent worker',[33] tend to support Marx's analysis of reification. Many workers, it is reported, understood the class structure of capitalism not as an 'historically created system of domination which had to be overthrown' but rather as 'a basic *datum* of social existence – *as a natural rather than as a man made phenomenon* which individuals had in the main to accept and adapt to'.[34] Indeed, the thesis is argued that the 'affluent worker', unlike the old traditional proletarian, is no longer ideologically committed to political struggles between capital and labour, rather he has become home- and consumer-oriented, rejecting political class consciousness in favour of 'commodity consciousness'. The 'affluent worker' is now 'privatised'. The result of this wholly pragmatic and instrumental orientation' to the social world is that the 'privatised worker' loses the strong fraternal nexus of the traditional working-class community. Leading an isolated, consumer-conscious existence the 'affluent worker' experiences work as intrinsically unrewarding apart from its economic rewards. Society, in short, is reified, comprehended as a natural phenomenon abetted by technology. The only viable proposition for those workers who grasp society in these terms is one of adaptation, to make 'the best of a bad job', to 'put up with it'.

Equally important is the stress which the 'affluent worker' places on money as the basic criterion of social class. As will be argued in Chapter 5, social stratification is not uni-dimensional but multi-dimensional and its structure does not hinge on one single factor of wages paid for the labour time expended in production. But it is a clear function of a reified social consciousness to understand the role of money in this way.[35]

There is, too, the crucial question of 'privatisation'. In the *Paris Manuscripts* Marx had drawn a distinction between 'species activity' and 'private activity', between man's 'consciousness of his species', and the cult of the individual based on the idealisation of the *abstract* individual.[36] The 'privatised' worker is indeed an 'abstract' individual : isolated, fragmented and leading a life which he acknowledges (to the interviewers) as 'dull'.[37] He seems cut off even from his class, except in his instrumental, calculative orientation to the trade-union movement as a means only for improving wages. This conclusion will be discussed in greater detail in the following chapter, but the important point to note here is the assumption, built into this as well as other sociological research, that the workers' private activity is a thing in itself and can be fully comprehended apart from the life activity of the class as a whole. For assuming 'privatisation' to be a genuine condition of modern labour, what causes it? Is it, for example, related to the fact that in bourgeois society the dominant ideology exalts 'privatisation' at the expense of communal political action or indeed any form of *praxis*?

There is, too, the question of whether the reified consciousness of the affluent worker flows *meaningfully* from the mode of production – private ownership of productive property – or from its mode of technology. Many industrial sociologists argue that technology, whether capitalist of socialist, is the major force in promoting work discontent and alienation. Yet by divesting technology of its specific economic content the concept of alienation becomes meaningful *only* as a reflection of a malfunctioning within the specific *work situation*, it becomes work bound. Thus for Blauner, in his study of the American factory worker, 'technology . . . determines the nature of the job tasks performed by blue-collar employees', shaping the precise ways in which they are alienated. In his analysis of various work situations (auto workers, print and chemical workers) Blauner separates the exploitive character of work in capitalism as a whole from the specific mode of work in particular industries. Thus, defining alienation in the technological sense of 'powerlessness' *on the job*, he shatters the notion of alienation as a total concept relating to the role of capital within capitalism as a whole and its close relationship with the organisation of society for the production of commodities. In this interpretation the worker's relation to technology – manual and machine operations involving mechanisation and technical knowledge – is seen as the major source of 'meaninglessness', 'powerlessness', 'normlessness', 'isolation', and 'self-estrangement', the categories of the contemporary sociological definition of alienation, which Blauner argues stem from 'standardised production and a division of labour that reduces the size of the workers contribution to the final product'.

This technological definition of alienation – an attempt to divest the critical and polemical elements from Marx's concept – employs categories which themselves refer to the process of reification. For the worker who experiences loss of autonomy, a sense of meaninglessness in work, who is isolated from other workers and himself, is indeed someone who has been turned effectively into an object, a thing : his social world is thus seen as external and dead apart from home and family. The categories of 'meaninglessness' *et al.* are in fact *aspects* of alienation but not alienation itself. Alienation is not defined by the subjective states of those experiencing it and is not to be equated with a sense of not 'belonging in the work situation' and an inability to identify with the organisation and its goals;[38]

its essence lies not in the consciousness of the worker but in the objective conditions of capitalist organisation of industry, of production which transforms man's labour power into an external and alien force. The work situation is only one *part* of the division of property and its control by the dominant class (capitalists) or bureaucracy (Soviet Union). In both cases the powerlessness which is seen as the major condition of alienation by many industrial sociologists, the 'expectancy . . . held by the individual that his own behaviour cannot determine the occurrence of the outcomes . . . he seeks'[39] derives from the laws of profit, investment and capital accumulation which flow from the need to appropriate surplus value from the labourer. When, for example, Blauner writes that 'alienation exists when workers are unable to control their immediate work processes, to develop a sense of purpose and function which connects their jobs to the overall organisation of production, to belong to integrated industrial communities . . .' he is in effect arguing that reification is *not* a function of alienation and thus of capitalist production. By defining alienation exclusively in terms of reification, that is, by aspects of control and authority in the work situation he ignores the total organisation of labour power in society as a whole. And focusing on the subjective states of workers in their different work functions he can conclude that a change in their different work functions in the *internal* organisation of industry can effectively eliminate the more extreme form of alienation. The norms of capitalist production, its goals and purposes, can thus be divorced from practical organisation of work on the shop floor. In effect this standpoint is utopian : it fails to grasp alienation genetically as an historical force; and identifying it with objectification it concludes that only a tempering, not an abolition of its inhuman consequences is possible.

IV

From what has been argued it might seem that Marx's theory of alienation is a form of determinism, that the worker and capitalist are trapped within irreversible social processes which they neither understand nor can change. This is certainly true of Marx's first discussion of alienation. But the whole weight of his later, mature work is against this interpretation. Foremost is an emphasis on the *dialectical* character of social development and social consciousness. Thus, while the division of labour may stupefy the consciousness of the individual worker, there are opposite tendencies generated by the division of labour itself which point clearly towards liberation. Thus modern machine production concentrates all initiative into collective effort making capital 'rich in social productive power' at the cost of the individual labourer who is converted to an 'automaton' and 'the special skill of each . . . insignificant operative vanishes as an infinitesimal quantity before the science, the gigantic physical forces, and the mass of labour that are embodied in the factory mechanism . . .'.[40] Yet at the same time this negative side is contradicted by a positive element :

> Modern Industry . . . imposes the necessity of recognising, as a fundamental law of production, variation of work, consequently fitness of the labourer for varied work, consequently the greatest possible development of his varied aptitudes. . . . Modern Industry . . . compels society, under penalty of death, to replace the detail worker of today, crippled by life-long repetition of one and the same trivial operation, and thus reduced to a mere fragment of a man, by the fully developed individual, fit for a variety of labours, ready to face any change of production, and to whom the different social functions he performs, are but so many modes of giving free scope to his own natural and acquired powers.[41]

The technical necessities of capitalist production, then, actually negate the tendency to turn man into a partial being; the worker becomes educated and many 'receive some little instruction in technology and in the practical handling of the various implements of labour'. Equally important is the fact that the worker, through social production, becomes aware of the need to defend his interests through the collective action of trade unions. But the worker remains exploited by capital and his full potential restricted by the fetishist forms which social relations embody. The forces of production are constrained by the social relations of production, by the requirements

106

of surplus value; it is this exploitative nexus which prevents the potentiality implicit within modern industry from being fully realised. Yet Marx is quite specific : the means for abolishing alienation exist within the very process which has created it.

It is this dialectical understanding which is the distinguishing cornerstone of Marx's social theory. The celebrated thesis of Max Weber of the increasing and ineluctable 'rationalisation' of Western society hinges on a one-sided and fatalistic conception of technology. In his discussion of bureacracy, for example, Weber argued that both capitalism and socialism require bureaucratic organisation. Discipline and control were equally important to socialism as to capitalism and in this sense some form of alienation is inevitable. For without bureaucracy capitalism itself would have been impossible; the development of capitalism, because it creates 'an urgent need for stable, strict, intensive and calculable administration', hinges on bureaucratic rationality.[42] In Weber's analysis the principle of rationality functions as a force external to and independent of human control. Moreover, rationalisation in this analysis transcends its specific historical forms to become a form of domination. In Weber's discussion rationality and technology have become reified : their impact on society may be modified but not brought under human will and subordinated to human purposes.

Weber's technological determinism is echoed in the contemporary writings of Herbert Marcuse. Rationality, he argues, has become the goal of modern industrial capitalism, pervading all aspects of social life. Weber had written of the rationalisation of culture, the parcelling out into different spheres of the varied activities of the human mind. For Marcuse a rationalised technology has created a world of artificial needs, mass consumption and irrational goals which men are too eager to accept. The exploitative relation of capital and labour is thoroughly hidden by the 'false consciousness' which flows directly from the 'one-dimensional' awareness of modern man. A technocratic and bureaucratic élite effectively controls the mass media and high, 'irrational' consumption : social differences become minimised through a levelling of consumption habits, leisure activities and social aspirations. The rationalisation of culture is complete and Marx's vision of proletarian revolution becomes utopian.[43] A 'repressive tolerance' characterises modern industrial society, and the technical apparatus of control guarantees that consumer-oriented 'slaves' are kept in a state of liberated conformity. Revolutionary *praxis* is therefore possible only through outsiders in this one-dimensional society, the blacks, and those with access to critical understanding, the students. The point here is Marcuse's emphasis on the overpowering structure of reification; and this emphasis is closely linked with his rejection of a *dialectical* understanding of capitalist development and society. For Marx's theory of alienation is not a theory of the *total* and pervasive power of reification in capitalist society as Marcuse interprets it, for if reification is the dominant condition of bourgeois society then how is it possible for man to free himself from this condition?

Marcuse's analysis of Western society in terms of reification owes much to Weber and Lukács. The all-pervasive power of reification is perhaps the major theme of Lukács's *History and Class Consciousness*, a left-wing analogue for Weber's 'rationalisation'. One other social theorist should be mentioned in this context : Georg Simmel, who clearly influenced Lukács's interpretation of Marx, was the first sociologist to emphasise the reified tendencies of modern society. For Simmel, the social world is made up of a vast variety of cultural objects – the products of a rationalised technology – which confront man as alien, immutable forms. These objects belong to man's cultural development, to his growing self-consciousness, are part of man himself; but now they attain a 'fetishistic' character as objects independent of man, becoming 'more and more linked to each other in a self-contained world which has increasingly fewer contacts with the subjective psyche and its desires and sensibilities'.[44] This split between product and producer is linked to the division of labour which for Simmel creates over-specialised work functions so that the individual becomes 'a mere cog in an enormous organization of things and powers which tear from his hands all progress, spirituality, and value in order to transform them from their subjective form into the form of a purely objective life'.[45]

Simmel's 'tragic vision' of Western culture is echoed in Lukács's similar treatment of reification. He argues that capitalist society transforms the commodity into a 'universal category' and as the worker's labour power is a commodity then 'the fate of the worker becomes the fate of society as a whole'. Reification means that society satisfies its needs through commodity exchange; capitalist development thus brings with it a deepening structure of reification which fatefully dominates social consciousness. Like Simmel, Lukács sees this process as total, stamping its 'imprint upon the whole consciousness of man' so that his various qualities and abilities cease to be his expression, but that of *another*, 'things which he can "own" or "dispose of" like the various objects of the external world'.[46] There is no escape :

> Reification is . . . the necessary, immediate reality of every person living in capitalist society. It can be overcome only by *constant and constantly renewed efforts to disrupt the reified structure of existence by concretely relating to the concretely manifested contradictions of the total development, by becoming conscious of these contradictions for the total development.*[47]

Lukács argues that the proletariat is saved because, as we have seen from the previous chapter, having been turned into a commodity it alone develops the standpoint from which a genuine understanding of society is possible. For since the proletariat is an *object* then its consciousness, developed historically through concentration in large-scale factory organisation which facilitates *class* identification, constitutes 'the self-consciousness of the object', a consciousness which automatically cuts through the fetishised and reified structures of its thought.[48]

But this is hardly tenable. It is untrue factually that the worker is transformed into a thing and his relations become those of things. The social world of commodities undoubtedly penetrates the workers' consciousness and yields a false because 'natural' understanding of societal forces, but equally, as Marx pointed out in *Capital*, there is always human, non-thinglike resistance to this process through trade unions and working-class culture. A dialectical relation exists between reification, alienation and class structure : the worker continually resists, through class organisation and activity, the process whereby his activity and himself become abstract entities, things. Marx himself argued, in the chapter on the working day in *Capital*, that the tendency of capital was to wring as much surplus value from the labourer as possible, and to effect this the hours of work were steadily increased from the eighteenth century onwards. But the working class resisted these tendencies : the Factory Acts which limited the hours of work and the age at which children could be employed were the result not of philanthropic intention but class struggle :

> The creation of a normal working day is . . . the product of a protracted civil war, more or less dissembled, between the capitalist class and the working class. As the contest takes place in the arena of modern industry, it first breaks out in the home of . . . England. The English factory workers were the champions, not only of the English, but of the modern working class generally. . . .[49]

In the most highly developed capitalist society in the nineteenth century the working class, on Lukács's terms, should have been totally dominated by reification : yet the British labour movement created the most powerful trade unions in the world and actually improved their social, economic and political status. The consciousness of the working class is not explained by postulating reification as a *total* process, for reification is, at all times, a 'moment' in the alienation of the worker. For there are always positive elements within every situation which move the proletariat away from total absorption into capitalist ideology and reification.

The argument of total reification is monolithic not dialectical : it fails to observe the first axiom of Marx's social theory – that the working class exists in specific societies with a consciousness compounded from local and national traditions, ruling-class ideology and working-class organisation (trade unions, etc.). It is an attempt to grasp the objective movement and contradictory elements inherent in social development. The theories of the reification and rationalisation of culture as uniform and total processes reflect a non-dialectical, ahistorical, theoretical standpoint.

Marx's theory of alienation became more precise because more scientific as he moved from the predominantly critical philosophical standpoint of the *Paris Manuscripts* to the mature social theory of *Capital*. In the *Paris Manuscripts* Marx had written of the 'inhuman power' dominating social life, frustrating man's essential powers and transforming him into mere object. In *Capital* Marx shows how the division of labour and factory production can ruin man's physical and intellectual condition, but at the same time create the conditions for working-class political practice. Stunted they may be : but the working class organise themselves into collective bodies and resist the 'inhuman power' of capital. This concept of *praxis* thus constitutes the link between Marx's early and later writings; *Capital* is as much about man creating the social world as is the *Paris Manuscripts*. But unlike the early work, the *Grundrisse* and *Capital* portray man's alienation in terms of the inner and contradictory movement in capitalist production itself, an alienation embodied in the transformation of labour power into a commodity, an exchange value.[50] Alienation is thus the specific, historical condition of labour within the capitalist mode of production and it is in this sense that the class struggle can be understood. *Praxis* means the class struggle : through this, man (i.e. the proletariat) changes himself and society, transforms his nature and develops his 'slumbering powers'.

5

CLASS STRUCTURE AND
CLASS CONSCIOUSNESS

'European sociology after World War II', writes the German sociologist Ralf Dahrendorf, 'started with a large number of studies in
industrial sociology. Most of these were devoted to the working
class and betray the disappointment on the part of their authors
with this class.'[1] The industrial working class, assimilated into capitalist society through the agencies of the Welfare State, political
representation at local and national level, and a rising standard of
living, had seemingly eschewed the revolutionary role ascribed to it
by Marx. Sociologists now argued that the sudden onset of affluence
within advanced industrial capitalist societies was largely responsible
for the lessening of class conflict and the virtual eclipse of working-
class political consciousness. Marx's theory of class, elaborated largely
with reference to nineteenth-century British capitalism, was summarily rejected, both for its predictive failures and oversimplified
conceptions of stratification.

This chapter will discuss Marx's theory of class stratification in
the light of these criticisms, as well as some contemporary sociological research into the nature of the modern working and middle
classes.

I

In the *Paris Manuscripts*, *The Poverty of Philosophy* and *The
Communist Manifesto* Marx outlined his first theory of class. In
these early writings Marx proclaimed the proletariat and bourgeoisie

as the two decisive classes of modern society and the proletariat as the universal negation of alienation. A simple, two-class model is characteristic of these early pronouncements, a theoretical position which implied that revolution flowed directly from obvious antagonisms and inequality. It must be emphasised that Marx's first theory of class derives its force, not from the analysis of 'surplus value' embedded at the heart of his mature theory, but from a more speculative, philosophical understanding of social development. But the elements of Marx's *general* theory of class are none the less clearly evident. Class for Marx was not defined in terms of work function, income or consumption, but rather by the relations it bears with the mode of production. 'Large-scale industry', he wrote, brings together many groups of workers and unites them into definite class groupings against the capitalist : 'This mass is thus already a class as against capital, but not yet for itself. In the struggle . . . this mass becomes united, and constitutes itself as a class for itself. The interests it defends become class interests.'[2]

Marx here expresses his well-known distinction between class 'in itself' and class 'for itself'. For Marx, a class 'in itself' was one in which the various strata, although engaged in dissimilar work activities, are united by their broad social and economic ties; objectively they form a class against capital, but remain non-conscious of the antagonistic relation with an oppressing class. A class 'for itself' is a class in which the members have become profoundly aware of their objective, conflictive connection with another class thus developing the appropriate consciousness and action necessary to defend its interests :

An oppressed class is the vital condition for every society founded on the antagonism of classes. The emancipation of the oppressed class thus implies necessarily the creation of a new society. For the oppressed class to be able to emancipate itself it is necessary that the productive powers already acquired and the existing social relations should no longer be capable of existing side by side. Of all the instruments of production, the greatest productive power is the revolutionary class itself.[3]

It follows that the emancipation of the proletariat requires the abolition of all other classes, substituting 'for the old civil society an association which will exclude classes and their antagonism', a community which specifically eliminates political power, 'since political power is precisely the official expression of antagonism in civil society'. The system of production for private profit necessarily generates classes and antagonisms between them. The economic relations of production bring men together in the areas of production, consumption and administration. But the mode of production conditions the social relations which arise on the basis of purely economic relations. These personal relations are the primary agency of social consciousness. But they are not autonomous forces, their character is forged by economic factors : change arising in the productive forces of men necessarily affects a change in their relations of production.[4] A social class is thus defined both in terms of property ownership or non-ownership and thus the degree of control over, or subservience to, exploitation, and the degree of personal freedom its members enjoy. This latter element is crucially important for understanding the evolution of class consciousness in a modern capitalist society, for in slave-owning or feudal societies the dependent class exercised little effective personal freedom. The slave is an object, owned by his master; the modern worker may not own the means of production, but his person, his self, is not owned and he is free to sell his labour power to the highest bidder and free to withdraw it. The serf, too, owns nothing and cannot exploit the labour of others; but he is bound legally to the land and his lord : 'Personal dependence here characterises the social relations of production.'[5] Wage labour is thus free labour; the worker's social consciousness will therefore reflect his 'formally' free status.

Marx's theory of class, therefore, emphasises the economic relation between the mode and relations of production, and the subjective awareness by the worker of his freedom, his similarities with other workers and the authority and power of a dominant class. It is the conjunction of these two components, the objective and subjective, which creates class consciousness. A frequent and serious misunderstanding of Marx's theory of class is one which minimises this element of consciousness so that the concept becomes merely a matter of statistics – money, consumption patterns, education etc. – when the whole point lies in the relations of domination and subordination with other classes. Class consciousness flows from an awareness of the common aims of a class as against another class. This is why Marx argues, for example, that the peasantry are not a class in the full sense of his concept :

Their mode of production isolates them from one another instead of bringing them into mutual intercourse. . . . In so far as millions of families live under economic conditions of existence that separate their mode of life, their interests and their culture from those of other classes and place them in opposition to them, *they constitute a class.* In so far as there is only a local connection between the small-holding peasants, and the identity of their interests *begets no community, no national unity, and no political organisation,* they do not constitute a class.[6]

Classes, therefore, are clearly distinct from estates, slaves, castes (class, in other words, must not be identified with stratification). The modern proletariat is the first 'underclass' to develop its own large-scale organisation (trade unions) which foster class identifications and class consciousness.

But the mode of production is not a homogeneous structure. Like other elements in society its development is dialectical; each society will contain survivals of a previous mode of production, residues which strike at the heart of a *pure* class model. It is important to grasp this aspect of Marx's thought since it is commonly assumed that the two-class model, outlined in the early work and based as it is on the simple criterion of property ownership, represents Marx's final position on class stratification; that the logic of the capitalist system was to obliterate the middle classes as a class, transforming them into proletarians or bourgeoisie. Thus in *The Communist Manifesto* Marx and Engels write that : 'Our epoch, the epoch of the bourgeoisie, possesses . . . this distinctive feature : it has simplified the class antagonism. Society as a whole is more and more splitting up into two great hostile camps, into two great classes directly facing each other : Bourgeoisie and Proletariat.'[7]

In his more polemical works Marx clearly offered an oversimplified view of capitalist stratification and its possible developments such as the phenomenon of social mobility. In his other more scientific and historical texts Marx repudiates such a simplistic class model. In the historical study, *The Eighteenth Brumaire of Louis Bonaparte* he distinguishes between the financial bourgeoisie, industrial bourgeoisie, petit-bourgeoisie, proletariat, landlords and free farmers, while in other studies of France and Germany he notes bourgeoisie, petit-bourgeoisie, farmers, peasants, serfs, agricultural workers, lumpen proletariat and feudal lords. In these writings Marx never articulates a simple two-class model as an *historical* fact, and he is at pains to emphasise the one category his earlier analysis had denied, the existence of the middle class.

Marx's second theory of class is highly complex, embracing proletariat, ruling class, middle class. The category of the middle class is especially important. It consists of variegated groups such as the small producers, the petit-bourgeoisie (employers of small fractions of labour); those engaged in the 'circulation of commodities' (marketing, buying, selling); the middle men (wholesalers, shopkeepers, speculators); those who 'command in the name of capital' (managers, etc.) and their assistants, supervisors, secretaries, book-keepers, clerks; and finally an 'ideological' group embracing lawyers, artists, journalists, clergy and state officials such as the military and the police.[8] The simplified model of the early philosophical/polemical works has disappeared. Indeed, Marx argues that the tendency of capitalism is not necessarily towards class polarisation but rather to augment a new middle class, what he calls the 'servants of the public', those who perform important 'social functions' – professional groups, magistrates, entertainers – who exercise an increasingly significant role in the maintenance of bourgeois society. As capitalism develops its productive forces this class increases in size and influence. Marx even suggests that with the growth of corporations and the gradual diffusion of the division of labour to all sectors of industry and commerce, managers and supervisors increase in numbers.[9] He is quite explicit : '. . . the constantly growing number of the middle classes which, situated between the workers on the one side and the capitalists and landlords on the other side, live mainly and directly on revenue . . . press like a heavy burden on the labouring class, enlarging the social security and power of the upper ten thousand.'[10]

These statements clearly contradict the view that Marx analysed class dichotomously, rather they suggest an awareness of the essential nature of capitalist development. Writing of Malthus, Marx argues that Malthus's hope 'that the middle class will grow in size and that the working proletariat will make up a constantly decreasing proportion of the total population' is no more than 'the course of bourgeois society'.[11]

What can we make of these statements? It is true that Marx never analysed in any one text the capitalist class system except in general historical terms. The final chapter of *Capital*, called simply 'Classes', paradoxically breaks off at the point where Marx approaches a close analysis of the English stratification system in the nineteenth century. This fragment occurs at the end of his work precisely because, as has been argued in Chapter 2, Marx's method was to work dialectically from the parts to the whole, and from the whole to the parts. His analysis of capitalism was initially based on a 'pure' model purged of all complicating historical factors, such as foreign trade, monopoly, colonialism and trade unions, a model dominated by the capital–labour relation. Of course, as the work unfolds, more and more complicating elements are re-introduced as Marx moves towards a full understanding of the actual historical functioning of the capitalist system in England. Unlike France and Germany, England enjoyed a far more advanced industrial base and more clear-cut class structure (no peasantry). Marx's comments suggest, however, that even here the class structure is not as polarised as many of his commentators have argued.

He begins by identifying three broad classes – the owners of labour power, capital and land – arguing that they constitute the 'three big classes of modern society based on the capitalist mode of production'. But : 'In England modern society is indisputably most highly and classically developed in economic structure. Nevertheless, even here the stratification of classes does not appear in its pure form. *Middle and immediate strata* even here obliterate lines of demarcation . . .' Marx adds that this tendency of capitalism to propagate a complex not simple class stratification is 'immaterial for our analysis', because the general trend of capitalist production lies in concentrating more and more property in fewer and fewer hands. In capitalist society the bourgeoisie (industrialists, bankers, etc.) constitute the dominant class while the petit-bourgeoisie are forced into a middle stratum although ideologically bound to the dominant class. The tendency to a concentration of property does not imply a simple dichotomic class structure based on wage labour nor a total proletarianisation of society.[12] In *The Communist Manifesto* Marx had predicted a sharp polarisation, a prediction made before his detailed analysis of the historical development of capitalism. As was argued in Chapter 1, there are no unconditional prophecies in Marx's mature social thought, only tendencies based on certain economic laws. It is crucial to grasp that Marx's social theory is not a deterministic theory of capitalist breakdown. As *Capital* unfolds it becomes increasingly obvious that the tendency for the rate of profit to fall as a result of the rise in the organic composition of capital (one of Marx's 'iron laws') is offset by factors such as increasing productivity of labour and intensive use of machinery. An economic crisis is not the same as breakdown : 'From time to time the conflict of antagonistic agencies finds vent in crises. The crises are always but momentary and forcible solutions of the existing contradictions. They are violent eruptions which for a time restore the disturbed equilibrium.'[13] Crises *alone* do not develop revolutionary class consciousness; without the active intervention of man (the proletariat) capitalist equilibrium is re-established.

Marx's emphasis on consciousness and community clearly suggests, therefore, a complex rather than uni-dimensional theory of class. Class is never a single homogeneous structure, but rather a cluster of groups which, sharing a similar work function, values, aspirations, interests, will frequently diverge on particular specific issues. Thus the ruling class is never a simple homogeneous whole, but consists of contradictory elements – the representatives of heavy industry and light industry, finance capitalists – although the whole, the unity of the various competing elements, is held together by one overriding interest, the exploitation of labour power. Similarly, in some of its sections (or fractions) the working class may articulate a coherent revolutionary class consciousness, while other sections will develop ideologies which reflect ruling-class conceptions rather than genuine proletarian interests. To take one obvious example, the 'working-class' Tory, the worker who consistently votes for Conservative political parties, suggests that working-class consciousness is never a single unitary structure.

It follows that class consciousness is dialectical in its development and contradictory in structure. Marx himself argued that working-class consciousness is not a given datum, but is created in struggle, and struggle can take many forms, from trade-union and strike activity to direct political confrontations. Working-class consciousness is not to be identified with revolutionary class consciousness which is mediated only through a revolutionary political grouping or party. But Marx continually emphasised that the working class is only a class when it is organised for class action : 'There is one element of success that the workers possess : its great numbers. But numbers will weigh in the balance only when united by organisation and guided by knowledge.' The organisation was the labour movement; the knowledge, Marx's social theory.

II

Modern sociology has long since rejected Marx's concept of class : Dahrendorf has argued, for example, that while Marx's analysis was accurate for nineteenth-century society it is now obsolete for analysing what he calls 'post-capitalism'. Raymond Aron and S. M. Lipset echo Dahrendorf's view that modern industrial societies have become far more complex than that portrayed in Marx's two-class conflict model. They argue that class antagonisms have abated in intensity, largely through the extension of welfare services to all social strata, redistribution of income and wealth through progressive taxation, increased rates of social mobility, the extension of the franchise to the working class and widespread 'consumer consciousness'. Social stratification in the 'affluent society' is therefore 'diamond shaped', that is, while still containing the extremes of great wealth and poverty it increasingly approximates to a structure dominated by a large and increasingly homogeneous middle stratum, highly skilled and well paid, whose life-styles are middle class rather than proletarian. Thus Aron argues that while income inequality still persists, wealth differentials have narrowed considerably, so much so that 'in whatever sense the idea of class is understood, an industrial society does not tend toward the model of a *class* society'.[14] Clark Kerr is even more specific : 'Classes have merged, not separated, in developed capitalist societies,' and access to positions of prestige is less dependent on heredity privileges than on ability and education. Affluence breeds contentment, security and conservatism : the class-conscious worker disappears, and the workers 'become like everybody else on most issues most of the time'.[15]

This argument adumbrating a simple, mechanical one-to-one relationship between economics (wages) and life-styles (norms, values, and aspirations) has become known as the *embourgeoisement* thesis which asserts that the well-paid worker sloughs off his proletarian origins and moves towards a middle-class existence. (In itself a mis-nomer since all that is maintained is that the worker becomes not a bourgeois property owner but a non-property-owning middle-class individual.) Class consciousness is replaced by status consciousness and the concept of a militant and potentially revolutionary working class is presumed to be a Marxist anachronism. The argument is buttressed by evidence of decisive shifts in the labour force from manufacturing industry to the services sector, the expansion of clerical and professional occupations, the rapid contraction of old industries (coal, shipbuilding), and the consequent decline of the class-conscious and radical working-class communities whose members played such prominent roles in the growth of the labour move-ment. The factual decline of the working class is thus an important factor in mitigating and undermining working-class militancy and Dahrendorf concludes that 'the integrating process which is the chief characteristic of industrial society has now encompassed that class whose inability to integrate into the society was once supposed to destroy that society'.[16]

The destruction of working-class political consciousness is thus a simple product of affluence, social integration and increased mobility. The fact, too, that the 'new middle class' is not a bour-geois stratum but rather compounded from the technical professions, bureaucrats and clerical workers, none of whom own property, is sufficient for many sociologists to argue for a decisive change in the social structures of industrial society. No longer is it possible to regard class merely in terms of lack of property, rather class becomes bound up with status ('prestige') and authority. Sociologists thus turn from Marx to Weber for a more 'rounded' theory of social stratification. Paradoxically, neither Marx nor Weber completed a detailed analysis of stratification, yet Weber's short discussion of stratification as a 'multi-dimensional' structure embracing class, status and party is frequently cited as the basic source of modern stratification theory.

Superficially, Weber seems to follow Marx; property or the lack of it are 'the basic categories of all class situations', and the factor which creates class 'is unambiguously economic interest'. But the 'class situation' is differentiated 'according to the kind of services that can be offered in the market'. Writing of Marx's fragment on class, Weber notes that 'it was intended to deal with the issue of class unity in the face of skill differentials'. Thus Weber distinguishes between 'property classes', the working class whose labour is directly exploited by the capitalist, those 'who offer services' and finally the 'acquisition classes'. The tendency of capitalism is to expand the 'acquisition classes' – merchants, bankers, financiers, entrepreneurs, professional people – the owners of certain scarce skills which determine their more privileged social position.[17] A pluralistic class structure thus emerges involving complex differentiation within the dominant middle and working class. Weber also distinguishes between class and status groups, arguing that class situation differs from status situation by virtue of 'a specific, positive or negative, social estimation of honour' : a status group is defined in terms of its 'specific style of life', social distance and exclusiveness, the group's repudiation of mere economic factors (i.e. money) as a basis for membership and a commitment to patterns of non-utilitarian consumption : 'With some oversimplification, one might thus say that "classes" are stratified according to their relations to the production and acquisition of goods; whereas "status groups" are stratified according to the principles of their *consumption* of goods as represented by special "styles of life".'[18] Class and status are interrelated and competing structures of stratification relating specifically to the distribution of power in society. As with other of Weber's concepts his concept of stratification is directed against 'vulgar' Marxist theories which defined class in simple economic terms and capitalist society as a two-class structure. It is in this sense that Weber does not 'round out' Marx, rather he follows Marx's class theory closely in many details, but departs from it on the question of status and status groups. It is this dimension of Weber's theory which has been developed by modern sociology at the expense of its other aspects.

Weber's arguments have been developed in two distinct but related ways : firstly, that class is no longer determined by productive property but increasingly by consumption patterns (style of life); and secondly, that social stratification in modern industrial (capitalist) society is complicated by what Dahrendorf, following Weber, calls the 'service class' embracing bureaucrats, managers, judges and military officers, who exercise power, not through the ownership of property but as incumbents of specific occupational roles. A highly mobile stratum, the service class provides a 'bridge' between the ruled and the rulers, although as Dahrendorf acknowledges, they are themselves committed to the ruling norms and political conformism.[19] The service class, he concludes, is an index of the relative openness of industrial society. Other sociologists have argued that the complex character of modern society is due to the growth of 'the new middle class', a loose and baggy category embracing clerks, supervisors, managers, technicians, scientists, new professionals and those engaged in providing services (welfare, entertainment, and leisure), groups whose social status hinges on 'market skills', on their education, culture, and styles of life.

The concept of the 'new middle class' originated, like so many contemporary controversies, in the years immediately preceding the First World War. 'Vulgar' Marxism had postulated the inevitable decline of the middle class as capitalist society polarised around the bourgeoisie and proletariat : Karl Kautsky wrote that the 'iron laws of capitalism' eventuate in the proletarianisation of the middle strata. The most important study of the subject, however, was Emil Lederer's *The Problem of the Modern Salaried Employee* (1912) in which the term 'new middle class' was first used. Lederer argued that salaried employees were growing in size and establishing a distinctive social character and consciousness. He suggested that this new social stratum was too heterogeneous to command either a class consciousness or to accept the authority of the proletariat. In subsequent debates in Germany, England and America, Kautsky's crude line tended to predominate, that the proletarianisation of the middle classes would necessarily result in a revolutionary *rapprochement* with manual workers : in short, that the 'new middle class' were proletarians with a 'false consciousness'.[20]

There can be little doubt that the occupational structure of industrial societies has changed dramatically since the 1860s : for Britain, in 1851, 1 per cent of the working population was engaged in clerical work; by 1961 it was 12 per cent. Between 1911 and 1971 the percentage of professional workers more than doubled (4 per cent to nearly 10 per cent). In the United States professional and technical workers, who formed 2 per cent of the labour force in 1900, comprised 15 per cent in 1970; between 1958 and 1969 this category increased its members by 50 per cent, a growth rate common to both capitalist and non-capitalist industrial societies. Clerical labour in the United States rose from 0.6 per cent in 1870 to 15.2 per cent in 1962 while those employed as salesmen/women rose from 2.5 per cent in 1870 to 6.5 per cent in 1962. Between 1958 and 1969 white-collar workers increased by 10 million while manual workers increased by 4.9 million, and by 1970 the total white-collar sector was larger than the 'blue-collar' groups, a trend repeated less dramatically in Sweden, France, Japan, Austria and West Germany. If all these white-collar groups are added together they constitute approximately one third of the occupied population of individual industrial societies, proof surely that industrialisation compounds class complexity. Indeed, it has been estimated that in twenty years' time manual workers will be outnumbered by white-collar workers in all industrial societies.[21]

Yet what is the reality behind these statistics? The service industries, for example, are largely staffed by women working as usherettes, waitresses, barmaids, hairdressers and beauticians, occupations in which pay and working conditions are poor; there are few facilities for training, no educational qualifications are required and work is often done on a part-time basis. Indeed, of the two million

123

sales workers and the two and a quarter million personal service workers in Great Britain nearly one-half to two-thirds are women. The sales girl in the supermarket and the waitress in a small restaurant can hardly be claimed as members of a 'new middle class', for such diverse and occupationally scattered strata lack the necessary *internal* cohesion for a distinctive class. What then of clerical workers and the professions?

Within the clerical stratum it is important to note once again that women outnumber men and that the type of work performed requires minimum training and skill (the expansion of the number of machine operators during the past twenty years for example). Surveys have shown that the rapid growth in non-manual work has come largely from the increased numbers of employed women. In Great Britain between 1911 and 1961 the percentage of women in white-collar occupations increased from 29.8 per cent to 44.5 per cent, a pattern repeated in other industrial societies.[22] One result of this development is to free men for more 'exacting' work carrying higher remuneration, status and career prospects. It is in this sense that some sociologists have argued for a distinct, white-collar middle class, clearly differentiated by considerations of status, mobility and job security from the manual working class.

In the past there was truth in this argument : writing in 1916 the editor of *The Clerk* argued that while clerks 'suffer many economic disabilities, yet they have a great many economic advantages not enjoyed by manual workers . . . permanency of employment, periodical increases in salary . . . comparatively reasonable hours of work, and in certain sectors superannuation'.[23] It is true, of course, that such differences still exist and that the clerks rarely embrace a class consciousness : higher educational qualifications, smaller work units, better fringe benefits such as pension schemes demarcate clerical from manual work. Yet evidence suggests that the gap between the earnings of the clerk and manual worker has narrowed so much in the last fifty years that one writer has called it 'one of the most striking changes in pay structure during the twentieth century', although if male clerks alone are considered the difference is greater.[24] But this change has not yet resulted in class identification : the unionisation of white-collar workers in Britain increased marginally from 28.8 per cent to 29.0 per cent during the period from 1948 to 1964, and while it may be argued that white-collar collectivism will continue to develop in response to increasing fragmentation of work, larger and more impersonal offices, bureaucratic organisation of work, restricted internal avenues of upward mobility and low pay, there is little evidence to suggest that the clerk's ambiguous status is being supplanted by a positive class sympathy with manual workers.

What of the professionals? Traditional professions such as the Church, Army and Law, recruiting predominantly from the upper classes have been outstripped by the newer technical/industrial professions, a trend characteristic of all modern industrial societies. Between 1931 and 1961 professional strata in Britain grew from 840,000 to approximately $1\frac{3}{4}$ million. In the same period the numbers of mechanical engineers and electrical engineers doubled while those of lawyers and the clergy increased only slightly. Today the newer professions are twice as large as the older professions and their members are salaried employees of large organisations. It is important to note that within the professional strata school teachers, technicians and minor administrative officials have the fastest growth rate both in the United States and in Europe. In what sense, if any, are these groups to be analysed as a status hierarchy? Certainly they are not status groups in Weber's sense, but rather a series of strata recruited from the upper levels of the manual working class and clerical stratum whose prestige hinges on acquired educational skills, membership of professional associations and reasonably high remuneration. Weber's concept of status group and status honour seem irrelevant to the analysis of modern industrial society, referring more properly to pre-capitalist societies and those pre-capitalist social strata which survived into capitalism, residual elements increasingly eliminated by social and economic development. For, as Weber argued, status honour is decisively threatened by money, the great dissolvent of inherited prestige. The 'ideals' of the old professions – service to the client based on personal trust – are now an anachronism for the majority of professional workers. But like the clerical worker the modern professional enjoys educational status and certain economic advantages, distinctive elements in the status situation which insulate him from the working-class movement although influenced by the same economic forces. The argument advanced by some sociologists, notably Serge Mallet, that the revolutionary vanguard is no longer the manual working class but rather the new, technical stratum, must be rejected on the grounds that many technical workers, although unionised, tend to *identify* with managerial and not working-class values, resist similarity of treatment and strive to maintain strict lines of division within the work situation. Moreover, their supervisory work function is firmly set within a formal bureaucratic hierarchy, their role enmeshed with the administration of labour power and the extraction of surplus value.

None the less, ambiguity remains. The middle strata of professional, clerical and technical workers enjoy relatively high levels of mobility. The evidence from mobility surveys emphasises that approximately one-quarter to a third of those born into the manual working class in France, Germany, the United States, Sweden, England and Japan will move upwards into the non-manual white-collar stratum. However, the chances of moving from manual to high professional and managerial occupations are remote : a recent American survey corroborated previous research in pointing to a closed rather than open stratum at the apex of the social structure : 'The white collar strata nearer the top as well . . . have less dispersed patterns of occupational mobility, whatever aspect of mobility is considered. These differences reflect in part the prevalence of short distance mobility.'[25] Short-range, not long-range mobility patterns thus characterise the social structure of the advanced capitalisms, a fact which must be borne in mind in any discussions of the social implications of the 'new middle class'.

From this brief survey of the evidence for a distinct middle class within modern capitalism it is clear that the concept of 'new middle class' is used both imprecisely and often with polemical intent. For some sociologists the existence of this class acts as a 'buffer' between capital and labour, a powerful stabilising force easing class tensions through its advocacy of moderate political programmes. Others argue that the course of capitalist development will eliminate cultural, social and economic disparities between white-collar and manual workers resulting in the eventual proletarianisation of the middle class. Supporters of the first argument tend to define the middle class in terms of managers, professionals, higher technicians etc., while those defending the second standpoint emphasise sales staff, clerks, supervisors. C. Wright Mills, for example, has argued that white-collar work is increasingly approximating to manual work in terms of income, while the status elements 'which have enabled white-collar workers to set themselves apart from wage-workers, are now subject to definite decline'. Rationalisation lowers work skills making white-collar work 'more and more factory like . . .'. Mills's point, however, is that both manual and white-collar workers have not automatically developed a socialist consciousness, a fact which clearly suggests that 'propertylessness is not the only factor, or even the crucial one, determining inner-consciousness or political will'.[26]

It is interesting to note that in his analysis Mills uncritically accepts the erroneous view that Marx's class theory hinged on polarisation and confrontation. But as we argued earlier such mechanical formulations are merely caricatures of Marx's social theory which stresses the highly complex, *dialectical* development of social stratification. The capitalist division of labour, Marx argues, has the effect of removing the worker from the sphere of direct production : 'For example the unskilled labourers in a factory . . . have nothing directly to do with the working up of raw material. The workman who functions as overseer of those directly engaged in working up the raw material is one step further away; the works engineer has yet another relation and in the main works only with his brain, and so on.'[27]

The result is the expansion of those whose labour power, while not directly involved at the point of production – scientists, technologists, clerical workers – is essential for production and the extraction of surplus value. Marx's distinction between productive and unproductive labour is important in this context : for having defined productive labour as that which is 'directly transformed into capital [and] which creates surplus value', and unproductive labour as labour exchanged merely for money, he concludes that the trend of capitalist development is towards 'new ramifications of more or less unproductive branches of labour being formed . . .'.[28] Marx suggests that the increasing productivity of labour under capitalism must augment the ranks of unproductive workers and thus of the middle class (i.e. the expansion of professional categories such as librarians and teachers). At the same time the concept of 'productive labour' and productive worker is enlarged; the division of labour ramifies throughout production so that specialised occupations and professions (engineers, scientists) tied to capital emerge to function as the administrative arm of exploitation.

Thus while Marx's polemical standpoint led him to portray capitalist stratification in dichotomic terms, his scientific method leads away from polarisation to a pluralistic concept of class structure. But this does not mean the end of revolutionary politics and class consciousness. The middle class is enlarged both in its non-productive and productive branches, and through differences in education, pay and work situation a line of division, extremely tenuous at the base, is maintained between the two classes. Unionisation of white-collar labour and superficial similarities in work organisation do not imply the proletarianisation of these strata nor a political identification with the working class. Trade-union collectivism in itself is not necessarily socialistic : white-collar workers may use trade unions as service institutions merely to enhance their middle-class status. Objectively, the new professions, clerical and service workers, do not constitute a distinctive middle class as was the case in the nineteenth century .The convergence of incomes between skilled manual workers and lower-professional and white-collar workers points to economic polarity and the reasons for trade-union collectivism. But the white-collar strata are too diffuse, they lack strong labour traditions of class struggle and can rarely rise above an economic and status consciousness : in Marx's terms they cannot constitute a 'class for itself' for their internal structure is too contradictory, some strata are objectively linked to the working class, others to the dominant class while the vast majority resonate a conservative ideology. In a revolutionary situation these diffuse and heterogeneous strata will follow not their own independent leadership and revolutionary aspirations but the leadership and ideology of the proletariat.

But while Marx's theory of class stratification can account for the 'new middle class' what of the modern proletariat?

Many sociologists have argued that rising 'affluence' breeds a conservative working class whose political commitment is pragmatic and non-revolutionary. The curious irony of this argument is thus the implicit assumption that poverty and material deprivation induce radicalism, a correlation rejected by such different thinkers as Tocqueville, Marx and Trotsky : for 'the mere existence of privations is not enough to cause an insurrection, if it were, the masses would always be in revolt'.[29] Contemporary sociological studies of English, French and German workers have shown the conceptual and factual naïveté implicit in the view that the working class of industrial capitalism has become 'bourgeoisified'. In France and Italy, for example, the urban factory worker generally remains persistently left-wing in political choice (the Italian Communist party has increased its vote in every election since 1946), while in West Germany and Sweden the highly paid skilled workers are more radical than the semi- and unskilled. Available evidence suggests a close relationship between the growth of large-scale factory organisation, radical ideas, high income and firm commitment to social democratic and left-wing parties.[30] For if the working class was on the move towards a middle-class life-style then this process would imply a change in norms and the social acceptance by the established middle class of the aspiring proletariat.

The evidence from Goldthorpe and Lockwood's survey of 'affluent workers' in the British motor-car industry shows clearly that the modern factory worker lives apart from typically middle-class housing estates, votes consistently for the Labour party, fails to join or exercise influence on formal associations (apart from trade unions) or take white-collar workers as a reference group. There is thus no evidence of a normative and relational change in the class structure, and even the economic aspect of the *embourgeoisement* theory is doubtful : a recent study of employment conditions in British industry indicated that nearly 50 per cent of firms investigated had no form of sick-pay scheme for manual workers, while 90 per cent had schemes for managerial and clerical staff; there are still significant differences too, in the availability of pension schemes for non-manual over manual workers, holidays, loss of pay for lateness at work, and the amount of overtime worked.[31] However, while the *embourgeoisement* thesis has been shown to be sociological non-sense, it is now argued that a major change *is* occurring within traditional working-class communities, centred on old industries with their traditions of militancy and loyalty to the Labour movement, in favour of more diversified industrial enclaves associated with engineering and motor manufacture.

In the current debate on the 'new working class' it is emphasised that the old socialist dream of a united working-class movement involving the Labour party and the trade unions as the main agencies of social change has been subverted by the progressive decline of the 'traditional proletarian' (coalminers, dockers, shipyard workers) and the emergence of a 'privatised' and pragmatic worker, who, unlike 'traditional proletarians' is no longer committed to socialist ideals through the trade-union movement, but increasingly judges political parties in terms of their strict economic appeal. The political ramifications of this 'privatised worker' thesis are obvious : for while industrial disputes over wages and wage conditions will continue, they will not be cumulative, that is, promote a solidaristic class consciousness. An atomised economic consciousness, partial rather than unified, relating to particular problems, will thus come to characterise the industrial working class of advanced capitalist society. And since the future lies with factory organisations like those in operation in the car industry, the authors conclude that the worker is unlikely to develop political class consciousness : a dismal prospect indeed for socialism.

A major criticism of this argument is that since the worker is shown to have only a simple *economic* relation with the firm, then his commitment is basically unstable : 'The cash nexus may snap just because it is only a cash nexus – because it is single stranded; and if it does snap, there is nothing else to bind the worker to acceptance of his situation.'[32] There can be no doubt, of course, that the 'traditional proletarian', with his ideology of 'them' and 'us' was receptive to socialist ideals and supported the trade-union movement, not as a 'service organisation' designed to improve his wages but as a socio-political force. Traditional loyalty to the labour movement was burned into the very fibres of the old working-class 'closed communities', a loyalty dissipated by the rapid development of new, technological industries. This is a definite trend, and it is thus concluded that for 'the great majority of workers . . . unionism was far from being a central interest in their lives; and only very rarely was unionism understood in the sense of a socio-political movement'.[33] However, it may be asked if such an attitude necessarily implies a politically quiescent, monolithically apathetic political class consciousness. The 'affluent worker', after all, remains propertyless and exploited, and while his image of society is said to approximate to a more fluid model than the dichotomic model of the 'traditional proletarian', his political affiliation remains undisturbed. 70 per cent of 'affluent workers' consistently vote for the Labour party, a higher percentage than the national figure, and 60 per cent of those voting Labour saw it in strictly class terms, 'the party of the working man', even though for many respondents there were few important differences between the two main parties.[34] Thus a marked instrumental attitude to trade unions and the Labour party is seemingly contradicted by the intense loyalty of the 'affluent worker' to a party identified in class terms.

To understand these contradictions it is necessary to establish the influence of the dominant ideology and the continuity of cultural tradition on working-class strata. It is not sufficient to argue that class consciousness flows automatically from 'the more primitive forms of collectivism in which [the worker] is involved at the workplace, in the local union branch, in the working-men's club, and, at an even deeper level, in the communal sociability of everyday life'.[35] For class consciousness is equally the result of the reformist political traditions within the labour movement, traditions which can be broken only at decisive historical moments. The 1926 General Strike was not solely supported by 'traditional proletarians', nor can the French General Strike of May/June 1968 be explained in terms of a 'privatised', pragmatic working class.

The 'privatised worker', indeed, can hardly aspire to a class consciousness : concerned only with consumption and his own private life, working only for money, he comes to evaluate society increasingly in pecuniary terms. It is reported that over half of the 'affluent worker' sample agreed that money was now the basic criterion of class; the manual and non-manual line is thus discounted as a source of social differentation. Given the central role of money in a capitalist society, however, it is hardly surprising that workers think it so important and fetishise it. Money, after all, does hide the real nature of the exploitative relation between labour and capital; money can create illusions of equality and fairness between individuals unequal in terms of property, educational opportunity and social status. As the researchers note, models of stratification built around money provide an image of society based not on power (ruling class, subordinate class) but on individual differences. Money models yield a more optimistic vision of the future, a future seen in terms of 'automatic economic growth' no longer dependent on 'collective action', on 'social struggles in the industrial or political arenas'. But this is not proof of a connection between holding a *false* belief in the determination of social class (money as criterion) and seeing the trade unions and the Labour party in strictly *economic* terms. The latter is clearly connected with the role of unions in a capitalist society, as institutions largely concerned with pursuing purely economic goals for their members. The bureaucratisation of unions, their 'reformist' character, will clearly affect the context and scope of working-class consciousness and buttress an already existing tendency to see unions in strictly economic terms. For the simple fact remains : the 'commodity consciousness' of the 'affluent worker', his 'destructured image' of society and his belief in a new 'central class' consisting of skilled manual and white-collar workers earning approximately similar wages, must be related to the *class* image of politics held by these workers and the tangible correlation between consistent Labour party support and membership of trade unions. To conclude that 'commodity consciousness' is not a 'false consciousness' because the workers' experiences of rising economic rewards and full employment have a 'real' not 'false' basis is merely to eliminate all the contradictions contained within this 'commodity consciousness'. For if the 'affluent workers' were solely privatised, instrumentally collectivist and obsesssed by commodities, it would constitute, not merely a triumph for capitalist ideology, but embody a homogeneous structure of class consciousness inimical to socialism and class politics. More precisely, it fails to explain why the worker, with a consciousness linked with private and local issues (family and work) should retain his *class* attachment to the Labour party and perceive it in those terms. Of course, the worker is alienated and he tends to comprehend the social world in reified terms, but, as his political affiliations suggest, this is not a dominant structure within consciousness. Class consciousness is compounded from the most diverse contradictions embracing the fetishism of commodities, nationalist sentiments, political reformism *and* class identification.

IV

In his essay on 'class consciousness' Lukács has argued that :

> The first question we must ask is how far is it in fact possible to discern the whole economy of society from inside it? It is essential to transcend the limitations of particular individuals caught up in their own narrow prejudices. But it is no less vital not to overstep the frontier fixed for them by the economic structure of society and establishing their position in it. Regarded abstractly and formally, then, class consciousness implies a class-conditioned unconsciousness of one's own socio-historical and economic condition.[36]

Any study of class consciousness must indeed begin from an awareness of the role which a dominant class ideology exercises over the subordinate strata, a failure implicit in the monographic method employed by many sociologists. The whole is obscured by the part : the contradictions which characterise working-class consciousness, the results of the complex determinations of class structure are explicable only when related to the objective structure of capitalist exploitation, alienation and ideology. The worker who divorces politics from economics is clearly suffering from 'false consciousness' in the obvious sense that the labour movement represents the only effective way he has for defending the basic rights and privileges won by years of struggle. Marx himself was highly critical of those labour leaders who saw trade-union activity solely in terms of economics :

At the same time the working class ought not to exaggerate to themselves the ultimate consequence of these struggles. They ought not to forget that they are fighting with effects not with the causes of those effects . . . that they are applying palliatives, not curing a malady. They ought, therefore, not to be exclusively absorbed in these unavoidable guerrilla fights . . . instead of simultaneously trying to cure it, instead of using their organised forces as a lever for the final emancipation of the working class. . . .[37]

Thus to speak of a 'genuine' revolutionary class consciousness is meant a consciousness of the whole, of those actions necessary to defend and extend a definite interest. It is in this sense that the bourgeoisie and the proletariat may develop false consciousness : the long-term interests of British capitalism, for example, were not defended by the pro-European, anti-Communist faction of the ruling class which appeased Hitler in the 1930s; the nineteenth-century Russian bourgeoisie falsely believed that co-operation with the Tsarist government was the most effective strategy for defending and augmenting its interests, a 'false consciousness' profoundly shattered by the 1905 and 1917 revolutions. Lukács is right when he argues that the class consciousness of the bourgeoisie must always constitute a false understanding of reality, the class nature of society, its conflicts and inner contradictions. Ideologically this takes the form, as Marx noted, of obscuring and mystifying 'the true nature of surplus value' and of exploitation,[38] for to survive as a class the bourgeoisie must believe in its slogans, rhetoric and theories; there are no conspiratorial plans to crush the working class or turn them into willing dupes of 'consumer capitalism'.

But Lukács goes beyond such sound, sociological generalisations when he argues that nineteenth-century bourgeois ideology resisted *all* insights into the true nature of capitalist society and its class situation. Lukács's discussion of class consciousness is clearly based on the same misunderstanding of Marx's stratification theory and his method noted earlier in Kautsky and Wright Mills. The analysis assumes that Marx's 'pure model' of capitalism either equals the existing reality or one in the immediate future, and that meaningful sociological-cum-philosophical generalisations can be extrapolated from the two-class model. The proletariat, as the gravediggers of the capitalist system, are thus entrusted with the historic task of developing a class consciousness which strives to grasp society as a totality : 'For a class to be ripe for hegemony means that its interests and consciousness enable it to organise the whole of society in accordance with those interests.'[39]

In Lukács's interpretation bourgeois thought represents 'the most strenuous efforts to mask the real foundations of bourgeois society', failing to see society 'from the centre, as a coherent whole', while proletarian thought strives towards a historical understanding and confirmation of its role as negation of capitalism. When Lukács distinguishes between 'psychological' class consciousness and 'imputed' class consciousness he commits the grossest sociological error. 'Psychological' consciousness, the empirically, factually given ideas men form of their immediate situation is clearly equivalent to the 'commodity consciousness' of the 'affluent' worker. But this consciousness is in no sense an homogeneous structure : as was emphasised above, immediate consciousness is riven with contradictions, an 'obvious' Marxist point which Lukács ignores. For him 'genuine' class consciousness is 'imputed consciousness', the '*appropriate and rational reactions*' of individuals to particular situations, how they *ought* to feel about capitalism, how they *ought* to behave. Borrowing heavily from Weber, Lukács writes that 'the objective theory of class consciousness is the theory of its objective possibility'.[40]

But what is 'imputed consciousness'? It is more real than psychological consciousness but it is only *imputed* by those intellectuals who, from their privileged position 'really understand' the logic and meaning of the historical process. 'Imputed' proletarian consciousness is possible only because of Lukács's historicism; *History* is invested with a purpose outside the concrete determinations, and in this sense is fundamentally élitist and Hegelian : only Hegel's philosopher could genuinely interpret 'the ruses of history'. It has already been noted that Lukács does not discuss the proletariat from Marx's position, that is, in terms of its palpable, empirical consciousness and its struggle to go beyond this towards a genuine scientific understanding of society. For Lukács the working class is a *whole*, a fixed category, which philosophically strives towards totality. In the real world the working class is broken into distinct strata and strongly influenced by bourgeois ideology on the one hand and its own local and national culture on the other. It is this failure to appreciate class consciousness as a dialectical process which is the central weakness of Lukács's argument: 'imputed consciousness' is no more than an ahistorical, abstract 'ideal type' lacking all the concrete determinations of historical class structure. There are no 'pure proletarians', no 'pure class consciousness', only 'real, living men', with their illusions, dreams and class interest.

v

The essence of Marx's dialectical method is to penetrate beneath the surface of particular phenomena and disclose its contradictory movement and structure. Modern sociology has demonstrated convincingly the persistence of class inequalities within modern capitalist society and confirmed that the working classes remain exploited, dispossessed and a distinct strata. The 'affluent worker' is not the working class but a stratum of that class, a stratum moreover with a consciousness both pragmatic and yet 'left-wing' in its orientation to economic and political questions. It has often been said that trade-union consciousness is not political consciousness, that the worker can aspire only to a very limited vision of the social world and only in exceptional circumstances will he advance to a revolutionary class consciousness. It is in this sense that the distinction between 'real' and 'potential' consciousness has validity, for the latter is no more than the consciousness of a 'class for itself', a force which unifies the different strata within the proletariat towards revolutionary *praxis*. And this is not a 'pure consciousness' for in all historical circumstances specific determinations create both the potentiality for revolution and the prospects for defeat; the 1926 British General Strike and France in May/June 1968 illustrate the fragility of 'potential, revolutionary consciousness', for while the objective conditions were those of a revolutionary situation the specific determinations of reformist trade-union, Labour party and Communist party leadership meant a return to the capitalist *status quo*.

The working class, then, are very much alive in capitalist society, co-existing with an expanding middle stratum which, as we have seen, is split between those who command high economic and social rewards and clerical, sales and supervisory labour. The predominance of women in the latter stratum and the differences of education and promotion prospects among the men lead to the conclusion that this stratum remains distinct from the working class and cannot aspire to a class consciousness *on its own*. It is far too fragmented and lacks the labour culture associated with manual workers. The steady growth of 'mere labour power' within this stratum, the depersonalisation implicit in larger and larger work units and the bureaucratisation of work duplicate similar if not identical work and labour market situations to those of manual workers (although status elements remain) and thus pose a serious threat to capitalist authority. For when Marx wrote that 'the constantly growing number of the middle classes . . . increase the social security and power of the upper ten thousand', he had in mind a privileged stratum of professional workers, managers and clerks, not the somewhat anonymous mass which is today's 'new middle class'. In 1926 students and clerks blacklegged and ran trains and buses; no modern capitalist state can rest on such unswerving ideological support today. The profound crisis of contemporary bourgeois authority flows directly from the very facts which modern sociology has frequently cited as proof of social cohesion and the end of ideology : the development of an 'affluent' working class with increasingly heightened economic and social aspirations and a broad white-collar stratum enjoying few, if any, privileges.

6

POWER, AUTHORITY AND LEGITIMATION

The previous chapter examined Marx's general theory of class strati-fication and it was suggested that misinterpretations of his ideas flowed from a failure to appreciate his sociological method. Marx's conception of the distribution of power in society, his theory of the ruling class, has enjoyed a similar fate both from well-intentioned and hostile interpreters. For the unsophisticated, ruling class meant simply a conspiratorial group of capitalists and their hired political lackeys consciously exploiting and dominating the working class; while for others the social authority of the ruling class hinged solely on economic factors and afforded no weight to political elements. In general, Marx's theory of power is grasped as a *mechanical* theory, in which the economy determines absolutely the political structure. This failure to treat Marx as a dialectical thinker, however, is not wholly the result of theoretical confusion. It has been vigorously argued that Marx's theory of the ruling class is no longer appropriate for a modern, complex industrial society since the economic basis for such a group has been eroded by the 'decomposition' of 'laissez-faire capitalism' into 'post-capitalism', and the elimination of pri-vate property as the basic source of class division. Capitalism and the capitalist class have given way to a bureaucratic society in which power is diffused over many competing 'interest groups' and where managers, although non-owners of proprety, take all effective deci-sions. It is argued that Marx failed to predict the emergence of this distinct, functional stratum of managers and bureaucrats and that he misunderstood the dynamics of industrialisation in separating ownership from control in large-scale industry. In the Soviet Union,

Eastern Europe and the Western Democracies power has thus passed to the incumbents of bureaucratic positions and is no longer dependent on private property. A unified ruling class is thus a sociological anachronism and modern social theory prefers the more 'flexible' concept of 'élite': instead of a monolithic ruling class facing an 'impoverished', revolutionary proletariat, we have a complex structure of competing élites in a situation of social and political pluralism. The capitalist state has thus 'withered away' as the agency of class rule: neutral, benevolent and autonomous it functions merely as the 'umpire' in the peaceful conflict between 'élites' and 'interest groups', guaranteeing the rights of the individual and the dictates of the 'national interest'.

I

It was argued earlier that Marx's concept of a class is not a simple occupational category or one related to a money income. Class involved both the subjective factor of consciousness and the objective element of organisation, bound together by the relationship to the means of production. Discussion of Marx's theory of class domination has generally assumed a two-class model, the ruled and the rulers, in which the latter are fully alive to their class function. In *The Communist Manifesto*, for example, Marx and Engels wrote that with the advance of capitalism, the bourgeoisie '. . . conquered for itself, in the modern representative State, exclusive political sway. The executive of the modern State is but a committee for managing the common affairs of the whole bourgeoisie. . . . Political power . . . is merely the organised power of one class for oppressing another.'[1] The polemical standpoint of *The Communist Manifesto*, however, is no basis for judging Marx's theory of class domination and the dichotomic model adopted here finds no echo in his mature, more scientific writings, although it must be emphasised that Marx did not work out a satisfactory theory of power in capitalist society.

Marx argues that class domination flows directly from the class antagonisms inherent in those modes of production built on economic inequality. A division occurs between those who own and exercise control over the means of production and those whose labour power is purchased and exploited for surplus value. Marx emphasises that while economic inequality and exploitation characterise all modes of production beyond simple tribal communism, capitalism has the important effect of making all relations between people increasingly dependent on private property, on purely economic factors. In pre-capitalist societies, for example, the social relations of serf and land-owner functioned through a personal as well as an economic nexus : the class domination of the landowner was based on the feudal ties of bondage and vassallage as well as those related to the ownership of property. The capitalist mode of production, in contrast, destroys those personal elements and increasingly transforms 'the motley feudal ties that bound man to his "natural superiors" ' leaving only 'naked self-interest' as the bond between men : 'In one word, for exploitation, veiled by religious and political illusions, it has substituted naked, shameless, direct, brutal exploitation.'[2] It is in this sense that Marx writes of class relations under capitalism becoming 'simplified' and 'universalised' with the result that power, because it hinges so strongly on economic forces, is not randomly distributed but highly concentrated in the major economic, social and political institutions. Thus Marx writes of 'economic domination' and 'social domination' to refer to the influence which *capital* exerts on the functioning of certain institutions, while 'political domination' refers to the ways in which the state creates and maintains the legal basis for bourgeois rule. The term 'ideological domination' is not used by Marx, although the concept is implicit in his analysis of ideology and refers to these ideas which, disseminated through socialising agencies and institutions of the mass media (however primitive and partial) to all social strata, support and legitimise the *status quo*. Economic, political and ideological domination form the basis of Marx's theory of the ruling class. In order to clarify the complex nature of Marx's theory of power it is necessary to discuss briefly these three dimensions as separate categories, although it must be borne in mind that such distinctions are largely conceptual and in reality form a totality of class domination.

(1) *Economic Domination.* In the *Paris Manuscripts* Marx had linked the alienation suffered by the worker with the existence of private property and the power of capital to transform 'free activity'

into 'mere labour'. It is through capital, Marx argued, that the capitalist 'exercises his power of command over labour',[3] a theme which informs his early and later writings. The power of capital to dominate men, however, turns on the specific form of labour within each society : in pre-capitalist societies, for example, the worker's labour power is not transformed into capital in the total way it occurs under the capitalist mode of production. Under slavery, Marx notes, 'the capitalist relationship can only be sporadic and subordinate, never dominant', and it is only when capitalist production predominated in the economic structure of society with 'the capitalist directly appropriat[ing] the whole surplus labour and surplus product' that economic domination holds sway.[4] The worker's class position is exclusively dictated by his complete subordination to an economic system which turns labour into 'the property of someone else' to confront the worker as an independent force – capital.[5] The conditions of labour thus come to dominate the labourer and Marx emphasises that the 'domination of capital over labour' and 'over the workers as its instruments' is neither challenged by high wages nor by an increase in the productivity of labour and capital :

Even the *most favourable situation* for the working class, the *most rapid possible growth of capital*, however much it may improve the material existence of the worker, does not remove the antagonism between his interests and the interests of the capitalists. . . .To say that the most favourable condition for wage labour is the most rapid possible growth of productive capital is only to say that the more rapidly the working class increases and enlarges the power that is hostile to it, the wealth that does not belong to it and that rules over it, the more favourable will be the conditions under which it is allowed to labour anew at increasing bourgeois wealth, at enlarging the power of capital, content with forging for itself the golden chains by which the bourgeoisie drags it in its train.[6]

Extended economic reproduction, while superficially creating 'affluence', only augments the considerable domination of capital over the worker and, as the 'personification' of capital, the power of the capitalist class. The economic domination of the capitalist class thus flows directly from its legal right and physical ability to exploit the labour power of others.

(2) *Political Domination.* As noted earlier, *The Communist Manifesto* postulates a simple one-to-one connection between economic and political interests. The state in capitalist society is a capitalist state and its functionaries – judges, civil servants, the military, police – exist to uphold bourgeois rights. It is in this sense that the bourgeois state survives changes in the modes and personnel of government. Writing of the turbulent period in French history between 1797 and 1850, Marx argued: 'None of the numerous revolutions of the French bourgeoisie since 1789 was an attack on *order*; for they allowed the rule of the class, they allowed the slavery of the workers, they allowed the *bourgeois* order to endure, no matter how often the political form of this rule and this slavery changed.'[7] This distinction between the ruling and non-ruling factions of the dominant class is an important one. For at no point does Marx argue that political domination is exercised by an homogeneous, unified ruling class; rather, class domination is compounded from diverse elements including bureaucrats, political representatives and the various groups engaged in finance and industrial capitalism. In the *Grundrisse* Marx had noted that because profit comprises two kinds of revenue, the existence of finance and industrial capitalists 'express nothing other than this fact',[8] 'the *two great interests* into which the bourgeoisie is split'. In *The Eighteenth Brumaire of Louis Bonaparte* he argues that at different historical moments various sections of the ruling class come to exercise a dominating influence on government: during the Restoration period for example, 'big landed property . . . governed', while under the July monarchy the great bankers constituted the major political force.[9] Marx emphasises that this 'finance aristocracy' defrauded the state through floating enormous government loans to the detriment of industry, agriculture and shipping: it challenged the interests of the industrial bourgeoisie:

> Since the finance aristocracy made the laws, was at the head of the administration of the state, had command of all the organized public authorities, dominated public opinion through the actual state of affairs and through the press, the same prostitution, . . .

the same mania to get rich was repeated in every sphere . . . to get rich not by production, but by pocketing the already available wealth of others. Clashing every moment with the bourgeois laws themselves, an unbridled assertion of unhealthy and dissolute appetites manifested itself, particularly at the top of bourgeois society. . . .[10]

The 1848 revolution ended this domination : the bourgeois class *as a whole* entered 'the orbit of political power', but it did so in a society where industry and the industrialists had yet 'to dominate the bourgeoisie'. Marx argues that 'the industrial bourgeoisie can rule only where modern industry shapes all property relations to suit itself, and industry can win this power only where it has conquered the world market, for national bounds are inadequate for its development.'[11] In England the industrial bourgeoisie had conquered the entire bourgeois class, subordinating both finance capital and the landed interest to its domination. Of course, the old aristocracy retained some of its privileges as a governing stratum within the dominant class. In Germany, by contrast, capitalist development took place within a governmental and bureaucratic structure dominated by the landowning aristocracy, the Junkers and Kaiserism, a fact which relates to the political weakness of the bourgeoisie in accepting the old aristocracy as the governing class; at the same time the aristocracy were compelled through the demands of industrialisation to augment the economic interests of the bourgeoisie.[12]

In these analyses Marx is arguing for the political autonomy of the state, that the political sphere is not a simple reflection of the economic structure and therefore cannot be reduced to straightforward class interests. The relation of politics to economics is uneven and contradictory : the non-dialectical, polemical concept of the modern state as 'a committee for managing the common affairs of the whole bourgeoisie' (*The Communist Manifesto*) does not represent Marx's final position on its role in a modern capitalist society. In his scattered comments on bureaucracy Marx emphasised its semi-autonomous status and argued that in certain circumstances it may appear as a completely independent force (under Napoleon III for example).

(3) *Ideological Domination*. Class domination is possible without ideological authority in the sense that rule is enforced through dictatorial fiat. Bonapartist, Fascist and totalitarian régimes, however, frequently subsist through the anti-ideological legitimations of naked terror, physical elimination of political opposition, police and army, although even here the dominant class feels obliged to justify its totalitarian politics in ideologically universal terms by invoking symbolic myths of race, class and nation. But typically, capitalist society has developed the parliamentary shell for bourgeois rule, institutions which emerged historically in many European societies from the conflict between bourgeois aspirations and feudal absolutism. The result is that class domination is no longer legitimated by traditional authority and blind obedience to the existing political institutions, but rather through the rational authority of an elected parliament and government. But the process whereby the bourgeois class creates its own political instruments is also the process which generates opposition to its rule :

> The bourgeoisie had a true insight into the fact that all the weapons which it had forged against feudalism turned their points against itself, that all the means of education which it had produced rebelled against its own civilisation, that all the gods which it had created had fallen away from it. It understood that all the so-called bourgeois liberties and organs of progress attacked and menaced its *class rule* at its social foundation and its political summit simultaneously, and had therefore become 'socialistic'.[13]

Capitalist development brings into being both the capitalist and his opposite, the proletarian : the conflict between capital and labour turns into a total conflict only when the bourgeois class has subordinated the entire society to the domination of capital. In these circumstances the representatives of capitalism and socialism confront one another; and capitalist stability hinges increasingly on the ideological subordination of the working class. Marx frequently uses the term 'ideologists of the bourgeoisie' to refer to its representatives in politics and the press. He accepted that the dominant class would diffuse dominant ideas through society but at no point did he suggest a conspiracy in their genesis or a simple, non-dialectical relationship between dominant class, the fractions within it, bureaucracy and the state. Under Napoleon III, for example, the bourgeoisie, seeking a compromise with the emerging dictator, 'invited Bonaparte to suppress and annihilate its speaking and writing section, its politicians and its *literati*, its platform and its press, in order that it might then be able to pursue its private affairs with full confidence in the protection of a strong and unrestricted government'.[14] In this situation of extreme instability, bourgeois rule required protection from its own advocates : Marx is scathing in his criticism of the weak French capitalist class which, in order to preserve its own economic power, was forced to break its political authority, silence its own bourgeois Parliament and condemn itself to virtual political impotence.

These three dimensions, then, constitute the core of Marx's theory of class domination. As in previous chapters the *dialectical* element has been stressed, and this is particularly important in considering the concept of equilibrium in Marx's thought. The balance of forces between the classes is clearly the key to understanding class domination, for in some circumstances neither the bourgeoisie nor the proletariat are in a position to exercise domination. The periodic crises of authority which characterise the history of capitalist society reflect a profoundly unstable equilibrium, when the ruling class has only a material, coercive force to impose its will, when it no longer enjoys authority over civil society. In circumstances when neither radicals nor conservatives possess the strength for victory, the result is the emergence of a charismatic leader or the growth of bureaucracy (France, 1848–70; Soviet Union 1928 to the present; Germany, 1933). Writing of nineteenth-century Germany, Engels noted the coexistence of a powerful landowning aristocracy, a weak bourgeoisie in the process of development and an increasingly organised working class : 'Therefore, alongside of the basic condition of the old absolute monarchy – an equilibrium between landed gentry and bourgeoisie, the basic condition of modern Bonapartism, – an equilibrium between the bourgeoisie and the proletariat.'[15] Equilibrium is indeed the 'normal' situation in bourgeois society, although this does not mean that the balance lies between politically equal forces : one class may possess a source of potential power sufficient to induce an equilibrium of forces, such as the strength of an organised working-class movement which through its trade unions and political party may win concessions from the dominant class and place restraint on *total* capitalist domination. But such 'pressure' takes place within the context of a capitalist social, political, and economic structure in which the 'dominant ideological apparatus' expresses the ideas and values of the ruling class. There are thus definite limits to the pressures exerted by a subordinate class; it must obey 'the rules of the game' and thus repudiate a direct challenge to the interests of the dominant class.

II

The complexity of Marx's theory of power has rarely been acknowledged among sociologists who in the main represent the theory as crude economism. It is important to grasp the dialectical character of the theory, that an uneven, contradictory relation subsists between the economic and political spheres; the dominant class is not economically homogeneous, rarely is it politically united and in certain circumstances the state can exercise a degree of autonomy. Historically, the major sociological challenge to Marx's theory occurred in the work of Gaetano Mosca, Robert Michels and Max Weber. For Mosca and Michels power flowed not from the ownership of property but rather from political and bureaucratic organisations; Weber's theory of bureaucracy emerges as a more complex development of this theme.

Mosca superficially seems to follow Marx in his argument that 'in all societies . . . two classes of people appear – a class that rules and a class that is ruled'. His 'political' (or ruling) class enjoys legal and factual authority as an 'organised' minority dominating an 'unorganised' majority, a situation inherent in all social organisations but one which reaches its highest expression in what Mosca termed the 'bureaucratic state'. Here the state embodies specialisation, centralisation and the salaried official forms part of the 'political class'. Democracy, therefore, becomes the rule of an organised minority which 'in spite of appearances to the contrary, and for all of the legal principles on which government rests . . . still retains actual and effective control of the state'.[16] Mosca's pessimistic sociology is further adumbrated in the work of Robert Michels, whose *Political Parties* turns on the 'sociological law' of oligarchical inevitability : all organisations, however democratic their ideology (socialist political parties for example), become necessarily oligarchic and bureaucratic. 'As a result of organisation, every party or professional union becomes divided into a minority of directors and a majority of directed.' Basing his arguments on the bureaucratic tendencies of the German Social Democratic party, Michels sought to show, like Mosca, the inevitable trend to bureaucratic control of the state and how this process in itself flowed from the organisational requirements of a modern society. His 'iron law of oligarchy', working through social institutions, means the rule of the bureaucratic official over democratically elected parliamentary representatives and an authority based on position in a hierarchy of salaried officialdom and not as Marx had stressed, the ownership of private property.[17] Bureaucratic organisation becomes a kind of natural law determining the structure of both capitalist and socialist societies : within capitalism administrators acquire an authority 'at least equal to that possessed by the private owner of capital', while under socialism the idea of a classless society 'would perish in the moment of its adherents' triumph'. Bureaucratic organisation would now determine social life, an ineluctable process giving 'birth to the domination of the elected over the electors, of the mandatories over the mandators, of the delegates over the delegators. *Who says organization, says oligarchy*'.[18]

Max Weber shares Mosca's and Michels's rejection of the 'utopian' ideals of socialism. He argues that the highly specialised division of labour, which forms the backbone of a modern economy, must inevitably lead to greater bureaucratisation in a society based on state interference and control of the economy and social life. For Weber, the bureaucratisation of social life formed the dominant characteristic of capitalist economic development, 'the parcelling out of the human soul', a process which leads to great tension between the democratic trends associated with bourgeois society and the anti-democratic ethos of bureaucratic organisation. In Weber's analysis bureaucracy becomes the major source of authority; organisation is the locus of power in modern society compounded of hierarchical structures involving an administrative staff of permanent, salaried officials. Organisations, he argues, generate a distinct set of rules binding on the individual members; the rules of the organisation form the administrative order within which authority is located. Administration and authority are closely linked : 'Every domination both expresses itself and functions through administration. Every administration, on the other hand, needs domination, because it is always necessary that some powers of command be in the hands of somebody.'[19] This is what Weber called 'imperative co-ordination', the probability that commands will be obeyed irrespective of their particular content or degree of supervision. For unlike Michels, Weber argued that commands are obeyed because they carry the weight of legitimacy. Like Marx, Weber argued that power embodied a combination of material and moral (ideological) domination : 'It is an induction from experience that no system of domination voluntarily limits itself to the appeal to material or affectual or ideal motives as a basis for guaranteeing its continuance. In addition every such system attempts to establish and to cultivate the belief in its "legitimacy".'[20] He identifies three 'ideal types' of legitimacy : traditional, based on a belief in the authority of traditional norms and customs; charismatic, based on the prophetic pronouncements of oracles and great leaders invested with 'magical' qualities; and finally, legal–rational, with its basis in law. These three modes of 'social authority' form the bases of domination and power in society.

Weber distinguishes power from domination in terms of this typology of legitimacy : he defines power as the ability to impose one's will on another against opposition, while domination is 'imperative control', that is, it flows directly from the belief that authorised commands will be obeyed without the sanction of physical coercion. Domination thus hinges on legitimate authority and constitutes a special case of power. Weber portrays modern capitalist society as characterised by the legal–rational domination of bureaucracy and emphasises the important role which capitalism has played in its development. Capitalist production hinges on bureaucracy, for capitalism creates 'an urgent need for stable, strict, intensive, and calculable administration'. Capitalism, he concludes, 'is the most rational economic basis for bureaucratic administration', for the superiority of bureaucracy 'lies in the role of technical knowledge which, through the development of modern technology and business methods in the production of goods, has become completely indispensable'. In the field of administration, states Weber, the choice lies simply 'between bureaucracy and dilettantism'. In complex modern societies the bureaucratic domination of appointed officials (not elected, and here Weber differs from Michels) is inevitable. Socialist society would be no exception to this potential tyranny of the 'technical expert', to the need for 'stable, strict, intensive, and calculable administration'. To produce and distribute the goods necessary for a socialist economy necessitates a higher level of technical efficiency than under capitalism.[21] The question of control, then, is clearly important : Weber answers pessimistically that the bureaucratic machinery is largely under the control of the technical experts, although in a capitalist economy the entrepreneur maintains a 'relative immunity' from the dictates of bureaucratic knowledge while the 'masses' becomes more and more dominated by it. This exception to Weber's 'law' helps to explain his rejection of socialism : in an important passage, written after the 1917 revolution, he argues that bureaucratic administrative staff are completely separated from the ownership of both the means of production and administration. There exists, he suggests, at the heart of bureaucratic administration 'complete separation of the property belonging to the organisation, which is controlled within the sphere of office, and the personal property of the official, which is available for his own private uses'.[22] Unwittingly, Weber has described the essence of the bureaucratic domination exercised in the Soviet Union under Stalin and in the East European socialist societies since 1945. Weber was convinced that the spread of a functional efficiency to all spheres of life (law, economy, technology, music) must eventuate in a total bureaucratisation : 'The future belongs to bureaucracy', he once wrote, 'where once the modern trained official rules, his power is virtually indestructible, because the whole organisation of the most basic provisions of life is fashioned to suit his performance.' In Weber's view, therefore, a socialist revolution would prepare the groundwork for total bureaucratic domination. Writing of the 1905 Russian revolution, and with Marxist theory in mind, he suggested the result of socialist practice as 'a new bondage' and that 'all the economic weather signs point in the direction of diminishing freedom'.[23]

It is impossible to explore all the ramifications of Weber's theory of domination here, but in contrasting it with Marx's theory of class domination two points can be made : firstly, although both theorists distinguish power from authority Weber fails to give sufficient weight to the concept of ideology for legitimising power and underpinning social authority; equally Weber minimises its class element. In Weber's interpretation bureaucratic authority, for example, functions as an indepedent force whose legitimacy rests in legal rationality defined in universal terms. Yet one of the most highly bureaucratised societies was undoubtedly Nazi Germany, where the fusion of party and state bureaucracies flowed necessarily from the requirements of Hitler's imperialist foreign policy on the one hand, and the need to control every aspect of social life, the elimination of all opposition to the régime, on the other. 'Ideological domination', extending through the mass media, education, family and the Hitler Youth became the basis for legitimation : the existing, pre-Nazi bureaucratic machine responded positively to the Nazi conquest with the German judiciary transformed into an agency of violence, administering the Nazi racial laws, the laws against Communists, socialists and free trade unions. On one level Nazi Germany presented a complex mixture of traditional, charismatic and bureaucratic elements, but the bureaucratic organisation necessary for the functioning of a modern state tended to diminish the legitimising role of tradition and charisma. Yet the fact remains that the legal–rational mode of legitimacy fails to explain Fascist authority and while some commentators have argued that Germany had become 'a non-state, a chaos, a rule of lawlessness' to which Weber's categories were inapplicable,[24] the enforcement of both pre-Nazi and Nazi law remained : the race laws, of course, were a reversal to cultural barbarism – but they constituted law. Similarly, the bureaucracies which ran the concentration camps, the S.S. and the police, enshrined the very virtues of bureaucratic administration – precision, speed, discipline, strictness and reliability – yet functioned not in legal–rational terms, but rather as an essential component of the dominant ideology. Bureaucracy, then, cannot be seen as independent of class : under the Nazis, bureaucratic administration controlled and developed a capitalist economy increasingly dominated by big business interests. The Nazi ideology supported private property and the economic virtues of capitalist exploitation : for, once in power, Hitler quickly eliminated the 'left-wing' of the Nazi party and moved to a total commitment with the large industrial monopolies. In his analysis of Napoleon III's accession to power, Marx had argued for the semi-autonomy of the state and bureaucracy, suggesting that in certain circumstances the dominant class, in order to safeguard its interests, must destroy some of its own institutions and law. But, of course, 'state power is not suspended in mid-air', and behind Napoleon and Hitler lay the interests of the dominant class and the need to maintain bourgeois order.[25] In these circumstances ideological legitimation becomes of paramount importance.

The second criticism of Weber's theory relates to his argument that bureaucracy necessarily leads to the domination of the technical expert over society and that a socialist economy must eventuate in the despotism of total bureaucratic administration. The rise of the socialist bureaucracies of Eastern Europe have seemingly confirmed Weber's prognosis; critics go on to suggest, indeed, that Marx's neglect of the problem of bureaucracy 'stemmed from a perception that his early analysis of bureaucracy fitted badly into his economic interpretation of politics'.[26] But, as we have seen above, Marx was fully alive to the question of bureaucracy and its quasi-independence from the dominant class; and unlike Weber, he focused on the ideological and complex class content of bureaucracy and its historical supercession. The element of fatalism in Weber's thought is wholly anathema to Marx : bureaucracy, as part of the social world, is created by man and can thus be changed by men and, extending the concepts of alienation and reification to bureaucratic administration, it becomes possible to grasp the sharp differences between the two theories, although it must be emphasised that Weber's analysis of the formal properties of bureaucracy has a richness unmatched in any other social theory. For Marx, bureaucratic domination in a capitalist economy is one expression of alienation, a necessary adjunct to the domination of capital over man's labour power in which social relations become relations of things; bureaucracy reflects the discipline and strictness associated with the capitalist regimentation of labour, a repressive and dehumanised administration of men as 'things'. In his *Critique of Hegel's Philosophy of Right* (1843) the young Marx had written *philosophically*, but critically, of bureaucracy :

> The general spirit of bureaucracy is the official *secret*, the mystery sustained within bureaucracy itself by hierarchy and maintained on the outside as a closed corporation. Conducting the affairs of the state in public, even political consciousness, thus appears to the bureaucracy as high treason against its mystery. Authority is thus the principle of its knowledge, and the deification of authoritarianism is its credo . . . within bureaucracy spiritualism becomes a crass materialism, the materialism of passive obedience, of faith in authority, of the mechanism of fixedly formal activities, fixed principles, views and traditions. . . . The bureaucrat sees the world as a mere object to be managed by him.[27]

At this stage of Marx's development there was no theory of class domination, and bureaucracy is depicted as standing above class interests. In his later writings Marx retains this quasi-independent conception of bureaucracy while closely identifying the personnel and ideology of bureaucratic administration with the dominant class. The young Marx's concern had been with alienation, a theme which remained in his later work. It is reasonable to argue, therefore, that for Marx bureaucracy reflects the trends of alienation and reification inherent in societies dominated by private capital, the demands of an extended division of labour and the expansion of 'unproductive workers'.

But what of the Soviet Union? Here, it is argued, Weber was surely right, for does not a powerful and dominant bureaucratic apparatus control virtually every aspect of social life in a society where the capitalist mode of production has been abolished. Some critics go further : the Soviet Union and the East European socialist states are dominated by a new ruling class of bureaucrats whose political ambition is the restoration of capitalism. The question posed, therefore, is the value of Marx's theory for the analysis of socialist bureaucracy. Lenin had been in no doubt: in his *State and Revolution*, written on the eve of the 1917 revolution, he argued that proletarian revolution would smash the old capitalist state machine and instead of a privileged minority standing above the people – 'the essence of bureaucracy' – he envisaged an administration in which officials would be subject to recall, election and supervision by workers' deputies. The revolution would institute 'immediate introduction of control and supervision by *all*, so that *all* may become "bureaucrats" for a time and that therefore nobody may be able to become a "bureaucrat" '. Later, after the revolution and the inception of N.E.P. (New Economic Policy in 1921) which introduced a degree of private capitalism into Russian agriculture, and more particularly after it was clear that proletarian revolution had failed in the more advanced Western European capitalist countries, Lenin consistently warned of the grave dangers posed by bureaucracy. But of all the Bolshevik leaders it was Trotsky who analysed the bureaucratic phenomenon with the greatest prescience. In 1923 he wrote that bureaucratisation must separate the party from the masses, weaken revolutionary spirit, create a stratum of officials owing allegiance only to the administration and a career, and promote a profoundly conservative ideology. 'Bureaucratism', he argued, 'is not a fortuitous feature of certain provincial organisations, but a general phenomenon', rooted in the backward state of Russian culture, economy and technique, and the conflicting interests of peasants and urban workers.[28] In *The Revolution Betrayed* (1936) Trotsky argued that bureaucracy was not inevitable within a socialist economy, but now it had passed from what he called a 'distortion' to a *system* of administration. The essence of his analysis revolved around his concept of the Soviet Union as dual in character, socialist in its property relations, bourgeois in the economic and social inequality that flowed from severe scarcity. Bureaucratic tendencies in any case would 'show themselves after a proletarian revolution', but the rapid growth of the Soviet bureaucracy 'is a result of the iron necessity to give birth to and support a privileged minority so long as it is impossible to guarantee genuine equality'.[29] Under socialism the Communist party should have acted as a counterweight to these conservative trends, but with the triumph of the Stalin faction in the late 1920s the bureaucracy and party became virtually one, a fact of some importance for the question of legitimation.

Weber's concept of bureaucratic domination rested on the factual basis of legal–rational norms, but the Soviet bureaucracy in a way similar but not identical to the Nazi bureaucracy, based its 'social authority' on ideology. Ideological legitimation flowed from the claim of the leading bureaucrats that they ruled on behalf of the proletariat, that the bureaucracy alone was the heir to the 1917 revolution, and in its attempts to establish *continuity* with Lenin and the Bolshevik party. It is this which leads Trotsky to argue that the bureaucracy is not a new ruling class but rather a transitional régime between capitalism and communism and thus lacking secure class roots. He writes :

In no other regime has a bureaucracy ever achieved such a degree of independence from the dominating class. In bourgeois society, the bureaucracy represents the interests of a possessing and educated class, which has at its disposal innumerable means of everyday control over its administration of affairs. The Soviet bureaucracy has risen above a class which is hardly emerging from destitution and darkness, and has no tradition of dominion or command.[30]

Unlike the bureaucracies of capitalist societies, the Soviet bureaucracy enjoys no close family links with a dominant class or shares common interests; and while it exemplifies bourgeois norms and customs based on the economic and social privileges of its members, it has no social basis in a national bourgeois class. In this sense it is more than a bureaucracy : it is 'the sole privileged and commanding stratum in Soviet society'. It is not a class for the simple reason that its domination and legitimacy flow from its defence of state property; its members own no stocks and shares and are recruited on the basis of an administrative hierarchy; there is no right of property transmission to heirs. The bureaucracy plays no 'independent role' in the economy, it lacks 'independent roots' in the means of production and has no rights of property other than those vested in its function of administering state property. Of course, the bureaucracy appropriates surplus value to reinvest in state property and thus extend its own private advantages :

> It devours, wastes and embezzles a considerable portion of the national income . . . it occupies an extremely privileged position not only in the sense of having political and administrative prerogatives but also in the sense of possessing enormous material advantages. Still, the biggest apartments, the juiciest steaks and even Rolls Royces are not enough to transform the bureaucracy into an independent ruling class.[31]

The Soviet bureaucracy, then, exploits the working class, not as a class but as a parasitical stratum forced to defend the conquests of the October Revolution and protect its own unstable, but privileged position. Legitimised ideologically, given passive support initially by a population worn out by civil war and severe material deprivations, bureaucratic administration in what Trotsky called 'degenerated workers' states', is neither the rational nor technically superior and efficient mode of domination analysed by Weber. It is perhaps unnecessary to mention the 'illegal' purges of the 1930s and those which followed the ending of the Second World War. In Russia, Hungary, Czechoslovakia, the accession to power of scientific and cultural charlatans such as Lysenko and Zhadanov, the frequent mismanagements in agricultural and industrial production, attest to the inefficiency and corruption of Soviet bureaucratic administration. For Weber, development of bureaucracy resulted from its success 'in eliminating from official business, love, hatred, and all purely personal, irrational, and emotional elements which escape calculation', but it is precisely these features which distinguish Soviet bureaucracy.[32]

Bureaucracy, then, does not become a 'thing in itself', a force which stands above society guaranteeing efficiency and stability. Weber's concepts seem inapposite to the Nazi and Soviet bureaucracies unless these are regarded as highly abnormal deviations from his general theory. In contrast, Marx's general class theory, and especially the dialectical elements, grasps bureaucratic domination as one variant of capitalist rule in periods of profound crisis; its social base remains vested in property relations. Of course, there is not a mechanical relationship between property and political power and indeed, with régimes of crisis (Hitler's for example) they succeed only in aggravating the contradictions and tensions in society. The Soviet bureaucratic régime is equally characterised by crisis : its claim to legitimacy is founded on the factual control it exercises over socialised property and the ideological claims of a lineage with the revolutionary Bolshevik party. It dominates *on behalf of the proletariat,* its social roots lie within the working class, however paradoxical that may sound. But because the proletariat is not the dominant class the bureaucracy lacks hegemonic authority. Terror and ideological legitimation co-exist as a reflection of its dual character.

It remains merely to add that the theory of managerial hegemony, associated with the concepts of 'bureaucratic collectivism' (Bruno Rizzi, Max Shachtman, James Burnham) and the 'new class' (Djilas) which assumes that a cohesive bureaucratic class has *legally* appropriated state property and transformed itself into an exploiting class within a state capitalist economy, is manifestly untrue. Empirical evidence drawn from contemporary sociological studies of mobility patterns, educational opportunity and recruitment to dominant positions within the bureaucracy in Russia, Poland, East Germany and Czechoslovakia indicates that although the privileged bureaucratic stratum can transmit specific social advantages to its children it does not form a homogeneous category in terms of social background, educational attainment and political independence.[33] In December 1970 riots in a number of Polish cities over rising food prices quickly fanned into a series of confrontations between the Polish bureaucracy and the industrial working class : Gomulka and many of his administrative appointees were swept from power and replaced by the pragmatic Edward Gierek. In the fighting between workers, police and army there were many casualties but no evidence that the capitulation of the Gomulka régime to working-class 'pressure' constituted the actions of a dominant class.

III

The state capitalist argument falters over the question of the right of managers and administrators to allocate the resources they control to their private use; their privileges undoubtedly enhance their children's future status, but that is all. In avoiding the theoretical confusions implicit within the state capitalist positions, social theorists have adopted the concept of élite: the 'power élite' thus dominates through exercising state power and control over nationalised property. The theory of ruling élites rather than dominant class is now firmly entrenched as a fashionable cliché of modern sociology as an explanation of both Western and Soviet society. In essence, the theory rests upon the assumption that capitalist society has passed into 'post-capitalist' mass society compounded from a passive, fragmented mass and a complex range of élite groupings, while in socialist society the disunited mass is totally dominated by powerful industrial and political élites. Raymond Aron has argued that while Marx expected proletarian revolution to produce democracy the result has been the emergence and consolidation of undemocratic élites: 'The elite theory of Pareto', he explains, 'is better adapted to the interpretation of revolutions which claim to follow Marx than is Marxism.'[34]

Élite theory in this sense follows Mosca's thesis that an organised minority will dominate an unorganised majority for no other reason than one of superior technical, administrative expertise based on the undemocratic logic of large-scale organisation. The leading role of the working class is thus wholly disparaged both in Soviet and capitalist societies; both types of society are, in fact, in a process of 'convergence' with élites based in science and technology exercising domination. But although the concept 'élite' has come to be used widely in modern social theory, there exists a great deal of confusion and ambiguity on its exact meaning. Thus a recent Marxist analysis of the capitalist state concludes by arguing that while 'advanced

157

capitalist society' is characterised by 'a plurality of economic élites', they none the less constitute 'a dominant economic class, possessed of a high degree of cohesion and solidarity, with common interests and common purposes which far transcend their specific differences and disagreements'.[35] From a wholly different standpoint, Ralf Dahrendorf, surveying the contemporary West German political and social structure argues for a plurality of competing élite groups based on the civil service, judiciary, government, business, trade unions, mass media, the Church and the legal profession; the major élites, he suggests, do not form 'a monolithic political class', since they lack the confidence for leadership invested in traditional ruling classes.[36] What, then, is meant by élite?

Historically, the concept originated in the work of Mosca and Pareto where it functions as a concept wholly opposed to Marx's 'ruling class'. Both writers argued against Marx's view that economic factors largely determined the political 'superstructure', postulating instead the theory of a 'circulation of élites' which effectively determine the openness of the political class. Thus writing of Marx's theory of class struggle – 'one of the best war horses of all opponents of the present organisation of society' – Mosca argued that the reorganisation of society results from dynamic elements emerging from within the governed class and obtaining a share in government and in social influence previously denied them : the result is an improvement in the relations between rulers and ruled.[37] Plagiarising from Mosca's somewhat simplistic analysis and dividing society into two broad categories of 'higher' and 'lower' strata (the rulers and the ruled), Pareto distinguished between a 'governing élite' consisting of those who exercise political authority and a 'non-governing élite' encompassing other occupational categories, arguing that the history of human society lay in the conflict generated by 'the accumulation of superior elements in the lower classes and . . . inferior elements in the higher classes'. Aristocracies, therefore, are inherently unstable :

> History is the graveyard of aristocracies. . . . They decay also in quality, in the sense that they lose their vigour. . . . The governing class is restored not only in numbers, but – and that is the more

important thing – in quality, by families rising from the lower classes and bringing with them the vigour ... necessary for keeping themselves in power. It is also restored by the loss of its more degenerate members.[38]

The result is that governing élites exist in a continuous process of gradual transformation interrupted by the occasional violent disturbance. Pareto's point is that normally society exists in a state of equilibrium maintained by élite renewal and circulation. Marx's theory of equilibrium, noted above, is wholly different from Pareto's conception which assumes a functionally integrated society saved from potential inertia by continuous interchange within the governing élite, but largely self-regulating and unchanging. Revolutions, for example, never bring a new class to power but merely replenish the existing élite with new talent : 'A conquest or a revolution produces an upheaval, brings a new elite to power and establishes a new equilibrium',[39] a cyclical movement in which nothing new really happens in history, only that the rulers continue to rule through absorbing the 'elements of superior quality' rising from the dominated class.

Contemporary discussions of élite theory have tended to redefine the concept so broadly that it bears little resemblance to its classic initiators. Today the term has come to mean occupational groups bearing high social status and only rarely are these related to the broader questions of power and authority. While Mosca and Pareto stressed the inevitably undemocratic character and function of élites in the maintenance of power, modern élite theorists emphasise the democratic role which competing élites exercise for a modern, complex society. This is the theory of democratic pluralism in which power is scattered through a wide variety of élite occupations so that no one group can effectively dominate the others. Government thus becomes one of compromise, of mediating between the interests of different groups, a situation of balance and equilibrium.[40]

One of the most important, and influential studies of the last few years which attacks this position is C. Wright Mills's *The Power Elite* (1956). Mills attempts to show that far from exhibiting a democratic balance of forces American society is dominated by a triangular structure of powerful élites, the economic, political and military, which together form 'an intricate set of overlapping cliques' who share in major national decision-making. Mills attempts to show that these three élites form a unified power élite – a conclusion diametrically opposed to the theory of balance. The 'moving balance of many compelling interests', Mills argues, comprising a great scatter of individuals, interest and 'veto' groups, fails to distinguish between the different levels of power – the top, middle, and bottom – or raise the question of common interests and, like 'all such romantic pluralism', postulates 'a semi-organised stalemate' as the norm of political and social life. Balance of power implies equality of power and this is manifestly not the case with American society : some groups have a monopoly of overwhelming power, especially the military chiefs. For there is no longer in America an independent base of power, a stable and strong middle class of small entrepreneurs and professionals, but a subordinate, politically passive *mass* of propertyless white-collar workers.

Here, indeed, is Mills's basic theme around which he builds his pessimistic theory of power, the rise of 'mass society', the decline of an informed and independent public in favour of fragmentation and disunity; bureaucratised and manipulated by the media, the masses 'in a metropolitan society know one another only as fractions in specialised milieux : the man who fixes the car, the girl who serves your lunch, the saleslady, the women who take care of your child at school during the day'. Mills's vision is of a totalitarian society in which 'there is no effective countervailing power against the coalition of the big businessmen' and the military : the result is a 'managed consensus' in which 'manipulation', not force, 'is a prime way of exercising power'. Defining authority as power rendered explicit and voluntarily obeyed, Mills concludes that American society is now dominated by a power élite whose exercise of rule is secret and without 'publicised legitimation'.

Mills's concept of a power élite thus comes close to an organised conspiracy of the rich and the powerful against the 'people'. Indeed, he suggests that the élite manifest a greater degree of class consciousness than any other group and while fractions and individual conflicts of interest exist, 'more powerful than these divisions are the internal discipline and the community of interest that bind the power élite together, even across the boundaries of nations at war'.[41] This is reminiscent of Pareto's emphasis on élite cunning and his cynical assessment of the masses as passive tools of an all-powerful ruling élite : the degree of self-awareness which this involves combined with a consciousness of selfish interests can hardly constitute a sound basis for rule. Undoubtedly Mills's 'conspiracy theory' is false, for as we argued above, political domination in a modern society requires some form of legitimation through ideology and no group can rule – for long – if it believes only in its own private interests. This is perhaps the weakest element in Mills's analysis and contrasts sharply with his summary rejection of Marx's theory of ruling class on the grounds that here the 'big economic man' dominates the power structure to the exclusion of other groups. He dismisses class analysis in favour of three separate, although closely related, 'institutional orders', the 'big domains' from whose top men is compounded the power élite. Marx's theory, Mills argues, is too deterministic and cannot grant autonomy to anything except economics; the approach via separate 'domains' implies some independence for the major élites – for example, the powerful role of the military since 1945 and its domination over business and political élites. Yet the whole weight of Mills's evidence is against this interpretation : he demonstrates that recruitment to the three élites is based on certain families, schools and universities and thus on class; he shows the overlapping membership of certain high status clubs, frequent contact and intermarriage between members of the different élites. He shows also the very close relations between the 'political directorate' and the 'corporate rich' so much so that it is difficult to conceive of them as distinct 'domains'. 'Domainal élites', in fact, on Mills's own evidence, constitutes a fairly unified ruling class.

Evidence from British and German studies tends to support this view. Guttsman, for example, has provided substantial evidence that members of the Higher Civil Service and especially the Foreign Service, directors of large industrial and financial companies, academics and scientists who advise government, and judges, are drawn largely from the top echelons of the class structure. Members of the government advisory committees set up to deal with important questions of national policy, Royal Commissions and government committees are predominantly recruited from high-class occupations.[42] A more recent survey and comparison of élite groups between 1939 and 1970 – the judiciary, armed forces, Church of England, directors of clearing banks and the Diplomatic Corps – revealed the persisting influence of Oxbridge and the public schools. In 1970 83.3 per cent of top-ranking army officers attended public schools (the figure in 1939 was 68 per cent), an increase found also with bank directors (59.1 per cent to 71.8 per cent); the percentage of senior judges attending Oxbridge remained the same (80 per cent), while the percentage of ambassadors coming from public schools has never fallen below 73 per cent. The pattern is one of 'self-recruitment' to top-status positions.[43] Dahrendorf's summary of the German material is equally significant : 'German élite groups from 1918 to the present have been consistently recruited to a disproportionately great extent from middle and higher groups of the "service" class as well as from their own predecessors in élite positions.' Self-recruitment dominates the legal profession, the military and the 'cultural and communications elites'. As for business, 'self-made men and first generation entrepreneurs' are the exception at the apex of German industry with the majority of 'leading entrepreneurs' springing from the upper classes. None the less, like Mills, Dahrendorf can conclude that political domination in West Germany lies with what he calls 'an abstract elite', a 'mere category' rather than a definite stratum or class, lacking cohesion and authority.[44] His evidence, however, opposes such an interpretation and it seems clear that Dahrendorf is describing the characteristics of a dominant class : continuity of family backgrounds and social position, self-recruitment and pro-capitalist ideology. A cohesive rather than disunited class regardless of the fact that individual members may not mix socially : the broad support given to the Nazi party by such diverse elements as the Prussian military caste, the industrialists, bankers and leading professionals indicates that social distance is no barrier to common defence of the *status quo*.

A distinction between the concept of élite and class must be drawn at this point. It is evident that a dominant class consists of many separate but interrelated layers, a fact demonstrated by contemporary sociological research. The English aristocracy, for example, maintained their *political* influence long after their economic power had waned, by marrying into the rising bourgeoisie and joining them in industrial and financial ventures; it was not until the nineteenth century that the political representatives of industry and finance began slowly to dominate the political structure.[45] In élite theories the 'fractions' within a dominant class, its political representatives (Mosca's 'political class'), leading bureaucrats and professionals, top military men and diverse elements from industry and finance become independent strata divorced from the totality of social and economic relations. This is, however, more than a mere factual problem for it involves the function of concepts within social theory and raises the question : Is the concept of élite sociologically neutral and thus 'useful' for Marxist and non-Marxist social theory? Marx argued strongly against the uncritical importation of concepts into his general theory and the unfinished *Theories of Surplus Value* stands as a reminder that a rigorous critique of the ideological structure of other social theories and their concepts constitutes an indispensable element of Marxist analysis. This point can be emphasised by a brief examination of the theory of managerialism as a variant of élite theory.

The theory is deceptively simple : the rapid growth of large-scale industrial and financial organisations within capitalism has led inevitably to a separation between the owners of capital and the controllers – what Dahrendorf calls 'the decomposition of capital'. The result is the emergence of a new élite of managers who because they own a small fraction of the assets they control extend allegiance to the firm and its workers rather than to profit maximisation and a capitalist class. Arguing that 'post-capitalist' society is now composed of a plurality of 'imperatively co-ordinated associations'. Dahrendorf asserts that a divorce between ownership and control has created 'a significant change in the basis of legitimacy of entrepreneurial authority' which is based on some form 'of consensus among those who are bound to obey [managerial] commands'. Private property is no longer the main axis of authority in modern society as the capitalist class has virtually disappeared, leaving decision-making in the hands of a non-propertied managerial stratum whose commands are obeyed because of their position in the association (i.e. companies and firms).[46] The conclusion follows that this élite takes decisions in the interests of the whole community.

Many critics have pointed to the empirical weaknesses in this argument by showing the close social relationships between owners and managers and their common origins in the upper echelons of the class structure : the existence of a shared ideology in which the values and aspirations of the non-propertied director are indistinguishable from the owners; the high salaries enjoyed by managers, the concentration of share ownership within the managerial stratum itself and the fact that profit margins remain in the forefront of managerial decision-making. But this information, however valuable, does not disprove the managerial thesis : to demonstrate the common social backgrounds of managers and directors in itself is no rebuttal of the concept of élite, and many writers have uncritically accepted that a managerial élite exists but only as one element within the dominant class. However, non-propertied managers cannot form part of a dominant class since they own no property in the means of production; if they own capital they belong to the capitalist class by virtue of their exploitative function within capitalist production. Class position is determined largely by the objective position of definite strata in the productive system and not, as with the non-propertied managers, in terms of shared values and ideology with owners. As the administrators of capital they function outside the dominant class even though sharing its basic assumptions and aspirations (after all, working-class Tory voters share some of the values of the dominant class). It is crucial to distinguish between the 'agents' of capital and the owners. Marx was perfectly clear that the extension to industry of the division of labour would result in the rapid growth of a new stratum of non-propertied, non-capitalist managers, a social stratum far removed economically from the 'embodiments and personifications of capital', – the capitalist class. In a celebrated passage Marx wrote that the capitalist increasingly becomes superfluous in the productive process as capitalist enterprises become dominated by banks and mere 'money capitalists'. 'An orchestra conductor need not own the instruments of his orchestra, nor is it within the scope of his duties as conductor to have anything to do with the "wages" of the

164

other musicians.'[47] It is capital and its domination over labour which for Marx forms the axis of class power within capitalist society. The development of joint-stock companies during the latter half of the nineteenth century did not herald the demise of capitalism and the emergence of a new 'élite', rather they developed 'the antithesis between the character of wealth as social and as private' into a new form of domination, one which must elude the concept of élite and the social theories which gave rise to it.[48]

7

ANOMIE, HEGEMONY AND SOCIAL ORDER

A persistent criticism of Marx is that his predictions have been falsified : the proletariat, far from heeding the call to revolutionary *praxis* have too often yielded to nationalistic and patriotic ideologies and the reformist leadership of social democratic political parties and trade unions. Rather than forging a revolutionary consciousness necessarily out of inevitable contradictions within capitalism and thus guaranteeing the victory of socialism, the working class in all advanced capitalist societies accepts the values of the dominant class and prefers the certainties of consumption to the ambiguities of revolution. Modern sociology rejects Marx's concept of the 'proletariat' in favour of the 'new working class' which has neither revolutionary potential nor intentions. It is argued against Marx that his theory seriously under-emphasised the integrating elements of social development, the stress on conflict leading him mistakenly to see the future of capitalist society as one of mounting and sharpening class conflict. It thus follows that contemporary sociology – the work of Durkheim, Weber, Parsons – has not necessarily negated and rejected Marx through its emphasis on social consensus and normative integration, but is rather an attempt to provide a more *realistic* account of the processes of change and development in Western industrial society.

Marx's social theory is most heavily criticised for its failure to explain social order, the persistence of social consensus in industrial capitalism since the middle years of the nineteenth century. For how is order possible when according to Marx's theory society is composed of warring classes and factions struggling to impose their will on others. Force would seem to constitute the only viable foundation of social order for such a theory.

I

During the eighteenth century, Adam Ferguson had been one of many social theorists who emphasised the role of conflict in social life. But nineteenth-century sociologists were more preoccupied with the problem of social order than conflict : in the work of Saint-Simon, Comte, Tocqueville and Durkheim, social theory comes to depict social conflict as abnormal and dangerous. Talcott Parsons's painstaking reworking of nineteenth-century social theory in terms of the social action framework is perhaps the most extreme statement of this theme in modern sociology.[1]

The terms 'social consensus' and 'social order', however, are somewhat ambiguous. Does the term order mean *order in general* or does it imply a specific form – bourgeois social order? Parsons has argued that eighteenth-century philosophy – utilitarianism – failed to explain social order through its central precepts of the randomness of ends, the rational orientation of individuals to these ends based on knowledge of the situation, and an atomistic conception of society. It was not sufficient for Bentham and the classical political economists to cite a 'hidden hand' which fused individual ends with collective ends or as with the utilitarian sociologist, Herbert Spencer, to postulate a social contract between men as an explanation for social order. For Parsons the problem of order is traced back to the philosophy of Hobbes, whose problematic social vision was dominated by a conception of human nature – passions, pains, pleasures – which, if allowed full reign in society, must lead to anarchy.[2]

In describing the origins of a problematic conception of social order Parsons does not attempt to link the specific theories with social, political and cultural forces, but treats them as independent of such elements, and it is quite clear that for him social theory develops independently from class and group interests.[3] This is a methodological point of some importance : social theory does not develop immanently; it is not impelled solely by an internal necessity for more exact scientific knowledge or logical consistency. Theories about the social world develop dialectically as both a response to the problems faced by a particular group or class *and* those of an intellectual character. But in Parsons's schema the development of social theory is treated as a simple response to the internal philosophical and sociological inconsistencies of utilitarianism : he omits any discussion of the conflict theories of Ferguson and Millar or the crucial contribution of Marx, all of whom were anti-utilitarian, and equally aware of social order.

Parsons argues that during the eighteenth century a specifically utilitarian rationality emerged which, based on *individuals*, was atomistic in structure, postulating an actor, an end, the notion of utility and an adequate knowledge of the ends and means available in any given situation.[4] Social order is thus possible through (1) the rational recognition of a natural identity of interests which thus neatly sidesteps the problems of a possible conflicts of ends; and (2) the necessary postulate of a social contract, in which men realise the utility of government and social stability. Parsons argues that the whole utilitarian doctrine was built around its atomistic conception of society and notion of rationality, for a rational norm is necessary in the absence of 'any other positive conception of a normative element governing the means-ends relationship'. All 'departures from the rational norm' are seen by the utilitarians as fundamentally irrational, especially ritualism. This is combined with the utilitarian emphasis on the randomness of ends, for the theory has little to say about relations of ends to each other. The ends which men seek are equally atomised.[5]

This utilitarian structure was clearly inherently unstable and Parsons shows how, in nineteenth-century political economy especially, the belief in a natural identity of interests breaks down and with it the entire utilitarian edifice of order. But the point here is that utilitarianism was not the only social theory developed in the eighteenth century. As suggested in earlier chapters, Smith, Ferguson and Millar developed an anti-contract, anti-rationalistic and fundamentally anti-utilitarian social theory in which social conflict and the unintended consequences of actions (the dialectical element) were especially prominent as important components in explaining change and persistence. It is this line of thought which leads to Marx; but Parsons's emphasis (or omissions) must end with Durkheim. Force, conflict and dialectical development constituted the elements of the anti-utilitarian social theory of Ferguson and Millar which Parsons totally ignores. It is only in the work of Marx that this theory is recovered and developed so that it provides an explanatory framework for analysing other theories and ideology as well as the complex historical development of society itself. For Parsons, however, a sociological theory of 'order' is traced through Durkheim and Tocqueville back to Comte.

II

Comte's concern with social order is paramount. While society is disintegrating into anarchy the essence of man is unity and not the conflict of interests which contemporary socialism preached. His vision of a new society is one in which the capitalist class suffused with Comte's positivist religion dedicate their lives selflessly to others. Comte argued that women's 'simple, tender, loving nature' would flood the social system with a contagious altruism which, through its moral influence, would bring an end to class conflict and egoism. Society once again would become a family in which the capitalists would look upon the workers in the same way as loving parents tend their children. Comte's social theory is concerned ultimately with an apparent decline in traditional modes of authority and the rise of secular dissent and socialism. His one-sided conception of human nature, that man when left alone produces only anarchy and disorder, leads inevitably to the conclusion that society, in the interests of order, requires a powerful mode of social regulation.

Comte's theories, however, cannot be understood adequately unless related to the work of Saint-Simon, whom Durkheim regarded as the founder of sociology : *The Division of Labour* must be read as a sustained critique of Comte's position in favour of Saint-Simon. For Comte had accepted the political economists' argument that the division of labour, on its own, creates specialisation and differentiated social interests; the division of labour practically undermines the consensus of moral beliefs on which social order rests and therefore a new form of regulation becomes imperative. In sharp contrast to Comte, Durkheim argued that *normally* the division of labour produces social reciprocity and shared moral values; it is only through its *abnormal* forms that dispersion of interests results. An unregulated division of labour, Comte maintained, must lead to 'a fundamental dispersion' of ideas, sentiments and interests : a system of 'spiritual power' was thus the only means for curing these 'evils'.

Unlike Comte, Saint-Simon had defined the 'fearful crisis in which all European society finds itself' as a crisis of regulation. The French Revolution had effectively undermined the legitimating function of religion and traditional institutions; science and industry, spreading a secular vision, had further created a moral vacuum of social deregulation. Durkheim's important concept of *anomie* can thus be traced to Saint-Simon's argument that the process of industrialisation brings with it 'extreme moral disorder' and 'egoism', *if* unregulated by some widely accepted normative structure. In his last writings, Saint-Simon proposed a 'new christianity', a secular religion capable of regulating economic activity by moral restraint and thus controlling selfishness and gratifying needs.

With Durkheim this problem is clearly stated : moral anarchy flows from a state of normlessness induced by the absence of adequate societal regulation, but unlike Saint-Simon, Durkheim introduced a one-sided, mechanical conception of human nature similar to that of Comte : man must be controlled because of his 'insatiable appetites' : 'There is nothing within an individual which constrains these appetites . . . [they must] be contained by some force external . . . or else they would become insatiable – that is, morbid.'[6] Durkheim's one-dimensional conception of human nature lies at the heart of his discussion of social order. For Talcott Parsons, order 'is Durkheim's central problem from an early stage', and he links Durkheim's theory directly with the philosophy of Hobbes.[7] But the line is rather from Saint-Simon and Comte, for the problematical conception of social order is bound up with the rejection of the achievements of eighteenth-century political economy and to the subsequent development of a social theory which assimilated all contradictions and negative elements through a call for moral regulation. It is in this sense that anomie must be understood, as a concept operating within a profoundly conservative theoretical structure.

Like Saint-Simon, Durkheim saw the crisis of society as one of authority. Unlike the utopian socialists, however, Durkheim was writing *after* not *before* the bourgeoisie had conquered state power and defeated the aristocracy. Durkheim argues that a state of anomie ('normlessness') occurs when '. . . society is disturbed by some painful crisis or by . . . abrupt transitions. . . . In the case of economic disasters, indeed, something like a declassification occurs which suddenly casts certain individuals into a lower state than their previous one.'

Anomie is normlessness and Durkheim quite clearly links it with the economy. In the sphere of trade and industry social life is in 'a chronic state'. Economic development has severed industrial relations 'from all regulations', from the discipline exerted by religion, government and 'occupational groups'. Appetites have thus been freed 'and from top to bottom of the ladder, greed is aroused', aspirations are no longer contained and no one recognises 'the limits proper to them'. With economic development and the resultant prosperity desires multiply and 'at the very moment when traditional rules have lost their authority, the richer prize offered these appetites stimulates them and makes them more exigent and impatient of control. The state of deregulation or anomie is thus further heightened by passions being less disciplined, precisely when they need more discipline.'[8]

Capitalist society (i.e. 'trade and industry') by promoting 'the malady of infinite aspirations' directly conduces to the spread of pessimism and mental anguish, to the growth in particular, of anomic suicide. Anomic suicide occurs, writes Durkheim, because the presence of society within an individual has become so weak that it can no longer constrain the 'passions' 'thus leaving them without a check-rein'. For individual passions can only be held in check by an authority which everyone 'respects and to which they yield spontaneously'. Only society has this power 'to stipulate law and set the point beyond which the passions must not go. . . . It alone can estimate the reward to be prospectively offered to every class of functionary, in the name of the common interest.' In the 'moral consciousness' of societies, argues Durkheim, the limits are vaguely fixed and accepted : the worker usually knows his position and 'realises the extreme limit set to his ambitions and aspires to nothing beyond. At least if he *respects regulations* and is docile to collective authority, that is, has a *wholesome moral constitution*, he feels that it is not well to ask for more. Thus an end and a goal are set to the passions.' Not that these goals are rigid : within limits some improvement is possible but the whole point is 'to make men contented with their lot, while stimulating them modestly to improve it'.[9] It is, in short, a theory of compliance with the existing institutional structure. Let us now examine the concept of anomie more critically.

III

According to Durkheim anomie is social declassification but lacking the restraints of traditional normative regulation. But what does this actually mean in the world of industry and work – the division of labour – where this anomic condition is supposedly most pronounced? The working class in the factory system were regulated by both bourgeois work norms as well as those norms which exist within working-class communities and trade unions – mutuality, co-operation, solidarity. The employers and business organisations, on the other hand, were wholly dominated by bourgeois norms. Thus a lack of norms can mean only an absence of traditional 'bourgeois norms', of bourgeois work discipline and ideology, not of norms in general, for norms are specific to a particular group and class structure. The dominant ideology will also generate ruling-class norms, and a contradictory balance exists between these and those sustained within working-class institutions and culture. The call for an external authority to regulate institutions and impose norms can mean only bourgeois authority not an abstract general authority. Indeed, it seems almost inconceivable that a 'normless state' could have characterised nineteenth-century industry and society : for the evidence adduced by Durkheim in support of his *initial* conception – the anomic division of labour creating class conflict and industrial crises – is precisely the opposition mounted by the working class against capitalist regimentation and exploitation. A strike of industrial workers is not evidence of anomie, of 'normlessness': but rather 'normal', 'healthy' opposition to capitalist exploitation through the agencies of working-class struggle.

But, of course, there is always *human nature*. Superficially, Durkheim's presentation is couched in Hobbesian terms, but with one crucial difference. It is important to note that the function of egoism in bourgeois thought changes in the course of the eighteenth and nineteenth centuries : in the philosophy of Hobbes and Mandeville egoism is used polemically to criticise residual feudal institutions and ideology and to glorify capitalist enterprise and effort. Its function in early critical philosophical materialism demanded a one-sided characterisation of human nature which, in the writings of later eighteenth-century thinkers became increasingly problematical : with Adam Smith, for example, both egoism and altruism are conceived as essential components of man's nature and are thus articulated within a theoretical structure which fails to unify them as a whole. Eighteenth-century political economy, in fact, forced the concept of human nature into the background, as a mere support for the more important economic and historical theory. Its resurrection as a pivotal element in bourgeois thought occurs in the work of Burke, Comte and Durkheim, no longer as criticism of dominant institutions but rather of the potential threat from the working classes and socialism in a society which seemed to lack a strong bourgeois authority. Durkheim's description of society in terms of a 'malady of infinite aspirations' can mean nothing more than a cultural force, not something which springs from within man autonomously : such aspirations are therefore bourgeois in so far as the ideology of the ruling class – individualism – sanctioned private egoism and greed. But it is difficult to understand how an essentially bourgeois value can dominate all social strata to the extent that widespread anomie necessarily results. For the working class neither possessed the means nor the desire to aspire egoistically : on the contrary, their culture exemplified all the virtues which Durkheim himself admired, solidarity and mutuality and through the trade-union movement, their activities were 'morally regulated'.

Durkheim, in fact, never analysed social stratification in a way which would have filled out or negated his general social theory.

173

Instead, the concept of anomie is illustrated, statistically, through his study of suicide. But he intended this analysis not merely as a closely argued monograph on a specific problem but as applicable to the whole society. Anomie was a general social and cultural condition. It is quite clear that the statistics on the various suicide rates in different groups are used polemically against the nature of modern (capitalist) society. He argues that 'suicide varies inversely with the degree of integration of the social groups of which the individual forms a part', and that Protestants have a much higher suicide rate than Catholics for the following reasons :

(1) Catholic communities possess the strong traditions and shared beliefs conducive to an integrated 'state of society' and 'a collective life' which restrains the suicidal tendencies endemic in modern society.

(2) The cause of suicide lies in the weakening of the power of 'collective representations' through the collapse of 'traditional beliefs' and cohesive communities in the face of industrialisation and social fragmentation.[10]

Durkheim argues that a positive statistical relationship exists between suicide rates and external associations, especially religion and education. The latter is important because the more educated a group the more it is prone to question tradition and thus authority. Durkheim also provided an explanation of the different suicide rates in terms of the consciousness of those committing suicide, that is, through the concept of 'collective representations'. But to appreciate the extent of his thorough-going concern with social order it is necessary to note his analysis of the different suicide rates among Protestants, Catholics and Jews.

His argument is simple : the state of society creates strong suicidal currents and the extent to which an individual is thus affected hinges on the degree of integration of his social group, his collectivity. Discussing 'egoistic suicide' Durkheim produces evidence to show that education and suicide are closely connected. Protestants are more educated than Catholics, who kill themselves less frequently. But Jews are more highly educated than Catholics, yet their suicide rate is markedly lower. At this point in his argument Durkheim might have attempted to show that among Jews, those with higher education kill themselves more frequently than those with lower education. In this way he could have saved his correlation. But he did not do this, for to do so would have meant cutting right across his main argument that the lack of integration within a religious society is the fundamental cause of suicide and more particularly the break with tradition which the 'spirit of free enquiry' (education) engenders. Durkheim's failure here is a measure of his ideological commitment to social order.

Durkheim goes on to argue that free enquiry is especially marked among Protestants but this in itself is not the cause of suicide. The need for 'free inquiry' he suggests, has a cause of its own, 'the overthrow of traditional beliefs', the questioning and criticism of established authority : '. . . for ideas shared by an entire society draw from this consensus an authority which makes them sacrosanct and raises them above dispute.'[11] Suicide rates are high, then, because morality is weak. And morality, for Durkheim, is closely bound up with religion. His explanation of the low suicide rate among English Protestants is particularly illuminating. Here were statistics which clearly threatened the whole of Durkheim's analysis : what to do about it? He argues that simple statistics are not what they seem, for in England there are laws which 'sanction religious requirements', there is the power of Sunday Observance and the prohibition of religious representations on the stage, all proof of a cohesive religious society. In England, moreover, respect for tradition is 'general and powerful'. In a passage which betrays Durkheim's polemical, not scientific intent, he writes that in England, 'Religious society . . . is much more strongly constituted and to this extent resembles the Catholic Church.'[12]

Durkheim encounters similar problems in his interpretation of Jewish suicide statistics. For having claimed an external link between the decline of traditional authority and education (the Protestants in France), he is forced to analyse the Jewish case as an *exception*. For religious minorities, he argues, suffering from continuous persecution use knowledge 'not . . . to replace [their] collective prejudices by reflecting thought, but merely to be better armed for the struggle'. In other words, education has a different meaning for Jews than for Protestants and therefore Durkheim can conclude that a high degree of education does not imply any weakening of traditional authority among the Jews. His approach then, can be summarised :

(1) Statistics do not support his theory at all points.

(2) Durkheim thus supplies 'intermediary meanings' to bring these exceptions into line with his general theory. These meanings are Durkheim's own (the attitude of the Jews towards education).[13]

(3) To explain the significant exception of English Protestantism he appeals to an 'abstract' control exercised by a traditional Church, a state of affairs 'generally known' (by whom is not stated).

Ultimately, therefore, Durkheim's argument is that the lack of 'shared moral beliefs' constitutes the root cause of high suicide rates; the 'moral constitution of society' has been subverted by anomie. This had been his starting-point in *The Division of Labour*, the collapse of traditional modes of regulation and the resultant problematical relationship between the individual and society. The capitalist division of labour lacks moral regulation precisely because it is 'forced', that is, based on widespread inequalities of occupation, income, status; it is therefore a transitional form, lacking the spontaneous regulation of a genuine social consensus.

Durkheim was not an opponent of capitalism and his proposals for a morally regulated, non-anomic society through occupational corporations eliminate the problem of exploitation and class domination. As with Comte the capitalist class remains as the educated guarantors of social stability, not the incumbents of an economically necessary, exploitative role. For Durkheim and Comte it was not a question of changing capitalism but merely of modifying its superstructure. In a passage of remarkable clarity, Durkheim writes that the 'pathological state' of modern society, with its 'morbidity', 'pessimism', its 'rising tide of suicide', its 'abnormal' (anomic) division of labour, can mean only that the 'social organism' has 'reached a degree of abnormal intensity'. The result is that anarchists, mystics and socialist revolutionaries share a hatred of the present and a 'disgust for the existing order' with 'a single craving to destroy and escape from reality'. For life is 'often harsh, treacherous or empty', and the function of social theory is to point to this inescapable fact, the necessity for 'collective sadness', and thus help to establish the collective authority which will prevent this sadness from reaching 'morbidity'.[14] Durkheim ends by advocating occupational corporations and moral education which in practice can mean no more than a 'humanised capitalism', one in which the state acts in a moral, not class capacity.

The concept of anomie, therefore, seems profoundly conservative : normlessness in Durkheim's analysis springs only from the *social* setting, never from the political organisation of society. Equally, it is not directly related to the *specific* functioning of the capitalist system. Alienation for Marx was a critical concept precisely because it pointed to the dehumanisation which the nature of capitalism – the transformation of use values into exchange values – necessarily engendered, and a society which had developed the most highly organised, disciplined mode of production in history necessitating strong, collective normative authority. Indeed, the essence of alienation lies in its emphasis on the ways in which capitalist norms embody significant aspects of alienation and reification; Durkheim, in fact, is arguing for normative regulation within a capitalist economic framework to support social harmony, the very target of Marx's criticism. It is thus extremely difficult to understand how many contemporary sociologists can accept anomie and alienation as similarly 'radical' concepts, 'ethically grounded metaphors for an attack on the economic and political organisation of the European industrial middle classes', describing essentially the 'same behaviour and discontents' although from different political perspectives. Anomie, such arguments suggest, is 'radical, historical and sociological', a trenchant criticism of 'economic individualism', a critical appraisal of those societies 'in which self-interest has been reified and raised to the level of a collective end'.[15] For while it is perfectly true that Durkheim criticised certain features of capitalist civilisation this fact *on its own* does not imply a radical overall criticism. Everything hinges on the point of view of the criticism : and it is clear that with Durkheim capitalism *as a whole* is not criticised.

This is the crucial point. The concept of anomie in Durkheim's social theory, unlike Marx's concept of alienation, does not refer to the economic organisation of society, the capitalist mode of production. It ignores this aspect completely. For with the development

177

of capitalism there can be only one clear, consistent standpoint of criticism and that is socialism. It is perfectly obvious that Durkheim had no sympathy with those socialists who claimed that capitalism had to be overthrown and socialism instituted in its place. In the final chapter of *The Division of Labour* he comes to grips, for the only time, with Marx's analysis of the capitalist division of work. For him the division of labour in modern society was abnormal, pathological, *not itself*: the central point here is that Durkheim made no attempt to analyse historically why the division of labour had taken this form, but rather argued that social order was threatened by its pathological formation and therefore other institutions must regulate it.

The differences, then, between Marx and Durkheim are clear. For Marx, capitalism was a society in which man was dominated by work norms exemplifying inhuman efficiency and external control, by processes which transformed him into an object; alienation was thus the acceptance of this external compulsion, of a passive adaptation to the dictates of highly regulated work processes, specialisation and the treatment of human labour as mere units. In sharp contrast to Marx's portrait of a systematic, regulated process of exploitation within a basically anarchical system of production, Durkheim proposed the metaphysical concept of an unregulated capitalism. For Marx, capitalism destroyed both man's inner creative potential and demanded that pleasure and desire be seconded to efficiency and profit. Durkheim understood that 'modern society' transformed man into a restless greedy individual, unhindered by the central fact of capitalist production : scarcity. These two thinkers can hardly be said to be describing the same phenomenon.

IV

Unlike Comte and Durkheim, Marx was more concerned with the actual historical processes of social change – through conflictive interests in society – than with social solidarity, consensus and order. History is class struggle and the propertyless proletariat constitutes the carriers of human emancipation from exploitation and alienation. But as was argued in Chapter 5 modern social theory has long abandoned the concept of revolutionary proletariat. Marcuse echoes many contemporary sociologists when he argues that modern capitalism is now so powerful that all oppositional thought and criticism is emasculated through a 'repressive tolerance' in which the mass media allows diverse points of view from fascist to communist to be aired, a situation in which 'stupid opinion is treated with the same respect as the intelligent one', with the effect of eliminating any potential revolutionary class consciousness.[16] The observation that the working class of capitalist society is non-revolutionary is neither new nor particularly relevant. In his novel *The Ragged Trousered Philanthropists*, written around 1910, the English socialist Robert Tressell portrayed the proletariat as patriotic, highly conservative, anti-socialist, the passive prisoner of 'The System'. The socialist hero pessimistically concludes that the real oppressors are not the capitalists but the apathetic and indifferent workers, 'those who not only submitted like so many cattle to the existing state of things, but defended it, and opposed and ridiculed any suggestion to alter it. . . . *They* were the people who were really responsible for the continuance of the present system.' During the 1930s, a period of massive unemployment, the proletariat again 'refused' its 'historic task'. George Orwell once observed that for the ordinary worker 'socialism does not mean much more than better wages and shorter hours and nobody bossing you about', and that in England, at the height of the Depression, the working class seemed totally resigned and passive. He recounts attending a socialist meeting in Wigan : 'I suppose these people represented a fair cross section of the more revolutionary elements in Wigan. If so, God help us. Exactly the same sheep-like crowd – gaping girls and shapeless middle aged women dozing over their knitting. . . . There is no turbulence left in England.'

A common theme, then, of novelists, sociologists and philosophers is that the worker is gullible, passive and too easily swayed by bourgeois propaganda and affluence. Both Orwell and Marcuse agree that the working class is more than non-revolutionary in that it actually supports the *status quo*, the repressive capitalist society and is partly to blame, therefore, for the failure of socialism in the West. If this is so then quite clearly there is no problem of social order :

Marx's social theory is false and utopian. But is Marx's theory of capitalist development predicated upon inevitable internal breakdown and the growth of an irresistible proletarian revolutionary consciousness?

It has already been argued in previous chapters that class consciousness and class action are mediated through the dominant institutions and ideology of society. If the proletariat lacks a revolutionary consciousness and revolutionary party it will never challenge bourgeois domination. The social authority of a particular class represents a crucial mediating force in the development of class consciousness. A dominant class, wrote Gramsci, 'should not count only on the material force which power gives in order to exercise an effective leadership', but must seek to create and diffuse through subordinate social strata an intellectual, moral and political hegemony. The great value of Gramsci's concept of hegemony lies in the emphasis given to domination within the 'superstructure' of society; hegemony lies not within the economic and political structure but in the sphere of 'civil society' (family, church, recreation, political parties, work) and domination is thus cultural not physical. Thus it is only when the working class has established its own hegemony, has subordinated other classes to its authority, that a successful proletarian revolution becomes possible. A crisis of hegemony occurs when a dominant class fails to carry through projects for which it has 'forcibly extracted the consent of the broad masses' (war for example) and thus activates the subordinate strata from a state of passivity into one of conscious opposition.[17]

Hegemony, then, focuses on the complex balance of class forces within society and suggests that only in exceptional circumstances will the proletariat, through its politically advanced sections, effectively challenge bourgeois authority. Both Marx and Engels, however, firmly believed in the revolutionary potential of the English proletariat, arguing that in England, in contrast to other European societies, capitalism was more advanced both in technique and class structure with a highly concentrated urban proletariat as the carriers of revolutionary change. Yet there was no revolution : the working-class movement paradoxically developed a revolutionary consciousness only in those societies at a lower level of industrial development

– France and Germany in the nineteenth century, Russia in the twentieth. Why?

Marx and Engels's writings contain many discussions on why the English working-class movement lagged behind that of Europe. Their analysis contrasts sharply with Durkheim's concept of anomie, for what they suggested was nothing less than a theory of social order, but one which emphasised the important role of consciousness. There are many passages which show their impatience with the English workers : in 1894 Engels despaired of the proletariat 'with their sense of imaginary national superiority', their bourgeois ideas and viewpoints, and their leaders corrupted by parliamentary reformism. Yet at the same time Engels could assert that 'the socialist instinct is getting stronger among the masses', so although the English worker 'will be the last to arrive' when he does so his 'contribution will weigh quite heavily in the scale'.[18] To explain the apparent contradiction between a highly advanced capitalist mode of production and the absence of revolutionary consciousness Marx and Engels emphasised the complex relation of economic factors to the specific forms of the cultural and political 'superstructure'. Social order, they suggest, is explicable in terms of economic conditions, ideology, national culture, trade-union organisation and political leadership.

They argue, for example, that after the potentially revolutionary threat of Chartism in the 1840s English capitalism settled down to a period of relative economic expansion and prosperity, a situation which facilitated the development of a 'class consensus' or equilibrium. Engels is somewhat crude in his argument that the workers were 'duped' by the representatives of the dominant class through the Liberal party and that the capitalist political parties in general were able to control the masses in the absence of a genuine working-class party. While this view contains an element of truth it must be rejected since it assumes a conspiracy theory. Of course, the dominant class is conscious of the potential threat posed by the working class to its authority but no ruling class is wholly aware of the need to subjugate a subordinate class. The most conscious representatives of a dominant class believe they rule not in the interests of a minority but for the whole society; to become aware of their class role as exploiters of labour power would lead quickly to political demoralisation. The social function of ideology is to prevent such processes from occurring. When Engels writes that the bourgeoisie has sense enough to realise that working-class representation in parliament is inevitable and therefore must be controlled by bourgeois parties thus 'chaining the workers politically still more firmly to the bourgeoisie' he is arguing that as a subordinate class in a society dominated by a persuasive ideology the workers find it increasingly difficult *on their own* to achieve a revolutionary class consciousness. They become bourgeoisified.

Equally important is the way in which the bourgeois class extends what were originally proletarian demands to the whole society. The Chartists had called for universal suffrage, secret ballot and the abolition of property qualifications, all of which were refused in the 1840s but enacted by bourgeois parliaments in the 1870s. Indeed, Marx wrote that to grant universal suffrage was equivalent to proletarian power, its extension implying the political supremacy of the workers. Here Marx was clearly wrong, for universal suffrage has meant the development of social democratic parties which, while based on working-class support, are reformist in ideology and seek merely to 'humanise' and not abolish capitalism. But it would be a great mistake to argue that the reformist nature of working-class parties is imposed from without : writing of the relatively privileged skilled working class in England at the end of the nineteenth century Engels was highly critical of '. . . the bourgeois "respectability" bred into the bones of the workers. The social division of society into innumerable gradations, each recognised without question, each with its own pride but also its inborn respect for its "betters" and "superiors", is so old and established that the bourgeois still find it pretty easy to get their bait accepted.' Tom Mann, adds Engels, one of the 'finest' of the labour leaders, is too fond of mentioning his lunch appointments with the Lord Mayor.

This penetration of bourgeois ideas into working-class organisations and consciousness remains a persistent theme in Marx's and Engels's writings; in 1858 Engels wrote : '. . . the English proletariat is actually becoming more and more bourgeois, so that this most bourgeois of nations is apparently aiming ultimately at the possession of a bourgeois aristocracy and a bourgeois proletariat *as well as* a bourgeoisie.' There had been no socialism in England, Engels concluded, because a 'privileged minority' had benefited from economic expansion. But perhaps more significantly this 'labour aristocracy' was organised within the most powerful trade-union movement in the nineteenth century. More than any other institution, it was trade unions which, while reflecting the class struggle in strikes, lockouts or simple wage bargaining, constituted an agency of social order. Engels argued, for example, that the English workers had never effectively used their trade-union organisation, being largely pragmatic, or to use a modern term, 'instrumentally oriented' to economic matters. This 'economism' is described by Engels as a 'vicious circle' of 'higher wages and shorter hours'. Trade unions became not agencies of social change but vehicles for improvement within the capitalist system : the 'ultimate aim' not one of propaganda and political organisation but the practical demand for more money and better working conditions. Engels was particularly critical of the 'new model unions' (the unions of skilled workers) which too quickly 'degenerate into mere sick funds and burial clubs'; they are 'conservative' and reject socialism. But this 'aristocracy of labour' cannot remain a privileged stratum within the working class indefinitely : the rise of the unskilled workers' unions – gas, dockers, general labourers – in the 1880s is seen as presaging a change to a more militant and socialist consciousness. Engels as always was optimistic : the working class will realise that fighting for higher wages and shorter working hours is only 'a very necessary and effective means towards a higher end : the abolition of the wages system altogether'.[19]

Thus the ways in which working-class consciousness is shaped by the trade unionism which forms such an important part of working-class culture helps in understanding the apparent paradox : the strongest labour movement in Europe constituted a major source of social order. When it challenged capitalism it did so from a partial, limited, pragmatic and non-revolutionary perspective.

In these circumstances – duplicated in varying degrees in most capitalist societies – revolutionary class consciousness and *praxis* is the exception rather than the rule. For given the social authority of the dominant class and the influence of ideology and alienation on working-class consciousness it is hardly surprising that many workers divorce economics from politics and use trade unions as economic rather than political institutions. It was Lenin who suggested that the working class would never achieve a socialist consciousness spontaneously but only a plebeian opposition to capitalism. However, this does not imply a passive adaptation of all proletarian strata to capitalism. Of course some workers are more politically conscious than others, but few are revolutionary. The majority accept the hegemony of the dominant class, and in this sense both the leaders and large sections of the working class bear a consciousness forged within the institutions of bourgeois hegemony. The result is that pristine socialist elements and components of working-class culture (solidarity etc.) frequently co-exist with elements of capitalist ideology. Thus the question of working-class leadership is clearly important. In 1874 Marx wrote that the workers must 'get rid of their present leaders' and four years later commented that the working-class movement 'had passed completely into the hands of the venal trade union leaders'. Discussing the 1868 election, which gave the urban workers the vote for the first time, he wrote : 'Once again the proletariat has discredited itself terribly. . . . Everywhere the proletariat is the tag, rag and bobtail of the official parties, and if any party has gained strength from the new voters, it is the Tories.'[20] Social order, therefore, seems guaranteed by the failure of the working class to develop revolutionary parties, its 'cringing to respectability' and the reformist quality of its leadership. Durkheim's fears of the collapse of authority in modern society seem acutely inapposite in the England described by Marx and Engels. In France and Germany the same processes which Marx and Engels saw as characteristic of the English working class came to dominate their labour movements, and the German Social Democrats and the French Socialists formed or were part of 'moderate' governments whose defence of bourgeois society was firm and acceptable to the bourgeoisie themselves. Indeed, the bourgeoisie requires both a proletariat and a labour movement cast in its own image.

'At a certain stage of their development', Marx wrote, 'the material productive forces come into conflict with the existing relations of production' a conflict which eventuates in an 'epoch of social revolution'.[21] But, as we have seen, capitalist society remained remarkably stable in the face of the potentially explosive conflict relations which its economic structure engendered. Marx was not an economic determinist : his social theory, with its emphasis on ideology and alienation, clearly focuses on 'superstructural' elements for explaining social order. Bourgeois ideology is all-pervasive, hegemonic; within capitalism the working class remains a subordinate class incapable of totally negating bourgeois influences on its thought, culture and action. Lenin wrote that 'bourgeois ideology spontaneously imposes itself upon the working class', its authority flowing from the fact that it 'is far older in origin than socialist ideology . . . more fully developed, and . . . has at its disposal immeasurably more means of dissemination'.[22] Thus within capitalist society a *sense* of equality is widely diffused and egalitarian strands can be found in bourgeois ideology itself. The modern emphasis on consumer norms tends further to flatten any sharp sense of inequality and succeeds in promoting an ideology of formal openness. Of course, capitalism is not an egalitarian social system but one dominated by great inequalities of income, wealth and power. In these conditions it becomes imperative for bourgeois society to find a legitimating ideology : the social authority of the dominant class springs largely from the political and educational socialisation of the subordinate strata – a process which is never total, but the influence and pervasiveness of ideology is such that social order becomes non-problematical. And from a purely theoretical standpoint, the concept of equilibrium discussed in Chapter 2 is further proof that for Marx social order, not disorder, constitutes a major tendency within capitalism.

In *Capital* Marx had written that 'the advance of capitalist production develops a working class, which by education, tradition, habit, looks upon the conditions of that mode of production as self-evident laws of nature . . . the dull compulsion of the economic relations completes the subjection of the labourer to the capitalist.'[23]

For Durkheim, the proof of anomie lay in industrial conflict, the defensive activity of the working class against the domination of capital. The important point here, of course, is that industrial conflict has increased both in extent and intensity since the beginning of the twentieth century in all advanced industrial societies. This might suggest unregulated relations and widespread anomie. But one writer has recently suggested that revolutionary conflict relations occur not out of the maturity of capitalism but emerge from its initial immature phases, at a time when the working class has yet to be integrated into the social and political structure; revolutionary class consciousness develops only when the potentially conflictive relations in industry are not adequately regulated.[24] This theory, which owes much to Durkheim, suggests that a politically disorganised nineteenth-century proletariat possessed a revolutionary class consciousness independently of a revolutionary party and thus posed a threat to bourgeois society. Such fiction needs stern correction : capitalism has been challenged by the proletariat *only* in the twentieth century – Italy, Germany, Hungary in the period after the First World War, Germany and France in the 1930s and France again in the 1960s – when it possessed the strength and party organisation necessary for revolutionary *praxis*. The ultimate failure of these movements should not blind us to the very real threat to bourgeois hegemony posed by the working class in this century, and the ways in which Communist parties have transformed themselves from revolutionary into reformist and parliamentary organisations, without doubt exercising the same role for the development of consciousness as the social democratic parties.

Durkheim's concept of anomie and his general theory of deregulation must fail as an explanation of social order : his ideas suggest the existence of potential disorder, conflict and a lack of equilibrium. In contrast, Marx's social theory is both an analysis of the social, economic and political sources of conflict and the forces promoting integration. And this is possible because Marx, unlike Durkheim, grasped the concept, the fact and the social power of ideology, of hegemony.

8

FUNCTIONALISM: CHANGE, CONFLICT AND SOCIAL ORDER

One of the striking themes of modern social theory is the argument that a 'crisis' in sociology has emerged because of an artificial separation of sociology from Marxism in the course of their development during the nineteenth and twentieth centuries. Central to this argument is functionalism : as a dominant sociological theory it has often been described as profoundly conservative, an ideological legitimation of capitalist hegemony. None the less, in order to transcend the 'crisis' in sociology resulting from the hiatus between sociology and Marxism, a theoretical convergence is claimed for Marx, Weber, Durkheim and functionalists such as Talcott Parsons.

The question of crisis in sociology will be left to the final chapter together with the related problem of 'critical' and 'radical' sociology. This present chapter will attempt to explore the relationship between sociological functionalism and Marx's social theory with particular emphasis on two major problems : firstly, the stress placed by functionalists on 'normative order' and social cohesion, and the implication that Marxism fails to explain social consensus; and secondly, the question of social change and the equilibrium models of society used by functionalists. By thus focusing on what is commonly accepted as the strength and the weakness of sociological functionalism the character of the relationship between Marxism and functionalism should clearly emerge.

Functionalism as a distinctive method and theory in the social sciences originated in attempts made by nineteenth-century anthropologists to understand the persistense of 'irrational' cultural residues ('survivals') in primitive societies. It is unnecessary to review the development of functionalist theory in any detail for the purposes of this chapter, but it is important to grasp its general features as they emerged in the work of Durkheim, Malinowski and Radcliffe-Brown. Durkheim, for example, is frequently cited as the founder of sociological functionalism because of his argument that social institutions exist for the purpose of fulfilling social needs. Thus 'all moral systems practised by peoples are a function of the social organization of these peoples', and that, apart from 'abnormal cases' every society develops a morality necessary for its proper functioning.[1] Institutions contribute to the unity and integration of the whole society except, as with Durkheim's analysis of the division of labour, when they become anomic. Durkheim went on to argue that criminal behaviour, like religion, must fulfil a particular need because it has always existed; it is therefore analysed as a necessary and 'integral part of all healthy societies . . .'.[2] In a similar vein Malinowski argued that magic fulfilled 'an indispensable function' in primitive societies through satisfying a need 'which cannot be satisfied by any other factors of primitive civilisation', while for Radcliffe-Brown the function of the funeral ceremony 'is the part it plays in the social life as a whole and therefore the contribution it makes to the maintenance of the structural continuity'.[3]

Explicit in these formulations is a model of society as a functional unity, its constituent parts meshing together with a degree of harmony and consistency to prevent serious conflict from developing; and that such conflict must be seen as dysfunctional to the maintenance of the whole. The tendency to regard functionalist theory as conservative largely stems from its emphasis on integration and social order and the analogy of society as a human organism in which social 'health' is identified with order and 'disease' with conflict.

The question of social order is central to sociological functionalism. As we have seen in previous chapters, this is Durkheim's problem in *The Division of Labour*, to seek for a regulative normative structuring of desires and appetites so that men's actions will be normal, healthy and functional. The function of the division of labour is normally to create unity; the 'abnormal' form functions to create dissension and conflict eventuating in a widespread state of anomie. But contemporary functionalism is no longer identified with this particular emphasis. In his 1959 paper, 'The Myth of Functional Analysis as a Special Method in Sociology and Anthropology' Kingsley Davis proclaimed that functionalism was now the method used by all social scientists whether they call themselves functionalist or not.[4] Not everyone sympathetic to functionalism would agree with this extravagant thesis; none the less, modern functionalism does claim that its models and theory provide the most adequate explanations of man's social world.

But the rise of functionalism is seen also as part of a conservative and thus ideological response to industrial capitalism and socialism. It is usually argued that in seeking to explain social order, sociological functionalism fails to provide an adequate analysis of social change and conflict and constitutes no more than a sophisticated rationale for the *status quo*. Ignoring society as a *process*, its continued emphasis on order is

> . . . an ideology; it congenially resonates sentiments that favour the preservation of privilege. . . . A social theory that takes as its central problem the maintenance of social order is thus more ideologically congenial to those who have more to lose. . . . In practice, the champions of order often counsel the dominant elites to play a policy of restraint : nothing too much.[5]

The functionalist theories of Talcott Parsons present a particularly attractive target for those critics who argue that they both reflect the dominant values of American capitalism and also fail to take account of *power* in society. For the 'normative order', which Parsons suggests lies at the heart of every social system, fails to explain the simple fact that certain men make decisions while others do not. Parsons's assumption, critics argue, suggests that people virtually govern themselves : the facts, however, are different, for 'among the means of power that now prevail is the power to manage and to manipulate the consent of men'.[6]

In general, functional theorists *have* ignored the problem of social conflict and power in society, although Parsons claims that in explaining social order his theory simultaneously grasps those factors making for instability and thus for social change. It is in this spirit that R. K. Merton has argued that far from embodying a conservative ideology functionalism can be radical and critical, pointing to the failures and weaknesses, the 'malfunctioning' of specific institutions for satisfying the collective needs of society. The fact that it can be understood as both radical and conservative, he suggests, implies that functionalism is neither one nor the other but, like other forms of sociological analysis, is simply neutral, given an ideological colouring only by the polemically motivated.[7] What, then, is sociological functionalism?

I I

The *general* characteristics of sociological functionalism can be briefly stated :

(1) Societies are wholes, systems of interrelated parts. Each part has meaning only in relation to the whole; society is a 'system' of interdependent elements which contribute to the integration of the system. Social causation is thus multiple and reciprocal.

(2) The integration of all parts – or 'sub-systems' – while never 'perfect' none the less produces a state of equilibrium. Adjustments are made to both internal and *external* influences and the general tendency is in the direction of stability and inertia. The crucial role of social control mechanisms is thus obvious.

(3) Deviance, tension, strains exist as 'dysfunctional' elements which tend to become institutionalised or resolved in such a way that perfect integration, while remaining an unrealisable ideal, is none the less the dominant tendency within the social system.

(4) Social change is not revolutionary, but adaptive and gradual; if there is rapid change it occurs in the 'superstructure' of society thus leaving the basic institutional structure unchanged. Change

stems largely from external factors, through structural and functional differentation and through inventions and innovations by individuals and groups.

(5) Social integration is achieved through value consensus, 'shared cognitive orientations', that is, a widely diffused set of principles which legitimate the existing social economic and political structure.

A distinction is sometimes made between *general* and *normative* functionalism. The latter, associated with the work of Talcott Parsons, postulates 'shared value elements' for achieving social consensus and defines society as a *system* of interdependent parts. One of the basic postulates of normative functionalists is that value consensus contributes necessarily to the maintenance of an integrated, equilibrated social system. General functionalism, by contrast, minimises the functional integration of parts, postulating the dysfunctional consequences of different and sometimes opposing values. But this distinction seems spurious : the work of so-called general functionalists – Kingsley Davis and R. K. Merton for example – differs only in degree, not in kind, from normative functionalism. Both emphasise consensus as the normal, integrated condition of society; society is defined as a system in which the various elements function for its adaptation, adjustment and equilibrium. As will be argued later, both 'normative' and 'general' functionalists agree that social integration is a consequence of both normative and structural elements and cannot be reduced simply to one or the other.

The value of distinguishing two functionalist models is that it allows for a synthesis between functionalism and Marxism : class conflict and the contradictions within the infrastructure of society supply social change and an historical dimension, while norms and values generate consensus and social integration – the result is a dynamic equilibrium model encompassing both change and stability. However, this is not the only way in which functionalism and Marxism can be synthesised. One theorist has no doubt that both functionalism and Marxism are

. . . fundamentally based on an equilibrium model. . . . The dialectic conceives of society as going through alternating phases of equilibrium and disequilibrium; the thesis is the initial equilibrated

191

stage of the cycle; the emergence of the antithesis leads to the intermediated disequilibrated phase; finally, as the contradiction resolves itself in the synthesis, one enters the terminal, balanced stage of the cycle, which then starts anew.[8]

The conclusion is that both functionalism and Marxism imply integration and change, conflict and consensus since no social system is totally integrated or persistently breaking down. And, as we have argued in previous chapters, Marx's social theory does involve a concept of equilibrium. But in what way does this differ from the functionalists' concept? And is the Marxist category of totality *more or less* the same as the functionalist concept of system?

The work of one Marxist writer lends weight to the claims for synthesis. Bukharin's *Historical Materialism*, written some forty years before the current debate between Marxism and functionalism, postulates society as a system characterised by a dynamic equilibrium between technology and economy, social classes, society and nature. The system is not static but constantly disturbed by contradictions between labour and capital, capitalist and socialist ideologies, the private forces of production and the collective social relations of production. Bukharin suggests 'a law of mobile equilibrium' embracing conflict, contradictions and antagonisms through which social change occurs, the disturbed equilibrium corresponding to the concept of antithesis in the dialectical triad with a new and higher equilibrium emerging as a necessary synthesis. And in language strikingly similar to that of Parsons, Bukharin argues that equilibrium is maintained through the normative consensus of 'ideologies which serve as rivets to hold together the existing order'. Social norms, Bukharin writes, constitute the '*contradictions of equilibrium* for holding together the internal contradictions of human social systems . . .'.[9] The image of society is thus one in which adjustments and adaptations are made automatically to internal and external change, a self-regulating and closed system in which men make history only as the instruments of the law of 'mobile equilibrium'.

It is unnecessary to recapitulate the argument of earlier chapters that the concept of society as a system dominating its members is anathema to Marx's social theory, that Bukharin's presentation of the concept of equilibrium is mechanical and non-dialectical. His treatment of the dialectical triad as a ready-made, sequential formula to impose on historical and social forces eliminates the crucial factor in dialectical analysis, the contradictory and complex determinations of specific events. This is particularly illuminated in Marx's brief discussion of economic equilibrium and the related problem of capitalist breakdown. In those sections of *Capital* and the *Theories of Surplus Value* where Marx discusses the nature of capitalist economic crises, he appears to argue for a strictly functionalist position. Capitalist accumulation tends to promote a decline in the rate of profit and the growth of over-production, speculation and crises. As the average rate of profit falls the capitalist system adjusts by making capital more unproductive or simply destroying it : the 'equilibrium is restored' through the resultant depression and depreciation of capital values which thus create the conditions necessary for investment, profitable production and further capital accumulation.[10] Marx, then, seems to argue for a self-regulated economic system in which economic crisis function as a necessary restorative forces for the maintenance of continual capital expansion. Indeed, on this basis, Marx does not predict the inevitable economic breakdown of capitalism at all, only that the capitalist system, in order to maintain its economic momentum, generates periodic economic crises through which the whole structure is recharged. At one point, however, Marx goes beyond this model to suggest that the process of equilibration itself 'already implies as a pre-condition the opposite of equilibration and may therefore comprise crisis; the crisis itself may be a form of equilibration'.[11] Bukharin's simple, triadic formulae find no echo in Marx's economic analysis : equilibrium is not a 'thesis' transformed into a 'synthesis' but a complex structure of living forces.

That a crisis may function as equilibrium clearly has important bearings for any synthesis between functionalism and Marxism, since in specific circumstances social conflict may well constitute equilibrium and not disequilibrium. But the crucial element in Marx's analysis of crises is his apparent support for the functionalist model of society as a moving equilibrium. The similarity is merely superficial. Of course, he argues that capitalist crises become more and more catastrophic, but this *in itself* is insufficient to produce socialist revolution : capitalism does not collapse spontaneously and inevitably through the workings of its internal contradictions, but only through the class-conscious actions of the organised proletariat. Capitalist crises produce the pre-conditions for social change : ideology and organisation are the essential pre-requisites for the transformation of capitalist society into socialism and one of the most critical determinations in any historical situation.

Here, then, lies the major distinction between the functionalist and Marxist notion of equilibrium. Talcott Parsons, for example, argues that social systems possess an inbuilt tendency to 'self-maintenance' and 'an ordered process of change', the 'moving equilibrium'. It is clear that for him the system dominates its members :

The social system's own equilibrium is itself made up of many subequilibriums within and cutting across one another, with numerous personality systems more or less in internal equilibrium, making up different equilibrated systems such as kinship groups, social strata, churches, sects, economic enterprises, and governmental bodies. All enter into a huge moving equilibrium in which instabilities in one subsystem in the personality or social sphere are communicated simultaneously to both levels, either disequilibrating the larger system, or part of it, until either a reequilibration takes place or the total equilibrium changes its form.[12]

For Marx, capitalist equilibrium was inherently unstable because of economic contradictions and potential class conflict. A crisis does not occur in a vacuum : it produces political and social consequences – heightened class struggles and the development of class consciousness – which constitute major determinations on the way in which a new equilibrium is restored. It is not the system which adjusts and moves on but men, who, through their struggles create change. (The equilibrium forced on a defeated British working class in the 1930s was possible only because of the failure of the 1926 General Strike; similarly, the equilibrium which followed the defeat of Chartism in 1848 was broken only by the class agitation in the late

1860s.) Paraphrasing Marx, the system is nothing, it neither fights battles nor wins wars and it is only men, in definite, historical circumstances, who change the social world.

The imagery employed by Parsons reflects a highly mechanistic and ultimately fatalistic sociology. When Parsons writes of the 'inputs' and 'out-puts' of sub-systems and systems he moves away from his so-called 'normative' functionalism to what might be called 'cybernetic' functionalism in which society has become a self-regulating and equilibrating system. There is a strong element of this in Parsons's thought, of grasping human society in reified, dehumanised terms. Equilibrium becomes an external condition, a process which goes on independently of man's consciousness, ideas and struggle. This aspect is especially marked in Parsons's analysis of integration : for while he identifies equilibrium with social order his concept of 'moving equilibrium' embraces the fact that no system is perfectly integrated, that a scarcity of goods and unequal allocation of resources may produce disintegration. It becomes essential, therefore, to create institutions that mediate the conflict of interests : what Parsons calls 'the integrative sub-system' functions to adapt individuals to the 'goals of the social system' by generating legitimate values :

The integrative sub-system of the society regulates the cultural value-patterns to the motivational structures of individual actors in order that the larger social system can function without undue internal conflict and other failures of co-ordination. These processes maintain the institutionalism of value-patterns which define the main structural outline of the society . . . solidarity is the general capacity of agencies in the society to 'bring into line' the behaviour of system units in accordance with the integrative needs of the system, to check or reverse disruptive tendencies to deviant behaviour, and to promote the condition of harmonious co-operation.[13]

Thus for Parsons equilibrium of *all parts of society* comprises its normal condition and that conflict, while present, is simply a residual and abnormal element. It was argued in earlier chapters that the idea of a widely diffused set of norms regulating conduct formed a basic theme in the social theory of Comte and Durkheim. Parsons, in *The Social System*, clearly argues that a value consensus is a necessary pre-requisite for society :

> The problem of order, and thus of the nature of the integration of stable systems of social interaction . . . focuses on the integration of the motivation of actors with the normative cultural standards which integrate the action systems, in our context impersonally. These standards are . . . patterns of value orientation, and as such are a particularly crucial part of the cultural tradition of the social system.[14]

Parsons argues that society is characterised by 'value orientations' held by certain 'solidary groupings' (professional occupations such as scientists for example) which, over time, pass into the 'value system' of the whole society. The term 'value system' is defined as : '. . . the set of normative judgments held by the members of the society who define, with specific reference to their own society, what to them is a good society.'[15] This definition may seem tautologous as well as sociologically banal since it fails to explain the existence of counter-values and counter-ideologies except as 'deviations'. Parsons defines values as 'normative patterns' which, held by different individuals, evaluate for them the nature of the social system. Norms are 'generalised patterns of expectations which define differentiated patterns of expectation for the differentiated kinds of units within a system', or more simply, what the individual can expect and what others expect him to get from society. Norms, values and collective goals govern and control individual behaviour, and Parsons follows Durkheim in emphasising the need to control the individual; his social theory is ultimately a theory of social control. Thus he argues that goals are not personal but collective, that is, social, and that the individual is motivated and oriented to the social world through the goals of the social system. The individual internalises the collective goals which society generates and in this way social order is augmented.

Durkheim's great merit for Parsons was to point towards a

196

genuine theory of social control, one which could 'lead to a theory of the mechanisms by which solidarity is established and maintained'. Parsons's functionalism is in effect an attempt to develop Durkheim's theory of social solidarity through an emphasis on 'integrative sub-systems' and motivation through values. In Durkheim motivation to action counted for little; it is crucial for Parsons. Through socialising agencies such as the family, school and community, the actor internalises goals, norms and values so that social order is 'normal' not problematical. Parsons's emphasis on *socialisation* flows from a similar stress in Durkheim's work. For Durkheim restraint is not forced on the individual but flows from the collective conscience which is society. 'In this way', writes Parsons, 'the moral component of *the conscience collective* is social', comprising common, shared values which are internalised through socialisation by the new members of society.[16] Culture, then, is all important. In his essay on Marx, Parsons suggests that the great weakness in Marx's social theory was its lack of a theory of personality. Marx's material-ism, he argues, led him to misunderstand that action 'is a function of the *organisation* of behaviour and actions in terms of generalised codes that permit the programming of widely varying particulars'. It is these 'cultural codes' which underlie the 'normative components of societies'. For, contrary to Marx's ideas, society is not character-ised by perpetual conflict but rather by underlying order. Durkheim's conception of organic solidarity is more crucial for understanding modern society than Marx's conflict model. Lacking adequate con-cepts of order and personality Marx's social theory could never ex-plain what Parsons calls 'directionality of orientations to work and enterprise' – this being accomplished in Weber's work (the work ethic of Protestanism). Thus remaining 'psychologically naïve' Marx's social theory failed to come to terms with the overriding importance of cultural factors in the maintenance of social order, integration and equilibrium.[17]

Before looking at these arguments in more detail one important point must be made: for Durkheim, industrial society generated widespread anomie and it is this theme which Parsons repeats again and again in his many analyses of contemporary society: he writes for example that 'the large-scale incidence of anomie in Western society in recent times is hardly open to doubt'.[18] Presumably, therefore, *order is problematical*. But this is not his conclusion : for social order is guaranteed even though there exist mighty forces – as will be seen shortly these are largely cultural in character – ranged against it. It is thus odd that Parsons calls Marx's conflict theory *wholly wrong* and yet himself uses such phrases as 'strains' and 'tensions' in describing 'widespread anomie'. This is an important source of confusion in Parsons's writings, especially marked in his analysis of the breakdown of society, and helps to explain his emphasis on religious values and religion in general as the basis for social cohesion and solidarity.

Here again Parsons follows Durkheim's analysis of the disruptive functions of the 'forced' division of labour for creating, in Saint-Simon's phrase, 'a moral vacuum'. The problem of order is thus grasped in terms of the weakening hold of traditional religious beliefs in increasingly secular societies, and raises the question of the kind of 'shared moral beliefs' which should replace them. In his critique of Parsons, Alvin Gouldner suggests that functionalism ignored the possibility that technology and economic institutions could of themselves provide some measure of unity and stability. Order can be solved in terms of morality *as such*. The emphasis is thus on morality 'as the keystone of social order'.[19] And indeed Parsons writes that the values which constitute the structure of modern society 'are legitimised by moral sanctions and in the last analysis . . . are grounded in our religious attitudes'. Religious institutions are thus a crucial component of the 'integrative sub-system'.[20]

In his essay, 'Christianity and Modern Industrial Society', Parsons argues that 'the internalisation of religious values . . . strengthens character' and that modern society 'is more in accord with Christian values than its forebears . . .' through its Welfare State provisions against poverty, sickness and old age.[21] For Parsons, religion is clearly a functional bulwark against disorder by promoting 'value orientations' within the 'institutionalised normative culture' necessary for equilibrium. In an earlier essay on religion Parsons had agreed with Durkheim's correlation of morality with the sacred, noting his 'important insight' 'into the exceedingly close integration of the system of religious symbols of a society and the patterns sanctioned by the common moral sentiments of the members of the community'.[22] In short, religion fulfils a *need*, a view widely shared by 'normative' and 'general' functionalism. For example, two representatives of 'general' functionalism have written :

The reason why religion is necessary is apparently to be found in the fact that human society achieves its unity primarily through the possession by its members of certain ultimate values and ends in common. Although these values and ends are subjective, they influence behaviour, and their integration enables this society to operate as a system. . . . Even in a secularised society some system must exist for the integration of ultimate values, for their ritualistic expression, and for the emotional adjustments required by disappointment, death and disaster.[23]

Criticising this extreme functional interpretation of religion Merton argues that while religion can be both functionally unifying and dysfunctional, some kind of moral agency is functionally indispensable for society. He goes on to suggest 'the concept of functional alternatives or functional equivalents or functional substitutes', citing Parsons's remark that wherever uncertainty enters into the pursuit 'of emotionally important goals, if not magic, at least functionally equivalent phenomena could be expected to appear'.[24] Now it is important to note that both Merton and Parsons do not support the idea of society as a total functional unity of its separate parts; it has been noted above that Parsons emphasises the anomic state of modern society, arguing especially for the persistence of what he calls the 'malintegration of culture'. Both Parsons and Merton agree, however, that religion represents a powerful force for enforcing group solidarity.

In developing his own more general approach to functionalism, Merton has suggested that the functionalist and the Marxist theories of religion are broadly similar. Following Weber and Parsons he suggests that religion is no mere epiphenomenon but an active force which enables man to orient himself to the world and provides motivation to various activities such as work. Marx's remark that 'protestantism, by changing almost all the traditional holidays into work days, plays an important part in the genesis of capital',[25] as well as his overall dialectical method, clearly suggests that religion as an ideology exercises a strong 'motivational' orientation to the world and is in no sense simply a passive reflection of it. However, Merton argues that through the metaphor of 'opium of the people' Marx's theory grasps religion as a 'social mechanism for reinforcing certain secular as well as sacred sentiments among its believers'.[26] But this is a mere caricature : the essence of Marx's analysis of religion, as with all ideology, was in terms of alienation and reification, as a false, non-scientific orientation to the social world. To be sure, religion is an active force in the development of consciousness : it obstructs man's understanding of the world, and religion itself, as social, human products. Religion is alienated consciousness, and the young Marx had written that the beginning of all criticism was the criticism of religion, a remark directed against the Young Hegelians. But it should be clear from Marx's analysis of alienation and reification that his social theory does not treat religion as a simple emanation of a specific social structure but rather as 'false consciousness' and partly autonomous.[27]

But as ideology, religion is useful for the maintenance of social order and in this sense functional for society. However, the meaning of religion as a social product cannot be grasped solely within a functionalist framework, since the whole essence of functionalism lies in analysing immediately known forms and eliminating the 'hidden' elements – alienation, ideology, exploitation. Parsons's functionalism, therefore, fails to grasp the alienation and ideology which is religion : his argument that 'order is the internalisation of the normative culture in the personalities of its members and the institutionalisation of that in the normative structure of society' and that religious values underpin *general* value consensus[28] ignores not merely the fact that some values lead directly to conflict (Catholics and Protestants in Northern Ireland, Flemings and Walloons in Belgium), but that far from producing cohesion such values create dissension. Parsons has argued that value consensus exists, that societies tend towards a state of equilibrium 'when the expectations of the members . . . have been mutually met',[29] but at no point does he focus on the ways in which the 'value system' is actually articulated by the different social groups and classes. For example, it has been argued that pragmatic rather than normative acceptance characterises working-class life, that such 'values' as 'achievement motivation' have totally different meanings for working-class and middle-class children, and if value consensus does exist it does so to a greater degree within the middle class.[30] Parsons's concepts of 'value consensus' and equilibrium seem little more than ideology bound to a concept of the social world as external, dehumanised and fundamentally dead. The laws of equilibrium, which Parsons once described as analogous to Newton's laws of mechanics, form an organic part of a social theory which, while invoking Pareto's concept of society as a 'moving equilibrium', is fundamentally built around the principle of inertia.

III

Functionalism, argue its critics, cannot explain social change : the concept of moving equilibrium is far too imprecise as a viable explanation. Yet Parsons has not shirked from analysing the problems of rapid social change, of revolution and 'anomie'. In his discussion of German Fascism he described it as 'one of the most critical . . . social events of our time' ; in *The Social System* a substantial part of his chapter on social change is devoted to Russian Communism and the 1917 revolution.

The analysis of German Fascism is based on the assumption that modern society is in a chronic state of anomie which produces strains that result in disequilibrium. Equilibrium breaks down, writes Parsons, when 'strain in certain parts of the system has mounted to points which canot be coped with short of major alterations of the moving equilibrium state'. A revolutionary movement is one consequence of such strains which can gain ascendancy only if a number of specific conditions exist, such as '. . . the presence in the population of sufficiently intense, widely spread and properly distributed alienative motivational elements. . . . Such alienative motivation is a prerequisite of the development of a revolutionary movement.' If society cannot control a revolutionary movement it will organise itself into a 'deviantly sub-cultural group' and generate 'a set of alienative motivational orientations relative to the main institutional order'. In language closer to the K.G.B. and Orwell's 'Thought Police' than to scientific, 'value free' social theory, Parsons notes that 'Combining in a solidary group . . . enables the deviantly motivated to evade a large proportion of the sanctions of normal social interaction. . . . They reinforce each other's deviance by providing an alter for ego's expectations . . .'.[31] In short, conspiracy theory : on this definition the English trade-union leaders in the period 1799 to 1825 (when the Anti-Combination laws were in force against workers but not employers) would constitute 'a deviantly motivated group', as would resistance groups in Nazi Germany, as well as the contemporary opposition groups in the Soviet Union and Eastern Europe. To call these groups deviantly motivated does not help to understand their sociological significance; it suggests also a totalitarian conception of society. However, let us look at Parsons's analysis of Fascism in more detail.

His argument, which owes much to Weber, is that Germany never developed an independent bourgeois class but one dominated and 'feudalised' by the landowning Junker aristocracy, the bureaucracy and the German officer corps. This feudal-militaristic element was not effectively broken even after 1918 when, through the Weimar Constitution, German society was formally democratised. The Prussian bureaucracy, when fused with the feudalised bourgeoisie, produced an extremely rigid, hierarchical administration which 'would not brook the "democratic" type of control . . .'. These two factors, Parsons argues, were largely responsible for an extremely unstable situation which 'greatly limited the decisiveness of the influence of the parliamentary element'. In Germany also, more than any other Western democracy, norms of masculine superiority prevailed : women and wives were accorded a wholly subordinate status. This strict segregation of roles meant that the 'romantic love' component of American culture was effectively blocked. Relations between the sexes were thus unequal and undemocratic.

All this leads to Parsons's conclusion : for while 'external' factors such as the Allies' treatment of Germany after 1918 and the relations between capital and labour – which he admits is a 'tension . . .

structurally inherent in all capitalist industrial economies' – all played some part in the genesis and success of Fascism, it was the *cultural* ('superstructural') elements which exercised the more significant role. For it was not the fact that National Socialism was anti-Communist and nationalistic which accounted for its success, but the fact that German society was in the throes of acute anomie. It is important to note how Parsons explains the breakdown of social order : in 'our commonsense thinking about social matters', he writes, there is a tendency 'to exaggerate the integration of social systems' and underemphasise the elements of 'malintegration, tension and strain'. This sounds odd from a theorist who has criticised Marx for precisely this 'error'. However, the development of Fascism was basically the result of the too rapid industrial and technological changes in Germany which led to 'widespread insecurity' and 'a good deal of free floating aggression, a tendency to unstable emotionalism and susceptibility to emotionalised propaganda'. In short, the 'rationalisation' of society proved too much for the Germans : the 'secularisation of religious values' which 'rationalisation' entailed, together with 'the general tendency of rational criticism to *undermine traditional and conservative* systems of symbols', produced 'imperfectly integrated institutional structures, ideological definitions of the situation, and the psychological reaction patterns typical of anomie . . .'.

Parsons places great stress on rationalisation. Having undermined traditional legitimacy it is made responsible not only for National Socialism but also for German Communism and socialism. He sees both movements as exemplifying a 'romantic' revolt against 'the whole tendency of rationalisation in the Western World'. Thus both socialism and Fascism are explicable in terms of the same set of factors. What Parsons is actually saying is that rapid social change produces a state of instability, the norms are no longer capable of governing society adequately, anomie results and Fascism and Communism emerge as mass movements able to canalise the 'free floating aggression' engendered by technology, urbanism and industry.[32]

The first point to be made about Parsons's analysis is that although he accepts that businessmen supported the Nazi movement for its anti-labour and anti-Communist ideology he does not draw any attention to the important support given to the Nazis by bankers and industrialists, for without this the whole movement would have failed. Secondly, the Nazis failed to attain power in the 'Beer Hall' Putsch of 1923 when the same set of conditions noted by Parsons were present : one reason for this was that the Nazi party rejected the existing capitalist institutions and had set itself up as a 'revolutionary' party. Its later success was largely because the leadership established links with German industry and finance and guaranteed the continued 'rationalisation' of capitalism. It is in this important sense that Fascism was not an anti-capitalist, romantic 'revolutionary movement' which according to Parsons, produces 'a radically new type of society', for German Fascism was not revolutionary *at all*; the economic foundations of society were left intact. Capitalism, indeed, flourished, for Hitler had smashed the trade unions, the Social Democratic and Communist parties, the only effective organisations whereby the workers could oppose and struggle against capitalism. In his analysis Parsons ignores these factors, for his basic argument is to show that the economic structure of capitalism was not responsible for the success of Fascism, that pre-capitalist residues (the cultural elements) combining with rapid change (modernisation) created conditions in which movements which were anathema to the 'real' democratic trends of capitalism could flourish.[33]

There is, however, a curious paradox in Parsons's analysis. In *The Structure of Social Action* he had postulated a voluntaristic conception of social science, arguing that in the work of Durkheim, Weber and Pareto the mechanical elements implicit in sociological positivism were eliminated and a genuine theory of *action* developed. His later, more explicitly functional writings maintain this 'action' element in his concept of motivation through values and norms. Yet in his discussion of National Socialism a form of *cultural* determinism is apparent. He has criticised Marx for 'economic determinism' and failure to develop a theory of adequate motivation. Yet Parsons is arguing that a conjunction of general cultural forces determined that German capitalism, rather than evolving in the direction of 'liberal American capitalism', moved in the opposite direction. Cultural determinism it seems replaces economic determinism. The truth, however, is more complex. In 1933, when Hitler was legally installed as Chancellor, the German Communist party, at that time the most powerful in Europe, had persistently followed the Moscow-dominated Comintern policy which identified Social Democracy as 'social fascist' ('the final stage of capitalism') and effectively blocked the formation of an anti-Nazi Front. The German Communist party defined the real enemy as the Social Democrats not the Nazis with catastrophic results. Such political tactics must have influenced the orientations of the German workers, and become part of their motivational structure : the German Communists were demoralised and beaten; the millions of workers supporting the Social Democrats lacked the necessary leadership to fight the Nazis. Yet the 'voluntaristic' Parsons ignores this aspect of the situation : party leadership is apparently insignificant for the 'motivational orientations' of its members. Equally significant is the failure of Parsons's functionalist approach to comprehend the class content of 'value consensus'. By 1933 capitalist interests, the military, civil service and large sections of the middle classes were united on one fundamental problem – the means necessary to save German capitalism from Communism. Fascist ideology was not anathema to the dominant class, who reluctantly embraced it as the only effective bulwark of 'order'. To characterise the Nazis (and other Fascist movements) as 'deviantly motivated' ignores the overlapping of interests between bourgeois and Fascist ideology.

Parsons's interpretation of Bolshevism is couched in similar terms, of an equilibrium model which leaves no scope for human *praxis* : the events in Russia, as were those in Germany, were inescapable. He argues that 'the motivational composition of a revolutionary movement is . . . ambivalent in structure', an uneasy fusion of 'utopian' and 'realistic' elements. All revolutionary movements may begin from a perspective of total and uncompromising criticism of the existing social system, but all must come to terms with 'reality' after the revolution :

In a sense . . . the basic conflict comes to be transferred from the form, the movement versus society, to that between the 'principles' of the movement and the temptation of its members to use their control of society to gratify their repressed need-dispositions some of which are precisely *needs of conformity* with the patterns of the *old* society which they have tried to abolish. This process of the re-emergence of needs to re-instate elements of the old order under the guise of the revolutionary regime is one of the main sources of the tendency to 'mitigate' the radicality of the revolution.

The triumph of Stalinism, the political elimination of the old Bolsheviks and their replacement by bureaucratic careerists and the total disregard for 'revolutionary principles' in favour of anti-Marxist nationalism and conservatism is thus seen by Parsons as inevitable and realistic. 'Quite clearly it would be utterly impossible for a society to become stabilised on the basis that a fundamentally ambivalent motivational structure towards its central values and ideology became the norm.' The 'central values' of the old society re-assert themselves necessarily, and Parsons explains the retention of differential payments in industry and a rigid system of social stratification not as the result of a struggle between Left and the Right, or in terms of a bureaucracy *consciously* stifling revolutionary theory and practice, but as a functional necessity for social systems. Stalinism is explained as 'the need for adaptive structures in the light of fundamental functional requirements . . . and the re-emergence of conformity needs associated with the old society as such'. There is thus continuity in change, and Parsons concludes his analysis with the hope that industrialisation will bring with it a 'universalistic-achievement pattern' of motivation to transform the Soviet Union into the same type of society as contemporary America.[34]

It should be apparent that Parsons's functionalism is no more than a species of sociological fatalism. Capitalism as a social system is basically sound, although there is much free-floating aggression and widespread anomie. In the United States, however, a liberal political system has meshed with a liberal bourgeoisie with the result that rapid, social, technological change has not induced 'anxiety'. In Russia and Germany cultural forces subverted the *natural* tendency of capitalism towards harmony and integration. In the end, however, the 'normal' capitalist equilibrium will assert itself, since the pattern of development in all industrial societies is more or less the same. The passive role of man is thus built into the very structure of function-

alism; consciousness is eliminated as an important factor. Thus paradoxically, the 'voluntaristic' social theory which Parsons announced
in *The Structure of Social Action*, turns out to be no more than cultural and psychological determinism. Parsons, it is clear, sees society
as standing above and over the individual, an abstraction which
dominates him totally. The 'central values' of the social system can
mean only the 'dominant ideology' and like Durkheim, Parsons's in-
sensitivity to the fact of ideologies leads him to a social theory which
is in essence a reflection of the dominant values of the *status quo*.
Marx's theory was a theory of theory : it grasped the mode of existence of other counter-theories and ideologies, in terms of groups and
classes. Parsons's functionalism can neither locate sociologically
other theories and ideologies nor explain *its* mode of existence; it
must judge those theories and ideologies which oppose it as 'deviant'.

I V

Parsons's theory of change is conceived in mechanical terms as
constant re-adjustments to internal and external 'strains'. There is
no place for conscious action, for class struggle and class conflict as
important elements in social change; the charge has therefore been
brought against functionalism that it eliminates conflict as an important source both of change and cohesion.

As we have seen, Parsons has never denied the factual existence
of conflict : 'Class conflict certainly exists in the United States', he
wrote in 1949, adding, 'I believe that class conflict is endemic in our
modern industrial type of society.' It is not, however, the dominant
pattern, for social stratification, as a whole, functions as an important 'integrating structure in the social system'. His argument that
no social system is fully integrated and that 'every complex society
contains very important elements of internal conflict and tension'[35]
does not, however, lead him to examine more closely the bases of
such conflict. On the contrary, conflict is characterised as a breakdown of social control and normative integration, an abnormal and
dysfunctional component which threatens social order, a 'deviant'
response to inequalities of income, status, power : in language close
to Durkheim, Parsons writes that 'some set of norms governing

relations of superiority and inferiority is an inherent need of every stable social system'.[36]

It should be clear, therefore, that the distinction between equilibrium and a conflict model of society is artificial and theoretically misleading. Parsons's equilibrium model merely minimises the *importance* of conflict, it does not deny it; and similarly, sociological conflict models make reference to consensus and equilibrium.[37] The argument over 'conflict' versus 'consensus' is at bottom a dispute *within* orthodox sociological theory, not between competing theories. Conflict theorists are merely asserting that functionalism cannot explain both social change and conflict adequately from within their methodological framework. But, paradoxically perhaps, modern conflict theory is as much concerned with the question of social integration as functionalism and its general orientation equally as mechanical and fatalistic. Of crucial importance is *its* failure to explain social change.

Thus Coser, after criticising Parsons's static equilibrium model, argues that 'conflict, rather than being disruptive and dissociating, may indeed be a means of balancing and hence maintaining a society as a going concern'. Instead of tearing society apart conflict can function as 'a safety valve', and enjoy an 'equilibrating and stabilizing impact'. Conflict functions to create new norms and rules, to re-establish unity between different groups and to redress potentially disruptive inequalities in power and authority. Without conflict, society must ossify, stagnate : for conflict and social creativity, it is argued, are bound indissolubly together and without creativity there could be no technological change. The conclusion follows that those societies in which conflict is institutionalised and tolerated are more stable and integrated than those with rigid structures :

> By permitting immediate and direct expression of rival claims, such social systems are able to readjust their structures by eliminating the sources of dissatisfaction. The multiple conflicts which they experience may serve to eliminate the causes for disassociation and to re-establish unity. These systems avail themselves, through the toleration and institutionalization of conflict, of an important stabilizing mechanism.[38]

The functional approach to conflict thus praises its equilibrating powers, for cleansing social systems of archaic values in favour of the new and for its basic therapeutic character in unifying social antagonisms. But conflict theory tends towards what C. Wright Mills called 'abstracted empiricism' in its failure to go beyond trivial examples (usually small groups), mere ahistorical generalisations, and to approach a concrete dialectical analysis. Marx wrote that the conflict of interests within capitalist society did not necessarily imply disunity for through specific organisation, leadership and ideology equilibrium is achieved. But equilibrium in Marx's theory is nearly always unstable in that it contains *within itself* the elements of disequilibrium, the negative and the contradictory. This is the role of class conflict in social change, both in terms of a constant struggle mediated through working-class institutions such as trade unions to maintain and improve the workers' situation, and embodying as well the potential threat to bourgeois society through class consciousness and revolutionary political organisation. Gradual social change as well as the more dramatic, revolutionary change can both be grasped in terms of Marx's class-conflict model.

Marx, of course, locates the basic source of class conflict in a capitalist society within the productive system. It has been argued in previous chapters that the existence of the objective conditions for class conflict in itself cannot explain the fact of social stability and that it is necessary to invoke Marx's theory of ideology as an integrative mechanism : capitalist hegemony thus becomes the key to understanding the co-existence of both conflict and stability. The role of trade-union bureaucracies and 'reformist' socialist parties in supporting this hegemony is clearly an important element, for working-class consciousness is mediated through its own organisations which, if 'playing the rules of the game', act as brakes on any potential development of revolutionary consciousness. Indeed, revolutionary consciousness and action are impossible within the structures of trade unionism and labour parties. Therefore, while conflict is generated by the property system, its specific historical form is fashioned by the strength of dominant class ideology, the organisation and tactics of working-class leadership. Given the growth of working-class institutions within capitalist society it is hardly surprising that social theorists have concluded that such organisations 'contribute to the integration and stability of the society' and that trade unions in particular 'serve to integrate their members in the larger body politic and give them a basis for loyalty to the system'.[39] However, such integration is not spontaneously produced out of a conflict nexus, but flows concretely from a conjunction of dominant class ideology, 'reformist' trade-union and social democratic pragmatism and the reified belief of some workers in the inviolability of capitalist civilisation. It is not a question of counterposing conflict to stability : conflict remains within a stable social structure. It is the task of the revolutionary party and Marxist theory to break this hegemony.

Power and the norms associated with conflict situations, therefore cannot be seen as straightforward modes of integration and institutionalisation. The criticisms that modern conflict theory fails to grasp the totality of relations associated with conflict situations, and that models of society based primarily on conflict and coercion eliminate the sociological bases of consensus and integration, are undoubtedly correct.[40] For such theories cannot adequately explain why some conflict produces change while other forms do not : it is essential, therefore, so this criticism goes, for conflict theory to converge with 'normative' functionalism, since 'the nature of the value system is of signal importance for the genesis, intensity and direction of potential conflict', shaping the aspirations of different social strata for change or not. The argument here is that Marx's social theory, with its emphasis on conflict as a result of the contradiction between the material means of production and the social relations of production, is in effect a species of general functionalism : a 'functional incompatibility' exists between the system of commodity production and the class structure which evolves from it. Crisis is thus 'dysfunctionality', a 'lack of fit' between 'the core institutional order' (social class etc.), and 'its material substructure'. Marx, in short, explains conflict and crisis, but not stability, integration and the fact that capitalist society has failed to collapse from the workings of its own internal contradictions.[41] But Marx does provide an explanation for 'social integration' and not merely an analysis of 'system integration', through his emphasis on the dialectical relationship between ideology, alienation and reification, and political leadership. As was argued in Chapter 7, Marx provides an analysis of order as the 'normal' mode of capitalist society and open class conflict leading to civil war as 'abnormal'. This point cannot be over-emphasised : Marx's social theory is not *coercion theory* and thus in need of *consensus* theory. Such banalities can lead only to a sterile eclectic sociology. Social theory in the work of Comte, Durkheim and Parsons has not ignored change and conflict : the point is simply that their analysis is unsatisfactory. For social theory is also bound up with the role of human consciousness in shaping the world and the role of ideologies in legitimising social institutions. It is here that functionalism fails, for defining the social as a natural condition of man to which he must realistically adapt, and society as a system dominating its members can lead only to a theoretical justification for the *status quo*; functionalist theory must end, not with a concept of society as historical product, but with one in which ineluctable class inequalities function as essential components for the encouragement of 'effort' and 'initiative'. The great inequalities of income, status and property-ownership which characterise modern capitalism are *given*, immutable structures, the result not so much of definite social and historical conditions but rather of the natural and universal laws of the ahistorical needs of occupational differentiation. Parsons accepts that civilisation has run to its close in American pluralistic democracy and that only modifications and 'improvements' can be expected in the pattern of social inequality during the coming centuries. Nazi Germany and Soviet Russia are merely episodes on the way to the normal mode of a well-integrated and stable industrial capitalism.

9

SOCIOLOGY: RADICAL, CRITICAL OR MARXIST?

The previous chapter explored the differences between Marxism and functionalism, suggesting that although emphasising cognitive elements in its analysis of society functionalism was largely a mechanistic sociology focusing more on social order than on social change. Change occurs, of course, but it must be consistent with the prevailing normative equilibrium; it is *adaptive* change, quantitative and partial. Revolutionary change is abnormal and pathological indicating only that the 'value system' has broken down and that cultural institutions are no longer performing their function of filling men with healthy, consensual values. To follow Merton and postulate the concept of dysfunction and the unintended consequences of social action as the basis of a *general* functionalist theory of change is in effect to return to the pre-Marxist standpoint of Smith, Ferguson and Hegel and argue for the 'hidden hand' of rationality, which unconsciously synthesises different and complex actions in a functional unity of actions which is social change. The meaning of such actions is thus hidden from the actors themselves; change becomes non-conscious and man merely the vehicle for dysfunctional processes. Functionalism has failed to produce a genuine social theory of change, for its point of departure is the ongoing society (liberal capitalism) which it defines as the summit and the close of history : change is thus deviations from and adjustments to unavoidable strains and pressures. *Praxis* has been eliminated.

None the less, the dialogue between functionalism and Marxism continues. The emergence of serious structural conflict in the United States during the 1960s, combined with the resurgence of ideological cleavages within liberal democracy, focused attention on the failure of functionalism to explain contemporary society adequately. Functionalism has no theory of conflict and change: it must be synthesised with Marxism; and following this line of thought Gouldner has argued that an inescapable 'drift' towards Marxist ideas is actually found within functionalism itself, with the consequent need to 'liberate' these critical components from its ultra-conservative shell. This 'crisis' in modern sociology is reflected in other trends seeking reconciliation with Marxism, such as structuralism, phenomenology and humanistic sociology. The last few years have seen a rapid growth of 'radical' and 'critical' sociology inspired by a mixture of Marx's early writings and the Frankfurt school, especially Habermas, Lukács, Schutz and Husserl. Functionalism is rejected: a more committed and activist sociology is demanded both in terms of political values and methodology. Orthodox sociology, built around the search for objective knowledge and value-free scholarship, aimed to explain not criticise society. 'Radical' and 'critical' sociology develops in opposition to the positivist ideals of objectivity and neutral scholarship, and looks to a revitalised and potentially subversive social science.

I

To discuss and compare these new trends in social theory it is necessary to outline the basic elements of Marx's sociology as described in previous chapters. Perhaps the most important point is Marx's emphasis on man as the creator of the social world, who is then trapped by ideology, alienation and reification, processes against which he nevertheless maintains a stubborn and persistent struggle as part of a social class. In one sense Marx's theory represents the culmination of philosophy in that it absorbs and transcends the theoretical, empirical and critical content of previous philosophy. In the philosophy and political economy of the eighteenth century a genuine secular vision had emerged in which man's *potential* as a subject of history conflicted with a highly deterministic, materialist nexus, involving physical, political and economic factors which defined man as mere object. Hegel's great insight that philosophy mirrored its own epoch in thought appreciated concisely the dialectical relation between the philosopher who unwittingly portrayed the real world, however obscure the language or thought involved, and concrete history. The point is that Marx's social theory assimilated the critical elements within philosophy by grasping philosophy's historical and social roots and the alienation which was necessary for philosophy to exist as a 'theoretical practice'. Philosophy had interpreted the world when the point was *praxis*; Hegel's philosopher had stood back and summed up the meaning of history when history had meaning only in so far as men made it.

It is in these senses, then, that Marx's theory is not a critical or moral theory. His critique of the utopian socialists rejected their identification of socialism with ethics : the basis of socialism was contained within the capitalist mode of production itself; socialism was not an ahistorical, asocial, *a priori* imperative but flowed historically from *inner necessity*, that is, Marx was not concerned to demonstrate the moral superiority of socialist over capitalist production, only to show how the contradictions within the capitalist system were resolvable only through the class struggle. It was not a question of judging capitalism in ethical terms; the task was preeminently that of disclosing the laws underpinning capitalist development and its basis in exploitation. The theory of surplus value has nothing to do with morals, for the historical function of the capitalist class is to exploit the labour power of others – this is what makes them capitalists. Of course, a scientific approach does not preclude a condemnation of those servile ideologists who argued explicitly in favour of the more brutal forms of exploitation – political economists such as Nassau Senior, who, in the wake of the first Factory Acts, postulated the 'theory' that reducing the working day to ten hours must destroy the foundation of profit, this being created in the final hour's work. For such thinkers Marx's criticism is scathing, but in the many passages in *Capital* where he writes of capitalists he does so only in terms of their historic role : developing the mode of production, furthering human and social progress through capital accumulation, technology and innovation, and creating their own negation, the proletariat. This is in no sense a strictly moral standpoint.

This brief statement is necessary because of the widespread view

214

which situates Marx as merely a *critic* of capitalism and his work one of moral condemnation. His intellectual development from *The German Ideology* onwards was towards a scientific understanding of social change, to provide socialism with a scientific basis. His method was critical because it was dialectical. Of his dialectical approach to society and history Marx wrote :

> In its rational form it is a scandal and abomination to bourgeois-dom and its doctrinaire professors, because it includes in its comprehension and affirmative recognition of the existing state of things, at the same time also, the recognition of the negation of that state, of its inevitable breaking up; because it regards every historically developed social form as in fluid movement, and therefore takes into account its transient nature not less than its momentary existence; because it lets nothing impose upon it, and it is in essence critical and revolutionary.[1]

Marx's social theory is critical in its grasp of the contradictory nature of social, political and intellectual development. It is revolutionary in making the working class the subject of history and capitalist society the locus of class conflict and dynamic change. Against Proudhon, Marx had written that bourgeois thought was ahistorical, for as a class the bourgeoisie were incapable of envisaging any form of society other than the capitalist. For Marx, society constituted an ensemble of social relations, a totality, the different parts explicable in terms of the whole. Although similar to the functionalist category Marx's concept of totality is both *historical* and dialectical. It is not mechanical, for men make history and Marx emphasises consciousness and ideology as *active* elements. Parsons writes of norms and voluntarism, of men filling roles, of the motivation which flows from the cultural system; ideas as class consciousness, as ideology which strives to change the world find no place in functionalist theory.

Marx's sense of historical specificity is echoed in his analysis of social theory. No other nineteenth-century theorist had Marx's sensitivity to the notion of ideology, its rich dialectical content (brought out especially in his discussions of Ricardo and Malthus), the close relationship between the social position of a thinker, his *praxis* and social theory. Positivism had eliminated the concept, which the French Enlightenment philosophers had first created as a critical weapon, and preferred a scientific belief in a straightforward application of natural science methods to social study. The prevailing belief in an inevitable progress further prevented positivist thought from grasping the dialectical not uniform relation of society to social theory and the significance of ideology.

Ideology is linked with alienation, a concept which has become part of contemporary sociological folklore, vague, general and uncritical. Marx defined alienation as a process whereby exchange values come to dominate use values, in which the worker increasingly defines historically specific capitalist social relations as natural and inescapable. An alienated consciousness defines the social world as fixed and immutable and human action as marginal for change. To the alienated man, society seems to be what it claims to be in terms of the dominant ideology.

But men do make the social world; history is a record of man's struggle to develop and transcend the given, the existing social structure. Reification as a total process would simply paralyse all action. The history of bourgeois society is the history of the opposition to its dominant values and institutions mounted by working-class organisations and parties. It is often claimed that Marx's theory of social change is mono-causal, that all change derives from the economic structure of society, from the system of production, but such an interpretation minimises the profound subjective element of consciousness, of men making the world through their purposes and activity. There is neither fatalism nor economic determinism in Marx's social theory, only an awareness of the crucial role which class consciousness exercises both in the shaping and the maintenance of society.

II

The concept of crisis in sociology is not new : Weber's critique of nineteenth-century positivism and 'mechanical Marxism' and the development of a 'voluntaristic' social theory can be seen as sociology's first crisis. Between 1880 and 1914 new, challenging and frequently disturbing theories and innovations created a volatile climate within European culture : Bergson's theories of time and consciousness with their impact on literature (the stream of consciousness novel) and phenomenology; Husserl's phenomenological critique of science and consciousness; Freud and the discovery of the unconscious; the concept of will and the role of unreason in society exemplified in the development of pre-Fascist ideologies and the work of Georges Sorel; and the emergence, within the positivistic evolutionary traditions of the Second International, of a 'revitalised' Marxism (Trotsky, Lenin, Rosa Luxemburg). These and other important movements of thought occurred within the space of a few years and in virtually the same capitalist countries (Germany and France especially). The first crisis in sociology reflected this broader crisis in culture, for these new ideas shattered the rock-like complacency of nineteenth-century positivism. European sociology was thus forced to question its own assumptions, methods and general orientation : and it was at this point that Marx's thought, albeit distorted, began to penetrate 'bourgeois' social theory through the work of Weber, Sombart and Mannheim. The breakdown of the dominant nineteenth-century paradigm – positivism – and the rise of a sociology built around the subjective awareness of the individual researcher (Weber, Mannheim) is paralleled in the modern crisis of sociology. For here functionalism as the major sociological paradigm of the last thirty years is said to be collapsing, and as the demise of positivism heralded a more subjective sociology, so too does the present crisis : the new sociology is to be called 'reflexive sociology'.

Reflexive sociology refers to the problem of subjective values in the act of selection : the question, what to study, involves a value judgement and a *praxis* (what is significant or not) which demands from the researcher evaluation and criticism. 'Radical' sociology is reflexive and its most frequent jibe against 'bourgeois' sociology is that it purveys a conservative ideology which buttresses the domination of a capitalist ruling class. John Horton writes of the obvious 'conservative implications' of sociology, of science and objective knowledge serving 'the technological needs of the elite, the ideological verbiage that hides the exploitation of the ruling reality from the non-elite'. Sociology, he concludes, is like advertising, 'the burial ground' of radical thought in whose 'cemeteries the critical and human element of the language of protest has been laid to rest . . .'.[2] In contrast a radical sociology will base itself on 'explicit radical political values', by carrying out radical research (into poverty and power for example) and through practice (in political groups and movements) thus raising public consciousness. 'Radical' sociology criticises orthodox sociology for abdicating its responsibility and ignoring major issues and problems (racism, imperialism, etc.) and too readily accepting functionalist and consensual models of society in which conflict, exploitation and oppression have been eliminated and inequality defined as a natural and ineluctable condition. Sociologists become consultants, managers and administrators involved in pacification programmes for underdeveloped nations, enmeshed in the power structure of modern capitalism.[3]

While it is true that 'radical' sociology is not homogeneous, the basic features, common to most of its practitioners, can be summarised :

(1) A commitment to humanist values especially the idea of self-realisation. The social world is made by men through *praxis*, thus the attraction of phenomenology for 'radical' sociologists. The human agent enjoys a dialectical, not fixed relationship with society and other men.

(2) 'Radical' sociology opposes a mechanical conception of 'base' and 'superstructure' and Marxism and functionalism are critisised for defining consciousness as an epiphenomenon.

(3) A denial of value-free scholarship and impartial objectivity which in some cases becomes a rejection of objectivity altogether.

(4) A rejection of prediction and laws of society in favour of a scepticism which challenges *everything*.

(5) A firm 'moral' commitment to certain political values. These are not reformist, rather 'the politically radical sociologist challenges the structures which have supported the rise of bourgeois society'.

There have been few sociologists in the past who have subscribed to these ideas, but one contemporary sociologist who has identified himself with this movement is Alvin Gouldner. Although not sharing the extreme formulations of 'radical' sociology, he accepts the necessity for commitment and action. However, he argues for the synthesis of functionalism and Marxism, and in his book, *The Coming Crisis of Western Sociology*, attempts to show how such a fusion is both intellectually feasible and historically necessary.

Gouldner's main thrust develops around three basic points : firstly, the existence of two sociologies in the nineteenth century, both stemming from Saint-Simon's ideas, but whereas positivism through Comte appealed to a privileged stratum of scientists and bourgeoisie, Marxism based itself on the propertyless and alienated proletariat. A 'binary fission' thus occurred and the development of sociology was twin-forked. Secondly, within both types of sociology a 'methodological dualism' developed in which the observer (the social scientist) was superior to those being studied. Reflexive sociology is an attempt to unite subject and object and transcend the limitations imposed by positivism on sociology. Reflexive sociology is thus a self-conscious *praxis* which accepts the world as it is and how it should become; it is not value free. And finally academic sociology, notwithstanding its connections and sympathy with the *status quo*, contains a critical element, a potentially radical component buried within 'an encompassing conservative structure'. The potentially critical forces within sociology, its 'internal contradictions' must therefore be liberated. One source of this liberation is Marxism but only a Marxism purged of its deterministic and Messianic character.

Thus unlike some radical sociologists Gouldner does not write off 'bourgeois sociology' and he rejects the extreme view that all sociology is ideological, 'an instrument of American corporate capitalism'. Sociology is not a unified whole but contains many diverse and contradictory standpoints in need of liberation. He draws a parallel between this situation and Marx's critique of Hegelianism : 'Just as Marx extricated the liberative potentialities of a Hegelianism which was previously dominated by its conservative aspects, so too, is it possible to transcend contemporary Academic Sociology and to deliver from it a radical or neo-sociology.'[4]

Such comparisons, however, are somewhat spurious : Hegel was not simply a conservative philosopher with a radical content; his early writings were revolutionary and in many respects anticipate

Marx's materialist analysis of alienation. But the main point is that Marx did not 'liberate' the radical and critical elements from within Hegel's philosophy, but rather assimilated and developed certain concepts, and more importantly, created a social theory built around an entirely different epistemology. This is perhaps one of the basic weaknesses of 'radical' sociology especially in its relationship to Marxism. Gouldner writes, for example, that the only hope for modern academic sociology lies in 'the changing political *praxis*' of younger sociologists and the interaction between sociology and 'voluntaristic' Marxism. Other radical sociologists accept the need for Marxist concepts but reject 'sectarian' and 'dogmatic' Marxism. Both seem to define Marxism in a particular way, as a form of mechanical materialism in which knowledge is epiphenomenal and passive. Thus Gouldner sees Marxism almost as a unified whole tending to minimise the important links between Lenin, Trotsky, Rosa Luxemburg and Gramsci, as if the work of these great Marxists were at variance with Marx's mature theory. His understanding of the epistemology of Marx(ism) seems seriously at fault : both Marxism and positivism, he argues, were unreflexive, dominated by 'methodological dualism'. This, it seems, is the cardinal sin of the two sociologies :

> Methodological dualism is . . . based on the tacit assumption that the goal of sociology is knowledge conceived as information. Correspondingly, it serves as a powerful inhibitor of the sociologist's awareness, for it paradoxically presupposes that the sociologist may rightfully be changed as a person by everything except the very intellectual work which is at the very centre of his existence.[5]

In his *Theses on Feuerbach* Marx had pointed to the basic contradiction in materialist philosophy, that it posited an educator and those in need of education, thus splitting society into two parts – it is this which Gouldner now calls methodological dualism. Again, it is important to appreciate that Marx's subsequent development was away from precisely this mechanistic model to a social theory which stressed the dialectical relationship between subject and object. In short, Gouldner has rediscovered what Marx discovered 130 years ago – that a social theory is one which has to do with real living men, with a consciousness of men as both subjects and objects. Thus, when Gouldner writes that the basic weakness of positivism and much of modern sociology is that it celebrates 'man's failure to possess the social world that he created', and that much of academic sociology is 'an accommodation to the alienation of men' rather than a struggle to transcend it, he is saying nothing more than Marx's analysis of alienation and reification in the *Paris Manuscripts* and *Capital*. Gouldner writes, for example, that 'The core concepts of society and culture, as held by the social sciences, entail the view that their autonomy and uncontrollability are a normal and natural condition, rather than intrinsically a kind of pathology. It is this assumption that is at the heart of the *repressive* component of sociology.' Social theory is shaped by, expresses and resonates what Gouldner calls 'domain assumptions', a somewhat vague concept which seems to mean the values which unconsciously influence sociological analysis and work. They are different from Marx's concept of ideology, being more subjective and personal. For it is Gouldner's view that academic sociology and Marxism, as they developed separately in the nineteenth century, appealed to different social orders (the industrial middle class; the proletariat), and thus different domains, and because of this interest nexus, were not genuinely sociological. The solution is reflexive sociology in which functionalism and Marxism are synthesised and yet transcend domain assumptions. The role of the honest and socially committed intellectual is obvious, as is the extremely subjective character of this brand of 'radical' sociology.

What is reflexive sociology? Social theory is created by men as a *praxis*, is shaped and determined by the kind of lives they lead and, although Gouldner does not state this, by the social groups and classes with whom they are associated. But with 'radical' sociology it is above all else a *private* affair : the 'historic mission' of reflexive sociology, Gouldner notes, is simply to transform the sociologist, 'to penetrate deeply into his daily life and work, enriching them with new sensitivities, and to raise the sociologist's self-awareness to a new historical level'. Such a sociology must be radical and dedicated to transforming an alien world, 'moral' and yet deny the value-free bias of objectivist sociology, possess a 'distinctive awareness of the ideological implications and political resonance of sociological work' and an 'historical sensitivity' that 'alerts it' to the dogmatic ideologies of the past and the purposes of men in changing the world.[6]

There seems little real difference between this orientation and that proposed by Weber and Mannheim : the sociologist, as an individual and as an intellectual, assimilates a great mass of knowledge and critically evaluates the truth, a truth, however, which is partisan and radical. But the individual does not exist except as a member of a group or groups with their own ideology and he is thus liable to error unless corrected by a scientific methodology which exists independently of such groups. 'Radical' sociology, however, rejects such a standpoint, demanding that the sociologist 'purge his mind of everything sacred and established . . . and begin in the manner of Descartes',[7] a sceptical and individualistic orientation without parallel in the history of social theory. For knowledge is not given, but involves complex mediations which 'radical' sociology eliminates in a dangerously misleading subjectivism. One 'radical' sociologist has suggested that this sociology will affirm 'basic human values' through 'utilising the sociology of knowledge', by which he means developing 'a counter-definition of social reality' from orthodox sociology. This prescription means only that the sociologist, feeling himself to be oppressed, joins others and through theory and practice liberates himself and others by building a new and more human society.[8]

A complete identification is thus made between subject and object. There seems no way of falsifying propositions and one man's radicalism seems as good as the next. 'Radical' sociology is, in short, an ideology of disenchanted left-wing intellectuals for whom the proletariat is no longer the means of revolutionary social change. For how is the situation to be changed? 'Radical' sociologists make much of the social world as reified, of the ways in which man and the human sciences have become dehumanised. To overcome this requires *thought* : 'To think radically is to practise de-reification. That means being attached to the groups that are actually engaged in the revolutionary re-direction of education . . .'.[9]

In his writings after 1844 Marx had moved beyond a merely 'radical' position. His mature social theory is a revolutionary theory based on the objective laws of capitalist development, its internal contradictions and revolutionary class. His work was pre-eminently scientific and objective. The thrust was in no sense an individualistic clarification of the world, a 'know thyself' and thus egoistic radicalism, but a genuine linking of social theory with class exploitation and class *praxis*. Lenin, Trotsky, and Gramsci developed Marx's theories as part of this class struggle. It seems, therefore, that the second crisis in sociology is to be resolved in the manner of the first : a 'free-floating intelligentsia' of 'radical' sociologists committed to a subjective honesty and a dedication to man transcending the 'domain assumptions' which afflict the less-privileged and despised 'bourgeois' sociologists. And they do so as mere *individuals*. Of such is reflexive sociology.

III

Like 'radical' sociology, 'critical' sociology is also reflexive. In contrast, however, it has greater affinities with Marxism : Critical Theory, for example, developed its modern form from the philosophers of the Frankfurt School – Marcuse, Horkheimer and Adorno – although the term itself dates from the 1840s with the 'Left-Hegelians' and their attempt to apply Hegel's philosophy to social and political questions. In the work of the Frankfurt School, Critical Theory attacks the scientistic and objectivistic tendencies of 'vulgar Marxism' and strives to return philosophy to social theory, thus making it more dialectical and reflexive. However, Marx's argument in the *Paris Manuscripts* which had linked the abolition of philosophy with the *praxis* of a revolutionary proletariat is rejected, for Critical Theory takes its point of departure from the integration of the working class into modern capitalism. Although writing at a time of massive class struggles in France and Germany, the Frankfurt School concluded that the proletariat no longer constituted the historic agent of social change but rather largely conformist strata within advanced capitalist societies.

What, then, is the relationship between Critical Theory and Marxism? In his essay 'Traditional and Critical Theory' (1937), Horkheimer argued that the goal of traditional theory was not *praxis* and change but rather pure knowledge and technological mastery of nature, society and man. In contrast Critical Theory was the search for the 'negative' and the 'critical' elements in society, which formed the only basis for change. Traditional theory had made a fetish of the objective world, of facts, scientific prediction based on external social laws, and in so far as Marxism followed these tendencies it had to be rejected. For Critical Theory, scientific objectivity was not a guide to truth : only a theory informed by a dialectical epistemology and created by intellectuals self-consciously aware of their own methodological procedures could provide the necessary orientation for Truth.[10]

Critical sociology emerges out of these revisions of Marxism. The goal of the critical sociologist is freedom from the 'repressive' nature of modern capitalism, and the means is *Theory* : 'By reconstructing ideology by the analysis of societal restraints, theory develops at the same time a concept of possible social freedom, . . . which it can only win at all as the "real" utopian content of the false consciousness in this course of critique.'[11]

In the work of critical sociologists, theory is able to distance itself from the objective and external technological dynamic of modern capitalism and thus transcend the reified, technological consciousness which these processes generate.

One critical sociologist is Norman Birnbaum, yet his arguments are strikingly similar to those advanced by non-Marxist sociologists such as Dahrendorf and Bell. He argues, for example, that Marxist sociology (by which he means critical sociology) like 'bourgeois sociology' is in crisis, defining crisis as a situation in which the internal development of a theory has become and is seen to be exhausted and/or because the social conditions which the theory purports to explain have changed so dramatically that a new, thoroughly revised theory is necessary. Birnbaum points out that in the course of bringing a theory up to date to explain the changed conditions, it may borrow heavily from the 'bourgeois' theory so that it ceases to be Marxism.[12] Thus he argues that capitalism is more complex than that described by Marx's theory : the class structure is compounded of heterogeneous strata such as technicians and the technical professions; the state no longer fulfils *laissez-faire* functions but coordinates and directs economic activities; private property is now more concentrated and impersonal and the correlation of property ownership and political power is no longer viable; the working class are more skilled than their nineteenth-century counterparts, enjoy full employment and the advantages of the welfare state. Thus although inequalities still persist the general class situation is now wholly different from that which confronted Marx and many Marxists.

Birnbaum's main thrust against Marx's social theory, however, is his argument that the modern state is no longer the agency of class rule, but has become an independent force within society. Domination is no longer bourgeois domination, and he agrees with Weber that the rationalisation of all spheres of social life is the chief characteristic of the modern age, culminating in the existence of objective and external technical processes which control man almost completely. It is this theme which links Birnbaum with Habermas, in whose work a critique of an alienated, although human world dominating the individual has been developed. Like Birnbaum, Habermas defines Marxism as largely mechanical and draws much of his inspiration, not from Lenin and Trotsky, but from Lukács and the Frankfurt School. The focus is not on exploitation and class struggle within modern capitalism, but rather on the ways in which bourgeois science and technology create a specific type of knowledge which is instrumental in maintaining domination and repression. Following Horkheimer, bourgeois science is defined as non-reflective, authoritarian and oriented towards non-freedom. On the other hand, Marx's theory of class consciousness, and consciousness in general, was too narrow because too deterministic and incapable of encompassing a genuine, reflexive comprehension. By developing a dialectical communication theory, Habermas hopes to demonstrate the nature of the external restraints imposed on man by technology and the growth of a capitalist consciousness which takes the form of technical rationality. In this way consciousness is freed and man is again the active subject of history. Thus critical sociology becomes an immanent critique of bourgeois theory and strives towards a dialectic of self-reflection.[13]

The concept of theory divorced from the historically specific

225

determinations of class struggle and political practice within revolutionary political parties is thus common to all forms of 'radical' and 'critical' sociology. It should be clear from what has been argued in previous chapters that these tendencies have little organic connection with Marxism, but are bound up with the fate of disillusioned bourgeois intellectuals for whom socialism has become a utopia and Marxism merely a method of analysis and critique of other theories. Such tendencies are possible only during periods of capitalist stability and the degeneration of Marxist ideas and parties. Since the 1930s Marxism has stagnated and continues to do so : 'radical' and 'critical' thinkers having identified Marxism with Stalinism and Marxism with positivism have nothing left except their privileged subjectivity and intellectual integrity. The result is the utopianism which Marx attacked at the outset of his work, an individualistic, 'critical' standpoint which must ultimately fail to explain the basic point : if capitalism creates inequality, poverty, war, imperialism, exacerbates racial tensions, wastes economic resources and turns its science and technology into dominating forces that imprison man within a reified consciousness, then how is all this to be changed? Can it be changed? If so, how – through criticism, through reflexive sociology?

IV

Marxism is pre-eminently a revolutionary social theory enriched by the *praxis* of the revolutionary party and the international working class, and developed by revolutionary intellectuals. In periods of stagnation and defeat for the revolutionary movement Marxist scholarship and theory degenerate into dogma and eclecticism. In these circumstances 'Marxist intellectuals', many of them isolated from the working-class movement, substitute themselves for the revolutionary proletariat and call for intellectual clarification, critical and radical consciousness. This is not the *praxis* which lies at the heart of Marx's thought but a specifically bourgeois philosophical standpoint which, as has been argued above, constitutes a reversal to pre-Marxist *passive* materialism. The ultimate failure of 'radical' and 'critical' sociology lies precisely in its rejection of Marx's scientific and dialectical social theory in favour of his earlier, critical–

philosophical standpoint. Its emphasis on an overpowering reification eliminates the complex, contradictory nature of modern capitalism, ideology, consciousness, and *praxis*, reducing Marxism to a largely deterministic, intuitive, individualistic and non-dialectical sociology. This book has attempted to explore the ways in which Marx's social theory grasps society as a dialectical totality, an historical and human product acting on man and yet the result of man's own actions; and as a methodology alive to the contradictory relationship of ideas and knowledge to society, of the autonomy of thought and human action and yet their dependence on specific social forces, institutions and structure. For Marxism builds on the strengths not weaknesses of bourgeois thought and it is in this very general sense that the relation of sociology to Marxism can be understood. As we have seen, Marxism does not define *all thought* except itself as ideological, but rather rejects non-dialectical abstractions such as 'bourgeois theory' and 'proletarian theory', to postulate a dialectical, not mechanical link between thinker and class. The task of a Marxist social theory is to assimilate the strong side of non-Marxist thought and yet remain Marxist.

NOTES

Abbreviations: *Capital* (3 volumes), *Cap.*; Marx, *Early Writings*, *E.W.*; Marx and Engels, *The German Ideology*, *G.I.*; Marx and Engels, *Selected Works* (2 volumes), *S.W.*; Marx, *Theories of Surplus Value* (3 volumes), *T.S.V.*; Marx, *Writings of the Young Marx*, *W.Y.M.*; Marx, *Grundrisse*, *Gru.*; Durkheim, *The Division of Labour in Society*, *D.L.*; Durkheim, *Suicide*, *Su.*; Weber, *The Methodology of the Social Sciences*, *M.S.S.*; Weber, *The Theory of Social and Economic Organisation*, *Theory*; Lukács, *History and Class Consciousness*, *H.C.C.* See the Select Bibliography (pp. 241–3) for full details.

Place of publication is London unless otherwise indicated.

INTRODUCTION

1. A. Salomon, 'German Sociology', in *Twentieth-Century Sociology*, ed. R. K. Merton and W. E. Moore (New York, 1945).
2. Themes summed up in D. Bell, *The End of Ideology* (New York, 1961), with its suggestive subtitle, *On the Exhaustion of Political Ideas in the Fifties*.
3. D. McLellan, *The Young Hegelians and Karl Marx* (1969) pp. 18–20.
4. Ibid.
5. *W.Y.M.*, p. 144.
6. *G.I.*, p. 31.
7. Cf. D. McLellan, *Marx's Grundrisse* (1972) pp. 20–5; M. Nicolaus, 'Foreword', *Gru.*
8. *S.W.*, II, 486–506.
9. G. Plekhanov, *Fundamental Problems of Marxism* ([1908] Moscow, n.d.) pp. 67–82.
10. On the Frankfurt School see M. Jay, *The Dialectical Imagination* (1973).

CHAPTER ONE

1. P. Berger and T. Luckmann, *The Social Construction of Reality* (1966) p. 209; P. Berger and S. Pullberg, 'Reification and the Sociological Critique of Consciousness', *New Left Review* (Jan/Feb 1966).

2. P. van den Berghe, 'Dialectic and Functionalism', in *System, Change and Conflict*, ed. N. J. Demerath and R. A. Peterson (New York, 1967).
3. Marx, 'Theses on Feuerbach', *G.I.*, pp. 651–2.
4. L. Trotsky, *In Defence of Marxism* (New York, 1965) p. 140.
5. Lenin, *Philosophical Notebooks, Collected Works*, vol. 38 (Moscow, 1961) p. 180.
6. Engels, *Anti-Dühring* (Moscow, 1959) p. 194.
7. Engels, *Dialectics of Nature* (New York, 1940) pp. 206–7.
8. *Anti-Dühring*, pp. 187–8.
9. *Dialectics of Nature*, p. 164.
10. Lenin, *Philosophical Notebooks*, pp. 349–54.
11. Smith, *Wealth of Nations* (1895) books I and V.
12. A. Ferguson, *Essay on the History of Civil Society* (Edinburgh, 1966) p. 122.
13. *Wealth of Nations*, pp. 308–19.
14. Hegel, *Science of Logic* (1970) p. 439.
15. Ibid. p. 54.
16. Ibid. p. 166.
17. Ibid. pp. 57–60.
18. Ibid. p. 440.
19. Marx, *The Poverty of Philosophy*, pp. 111–13.
20. *Gru.*, pp. 146–51.
21. For details see my article, 'Comte, Marx and Political Economy', *Sociological Review* (Nov. 1970).
22. *D.L.*, p. 4.
23. *D.L.*, pp. 353–72.
24. *G.I.*, p. 55.
25. *Anti-Dühring*, p. 190.
26. K. R. Popper, *The Open Society and its Enemies*, vol. 2 (1945) 82.
27. *S.W.*, I, 34–65.
28. *Gru.*, pp. 495–514.
29. A. Gramsci, *Prison Notebooks* (1971) pp. 444–6.
30. Marx and Engels, *The Holy Family*.
31. *Cap.*, I, 178.
32. Popper, *The Open Society*, p. 186. Quoting *Cap.*, I, 644–5.
33. *Cap.*, I, 645.
34. Marx and Engels, *Selected Correspondence* (Moscow, n.d.) p. 507.
35. Lenin, *Philosophical Notebooks*, pp. 266, 359–60.

CHAPTER TWO

1. Marx and Engels, *Selected Correspondence*, p. 121.
2. Engels, 'Ludwig Feuerbach and the End of Classical German Philosophy', in *S.W.*, II, 360–402; and see *Cap.*, I, 19–20.
3. In his *Philosophical Notebooks* (*Collected Works*, vol. 38) Lenin noted that

'the simple form of value, the individual act of exchange of one given commodity for another already included in an undeveloped form *all* the main contradictions of capitalism . . .' (pp. 178–9).

4. Marx, *The Poverty of Philosophy*, p. 110.
5. *H.C.C.*, p. 27 (Lukács's emphasis).
6. Ibid. pp. 9, 30.
7. F. Hayek, *The Counter-Revolution of Science* (New York, 1955) pp. 25–35.
8. Marx and Engels, *Selected Correspondence*, p. 494.
9. A. Schutz, *The Phenomenology of the Social World* (1972) pp. 4–6, 37.
10. Hegel, *Science of Logic*, pp. 513–17.
11. A. Swingewood, 'Origins of Sociology', *British Journal of Sociology* (June 1970).
12. Montesquieu, *Spirit of the Laws* (New York, 1949) p. 293.
13. Smith, *Wealth of Nations*, pp. 308–19.
14. Marx and Engels, *The Holy Family*.
15. Marx, *A Contribution to the Critique of Political Economy* (Moscow, 1971) p. 189.
16. Ibid. pp. 20–1.
17. Ibid. pp. 204–5.
18. J. Millar, *The Origin and Distinction of Ranks* (Glasgow, 1779) pp. 2–3.
19. Marx, *A Contribution to the Critique of Political Economy*, p. 196.
20. *Cap.*, I, 8.
21. P. Sweezy, *The Theory of Capitalist Development* (1962) p. 11.
22. Marx, *Contribution to the Critique of Political Economy*, pp. 205–6 (my emphasis).
23. Ibid. p. 206.
24. Ibid. p. 207.
25. Ibid. pp. 189–93.
26. *Cap.*, II, 421.
27. Ibid., III, 172.
28. *Cap.*, III, 244.
29. Cf. L. Gumplowicz, *Outlines of Sociology* ([1885], Philadelphia, 1963) and from a different standpoint F. Tonnies *Community and Association* (1887).
30. *M.S.S.*, p. 103.
31. Ibid. p. 90.
32. M. Weber, *The Protestant Ethic and the Spirit of Capitalism* (1965) p. 29.
33. *M.S.S.*, pp. 53–4.
34. Ibid. pp. 72–6, 84.
35. Ibid. p. 107.
36. Ibid. p. 111.
37. *Theory*, pp. 107–9.
38. Marx, *A Contribution to the Critique of Political Economy*, p. 204.
39. Engels, 'Introduction', 'The Class Struggles in France' (1895), *S.W.*, I, 119–20.

40. Berger and Pullberg, 'Reification and the Sociological Critique of Consciousness', p. 66.
41. J.-P. Sartre, *The Problem of Method* (1963), pp. 43-4.
42. Ibid. pp. 68-9, 76-8.
43. Ibid. pp. 155, 159.

CHAPTER THREE

1. G. W. Remmling (ed.), *Towards the Sociology of Knowledge* (1973) p. 141.
2. K. Mannheim, *Ideology and Utopia* (1960) p. 278.
3. M. Weber, *The Protestant Ethic and the Spirit of Capitalism*, pp. 64, 55-6.
4. *G.I.*, pp. 37-8.
5. Marx, *A Contribution to the Critique of Political Economy*, pp. 20-1.
6. *S.W.*, II, 497.
7. *S.W.*, II, 488-9.
8. Ibid. p. 504.
9. Ibid. pp. 495-6.
10. Ibid. p. 397.
11. Ibid.
12. Marx, *A Contribution to the Critique of Political Economy*, pp. 214-17.
13. *Cap.*, I, 14-15.
14. *T.S.V.*, I, 153-5.
15. Ibid., II, 118-19.
16. Ibid. I, 290-2.
17. Ibid. II, 114-19.
18. Marx, *Theses on Feuerbach* (1845).
19. K. Mannheim, 'The Problem of a Sociology of Knowledge' (1925), *Essays on the Sociology of Knowledge* (1964) pp. 140-6. For the studies of 'Historicism' (1924) see ibid. pp. 84-133; 'Conservative Thought', *Essays in Sociology and Social Psychology* (1956) pp. 74-164; *Ideology and Utopia*, pp. 97-136.
20. Mannheim, *Ideology and Utopia*, p. 45; 'Conservative Thought', pp. 74-6.
21. Ibid. pp. 52, 278.
22. Ibid. pp. 66-7.
23. Ibid. p. 72.
24. Ibid. pp. 36, 84-5.
25. Mannheim, *Essays on the Sociology of Knowledge*, p. 184.
26. *H.C.C.*, pp. 20-1.
27. Ibid. p. 23.
28. Ibid. p. 156.
29. Ibid. p. 162.
30. Ibid. pp. 163-4.
31. Ibid. p. 66.
32. Mannheim, 'Conservative Thought'; 'Competition as a Cultural Phenomenon', in *Essays in the Sociology of Knowledge*, pp. 197-8, 272-3.

33. Berger and Pullberg, 'Alienation and the Sociological Critique of Consciousness', p. 71.
34. Berger and Luckmann, *The Social Construction of Reality*, p. 27.
35. A. Schutz, *The Phenomenology of the Social World*, p. 147; 'Concept and Theory Formation in the Social Sciences', in *Collected Papers*, vol. 1 (The Hague, 1962) 48–66.
36. Gramsci, *Prison Notebooks*, pp. 197–8, 328–33.
37. Schutz, 'Concept and Theory Formation in the Social Sciences'; *The Phenomenology of the Social World*, pp. 142–3.
38. Berger and Luckmann, *The Social Construction of Reality*, pp. 35–41, 82–3.
39. Ibid. pp. 85–7.
40. Gramsci, *Prison Notebooks*, p. 324.

CHAPTER FOUR

1. *E.W.*, p. 72.
2. Hegel, *The Phenomenology of Spirit* (1807). Cf. R. Schacht, *Alienation* (1971) pp. 54–5.
3. Quoted by Schacht, *Alienation*, p. 68.
4. *E.W.*, p. 122.
5. *Gru.*, p. 831.
6. *E.W.*, pp. 123–4.
7. Ibid. p. 123.
8. Ibid. p. 127.
9. Ibid. pp. 76–9, 132.
10. Ibid. p. 59.
11. Ibid. p. 178.
12. Ibid. p. 120.
13. *E.W.*, pp. 43, 51.
14. R. Nisbet, *The Sociological Tradition* (1967) p. 288.
15. *G.I.*, pp. 44–5.
16. *T.S.V.*, III, 271.
17. Ibid. III, 296.
18. *Cap.*, I, 316.
19. Quoted by Nisbet *The Sociological Tradition*, p. 279.
20. *Cap.*, I, 91 ff.
21. *T.S.V.*, III, 268–9.
22. *Cap.*, I, 176.
23. Ibid. I, 72.
24. *T.S.V.*, III, 508.
25. *Cap.*, I, 72–4. Cf. *T.S.V.*, III, 511–12.
26. *T.S.V.*, III, 514.

27. *Gru.*, pp. 831–2. Marx's language here is identical to that employed in the *Paris Manuscripts*.
28. *Cap.*, III, 259.
29. *E.W.*, p. 121.
30. R. Blauner, *Alienation and Freedom* (New York, 1967) p. 28.
31. L. Goldmann, 'La Réification', in *Recherches dialectiques* (Paris, 1959) p. 88.
32. *Cap.*, I, 333.
33. J. Goldthorpe and D. Lockwood, *The Affluent Worker*, 3 vols (Cambridge, 1968–9).
34. Ibid. III, 153–4 (my emphasis).
35. Ibid. p. 147.
36. *E.W.*, pp. 200–8.
37. Goldthorpe and Lockwood, *The Affluent Worker*, p. 102.
38. Blauner, *Alienation and Freedom*, p. 24.
39. M. Seeman, 'On the Meaning of Alienation', *American Sociological Review* (Dec. 1959).
40. *Cap.*, I, 361, 423.
41. Ibid. pp. 487–8.
42. M. Weber, *Economy and Society* (New York, 1968) II, 223.
43. H. Marcuse, *One-Dimensional Man* (1964) p. 32.
44. G. Simmel, *Philosophie des Geldes* (1900). Quoted by L. Coser in 'Introduction', *Georg Simmel* (New Jersey, 1965) p. 22.
45. G. Simmel, 'The Metropolis and Mental Life', in *The Sociology of Georg Simmel*, ed. K. Wolff (New York, 1950) p. 422.
46. *H.C.C.*, pp. 90–3, 100.
47. Ibid. p. 197.
48. Ibid. p. 178.
49. *Cap.*, I, 283, 299.
50. *Gru.*, pp. 243–4 especially.

CHAPTER FIVE

1. R. Dahrendorf, 'Recent Changes in the Class Structure of European Societies', *Daedalus*, vol. 93 (1964) 244–52.
2. Marx, *The Poverty of Philosophy*, p. 173.
3. Ibid. pp. 173–4.
4. Ibid. p. 109.
5. *Cap.*, I, 77. Cf. *Gru.*, pp. 163–5.
6. *S.W.*, I, 334.
7. Ibid. pp. 34–5.
8. *Cap.*, I, 446.
9. Ibid. ch. 13; *T.S.V.*, III, 476–97.

10. *T.S.V.*, II, 573 (translation modified).
11. Ibid. III, 63.
12. *Cap.*, III, 862–3.
13. Ibid. pp. 243–4.
14. R. Aron, *Progress and Disillusion* (1968) p. 11. See also A. Giddens, *The Class Structure of the Advanced Societies* (1973) ch. 3.
15. C. Kerr, *Marx, Marshall and Modern Times* (Cambridge, 1966) pp. 95–9.
16. R. Dahrendorf, *Class and Class Conflict in Industrial Society* (1959).
17. M. Weber, *Economy and Society*, 1, 305.
18. M. Weber, 'Class, Status, Party', in *From Max Weber*, ed. H. H. Gerth and C. W. Mills (1948) p. 181.
19. R. Dahrendorf, 'Recent Changes in the Class Structure of European Societies'· See the same author's *Society and Democracy in Germany* (1967) pp. 83–104.
20. See for example, H. Speier, 'The Salaried Employee in Modern Society' (1937), in his *Social Order and the Risks of War* (New York, 1952); F. D. Klingender, *The Condition of Clerical Labour in Britain* (1935).
21. From J. K. Galbraith, *The New Industrial State*, 2nd ed. (1972); A. Sturmthal, *White-Collar Unions* (Urbana, 1966); G. Lenski, *Power and Privilege* (New York, 1966); G. Bain, *The Growth of White Collar Unionism* (Oxford, 1970).
22. G. Routh, *Occupation and Pay in Great Britain* (1965) p. 26; Bain, *The Growth of White Collar Unionism*, pp. 14–15; Sturmthal, *White-Collar Unions*, p. 373.
23. Quoted by D. Lockwood, *The Blackcoated Worker* (1958) p. 40.
24. Bain, *The Growth of White Collar Unionism*, p. 54.
25. P. Blau and O. D. Duncan, *The American Occupational Structure* (New York, 1967) p. 423.
26. C. W. Mills, *White Collar* (1951) p. 297.
27. *T.S.V.*, 1, 398.
28. Ibid. 1, 149; II, 560.
29. For references see R. F. Hamilton, *Affluence and the French Worker in the Fourth Republic* (Princeton, 1967) p. 282.
30. Hamilton, *Affluence and the French Worker*, ch. 6 especially.
31. F. Parkin, *Class Inequality and Political Order* (1971) pp. 23–5.
32. J. Westergaard, 'The Rediscovery of the Cash Nexus', in *Socialist Register*, ed. Miliband and Saville (1970) pp. 111–38.
33. Goldthorpe and Lockwood, *The Affluent Worker in the Class Structure*, p. 170.
34. Goldthorpe and Lockwood, *The Affluent Worker: Political Attitudes* (Cambridge, 1969).
35. Ibid. p. 75.
36. *H.C.C.*, p. 52.
37. *S.W.*, 1, 446–7.

38. *Cap.*, III, 165.
39. *H.C.C.*, p. 52.
40. Ibid. p. 79.

CHAPTER SIX

1. *S.W.*, I, 36, 54.
2. Ibid. p. 36.
3. *E.W.*, p. 85.
4. *T.S.V.*, III, 414–20. Cf. W. Wesolowski, 'Marx's Theory of Class Domination', in *Marx and the Western World*, ed. N. Lobkowicz (1967) pp. 68–9.
5. Ibid. pp. 490–1.
6. *S.W.*, I, 98. Cf. *T.S.V.*, III, 497; *Cap.*, III, 858–9.
7. Ibid. p. 162.
8. Quoted in A. Giddens, *Capitalism and Modern Social Theory* (Cambridge, 1971) p. 39.
9. *S.W.*, I, 264–5, 272–3.
10. Ibid. pp. 142, 318–19.
11. Ibid. pp. 211, 148.
12. *S.W.*, I, 106–17.
13. *S.W.*, I, 287.
14. *S.W.*, I, 317–20.
15. Ibid. p. 605.
16. G. Mosca, *The Ruling Class* (New York, 1939) pp. 50–87, 331.
17. R. Michels, *Political Parties* (New York, 1962) pp. 61–3.
18. Ibid. pp. 333–56.
19. *Max Weber on Law in Economy and Society*, ed. Max Rheinstein (1954) p. 330.
20. *Theory*, p. 325.
21. Ibid. pp. 337–9.
22. Ibid. p. 331.
23. Cited in R. Pipes, 'Max Weber and Russia', *World Politics* (April 1955) pp. 377–8.
24. H. Gerth, 'The Nazi Party: Its Leadership and Composition', *Reader in Bureaucracy*, ed. R. K. Merton (New York, 1964).
25. *S.W.*, I, 302.
26. M. Albrow, *Bureaucracy* (1970) pp. 68–70.
27. Marx, *Critique of Hegel's Philosophy of Right* (complete English translation 1971); *W.Y.M.*, pp. 185–6.
28. L. Trotsky, *The New Course* ([1923], Ann Arbor, 1965) pp. 15, 21–2, 45–53.
29. L. Trotsky, *The Revolution Betrayed* (1967) pp. 54–9.
30. Ibid. p. 248.

31. L. Trotsky, *Writings 1933–4* (New York, 1972) pp. 112–13.

32. Weber, *Economy and Society*, III, 975.

33. B. Rizzi, *La Bureaucratisation du monde* (1938) was the first important statement of 'bureaucratic collectivism', a theory plagiarised by James Burnham in *The Managerial Revolution* (1943). The Yugoslavian critic, Milovan Djilas argued a similar theory in his *The New Class* (1957) – the Soviet bureaucrats constituted 'a special social category: the ownership class'. The failure to distinguish between bureaucratic officials and party bosses is a common weakness of these writers. See the evidence in D. Lane, *The End of Inequality: Stratification under State Socialism* (1971).

34. R. Aron, 'Social Class, Political Class, Ruling Class', *European Journal of Sociology* (1960).

35. R. Miliband, *The State in Capitalist Society* (1969) pp. 47–8.

36. R. Dahrendorf, *Society and Democracy in Germany* (1967) pp. 269–70.

37. Mosca, *The Ruling Class*, pp. 298–9.

38. V. Pareto, *The Mind and Society* (New York, 1963) para 2054.

39. Quoted in T. B. Bottomore, *Elites and Society* (1964) p. 43.

40. See, for example, J. K. Galbraith, *The New Industrial State*, new ed. (1972); T. Parsons, *Structure and Process in Modern Society* (1961); A. H. Rose, *The Power Structure* (1967); R. A. Dahl, *Pluralist Democracy in the United States* (1967).

41. Mills, *The Power Elite*, pp. 18, 243–6, 320, 316–17.

42. W. L. Guttsman, *The British Political Elite* (1963) pp. 319–56.

43. D. Boyd, *Elites and their Education* (1973).

44. Dahrendorf, *Society and Democracy*, pp. 228, 234–5, 256–9, 277–8.

45. Guttsman, *The British Political Elite*, pp. 109–37.

46. R. Dahrendorf, *Class and Class Conflict in Industrial Society* (1958) pp. 44–5.

47. *Cap.*, III, 379–80. Cf. *T.S.V.*, III, 476, 496.

48. Ibid. pp. 430–1.

CHAPTER SEVEN

1. T. Parsons, *The Structure of Social Action* (New York, 1961).

2. Ibid. pp. 100–1.

3. Ibid. especially p. 5.

4. Ibid. pp. 57–8.

5. Ibid. pp. 52–60.

6. E. Durkheim, *Socialism and Saint Simon* (1959) pp. 199–200.

7. Parsons, *The Structure of Social Action*, p. 307.

8. *Su.*, pp. 252–4.

9. Ibid. pp. 249–58 (my emphasis).

10. See the discussion in J. Douglas, *The Social Meanings of Suicide* (Princeton, 1967) pp. 43–5, 63–4.

11. *Su.*, p. 159.
12. Ibid. p. 161.
13. Douglas, *The Social Meanings*, pp. 64–6.
14. *Su.*, pp. 366ff.
15. J. Horton, 'The Dehumanisation of Alienation and Anomie', *British Journal of Sociology* (Dec. 1964).
16. 'Repressive Tolerance', in R. P. Wolfe, Barrington Moore, H. Marcuse, *A Critique of Pure Tolerance* (1969) p. 108.
17. Gramsci, *Prison Notebooks*, pp. 57–60, 77–9.
18. Marx and Engels, *On Britain* (Moscow, 1962) pp. 583–4.
19. Ibid. pp. 361, 488–9, 507, 522, 537–8, 555, 568, 575–6.
20. Ibid. pp. 554–5, 545.
21. Marx, 'Preface' to *A Contribution to the Critique of Political Economy*.
22. V. I. Lenin, 'What Is To Be Done', *Selected Works* (Moscow, 1950) I, 386.
23. *Cap.*, I, 737.
24. Giddens, *The Class Structure of the Advanced Societies*, pp. 152–3, 285–6.

CHAPTER EIGHT

1. Durkheim, *Sociology and Philosophy*, p. 56.
2. Durkheim, *The Rules of Sociological Method*, p. 67.
3. B. Malinowski, 'Anthropology', *Encyclopaedia Britannica* (1926) p. 136; A. R. Radcliffe-Brown, *Structure and Function in Primitive Society* (1952) p. 180.
4. K. Davis, in *System, Change and Conflict*, ed. N. J. Demerath and R. A. Peterson (New York, 1967).
5. A. Gouldner, *The Coming Crisis of Western Sociology* (1971) pp. 253–4.
6. C. W. Mills, *The Sociological Imagination* (1959) ch. 2.
7. R. K. Merton, *Social Theory and Social Structure* (New York, 1957) pp. 38–9.
8. P. van den Berghe, 'Dialectic and Functionalism', in *System, Change and Conflict*, ed. Demerath and Peterson, pp. 304–5.
9. N. Bukharin, *Historical Materialism* (Ann Arbor, 1969) pp. 136–42, 151, 239–56.
10. *Cap.*, III, 207–21.
11. *T.S.V.*, II, 521 (translation modified).
12. T. Parsons and E. Shils (eds), *Toward a General Theory of Action* (New York, 1951) pp. 226–7.
13. T. Parsons and N. J. Smelser, *Economy and Society* (1959).
14. T. Parsons, *The Social System* (1951) pp. 36–7.
15. Ibid.
16. Parsons, *Sociological Theory and Modern Society*, pp. 27–9.
17. Ibid. pp. 123, 132–5.

18. T. Parsons, *Essays in Sociological Theory* (New York, 1954) pp. 129, 137–8.
19. Gouldner, *The Coming Crisis*, pp. 250–1.
20. T. Parsons, 'Order as a Sociological Problem', in *The Concept of Order*, ed. P. G. Kuntz (1968) p. 377.
21. Parsons, *Sociological Theory and Modern Society*, pp. 417–20.
22. *Essays in Sociological Theory*, p. 206.
23. K. Davis and W. Moore, 'Some Principles of Stratification', *American Sociological Review*, no. 2 (1945).
24. Merton, *Social Theory*.
25. *Cap.*, I, 276n.
26. Merton, *Social Theory*.
27. Marx and Engels, *The Holy Family*.
28. Parsons, in *The Concept of Order*, ed. Kuntz, p. 379.
29. *The Social System*, pp. 205–6, 481–4.
30. M. Mann, 'The Social Cohesion of Liberal Democracy', *American Sociological Review* (June 1970).
31. *The Social System*, pp. 520–3.
32. *Essays in Sociological Theory*, pp. 104–41.
33. Ibid. pp. 116–17.
34. *The Social System*, pp. 523–33.
35. *Essays in Sociological Theory*, pp. 329–33, 246.
36. Ibid. p. 325.
37. R. Dahrendorf, 'Out of Utopia: Toward a Reorientation of Sociological Analysis', in *System, Change and Conflict*, ed. Demerath and Peterson.
38. L. Coser, *The Functions of Social Conflict* (1956) pp. 127, 153–5; *Continuities in the Study of Social Conflict* (New York, 1967) ch. 1.
39. S. M. Lipset, *Political Man* (1959) p. 113.
40. This argument is developed in D. Lockwood's article, 'Social Integration and System Integration', in *Explorations in Social Change*, ed. G. R. Zollschan and W. Hirsch (1964).
41. Ibid. pp. 248–52.

CHAPTER NINE

1. *Cap.*, I, 20.
2. J. Horton, 'The Fetishism of Sociology', in *Radical Sociology*, ed. J. D. Colfax and J. L. Roach (1971) pp. 175, 179, 185.
3. Ibid. pp. 12–20.
4. A. Gouldner, *The Coming Crisis of Western Sociology* (1971) pp. 11–15, 441.
5. Gouldner, *The Coming Crisis*, pp. 54–6, 495–7.
6. Ibid. pp. 53, 483–99.
7. Albert Szymanski, 'Toward a Radical Sociology', in *Radical Sociology*, ed. Colfax and Roach, pp. 102–3.

8. Ibid. pp. 104–6.
9. Horton, *The Fetishism of Sociology*, p. 189.
10. M. Horkheimer, 'Traditional and Critical Theory', in his *Critical Theory* (New York, 1972); H. Marcuse, 'Philosophy and Critical Theory', in his *Negations* (1968).
11. Albrecht Wellmer, *The Critical Theory of Society* (1969) p. 87.
12. N. Birnbaum, *Toward a Critical Sociology* (1972) pp. 116–28.
13. J. Habermas, *Knowledge and Human Interests* (1972), especially pp. 301–17; *Toward a Rational Society* (1971) ch. 6; 'On Systematically Distorted Communication', *Inquiry* (1970) pp. 205–18.

SELECT BIBLIOGRAPHY

The place of publication is London unless otherwise indicated.

WRITINGS OF MARX AND ENGELS

K. Marx and F. Engels, *Selected Works*, 2 vols (Moscow, 1958). This selection includes, by Marx, 'Wage Labour and Capital', 'The Class Struggles in France', 'The Eighteenth Brumaire of Louis Bonaparte', 'The Civil War in France'; by Engels, 'Socialism, Utopian and Scientific', 'Ludwig Feuerbach and the End of Classical German Philosophy'; as joint authors, 'The Communist Manifesto'.

K. Marx

Capital, 3 vols (Moscow, 1958).
Grundrisse: Foundations of the Critique of Political Economy, ed. and trans. M. Nicolaus (1973).
Marx's Grundrisse, ed. D. McLellan (1972).
Early Writings, ed. and trans. T. B. Bottomore (1963).
Writings of the Young Marx on Philosophy and Society, ed. L. Easton and K. Guddat (New York, 1967).
The Early Texts, ed. and trans. D. McLellan (Oxford, 1971).
The Poverty of Philosophy (Moscow, n.d.).
A Contribution to the Critique of Political Economy (Moscow, 1971).
Theories of Surplus Value, 3 vols (Moscow, 1964–72).
Critique of Hegel's Philosophy of Right, ed. and trans. J. O'Malley (Cambridge, 1971).

F. Engels

Anti-Dühring (Moscow, 1959).
Dialectics of Nature (New York, 1940).
Germany: Revolution and Counter-Revolution (1933).

K. Marx and F. Engels

The German Ideology (Moscow, 1965).
The Holy Family (Moscow, 1956).
Selected Correspondence (Moscow, n.d.).

WRITINGS OF DURKHEIM, LUKÁCS, PARSONS AND WEBER

E. Durkheim

The Division of Labour in Society (New York, 1964).
The Rules of Sociological Method (1964).
Socialism and Saint-Simon (1959).
Suicide (1952).
Sociology and Philosophy (1953).
Moral Education (1961).
'Pragmatism and Sociology', 'The Dualism of Human Nature and its Social Condition', in *Essays in Sociology and Philosophy*, ed.K. Wolff (New York, 1964).

G. Lukács

History and Class Consciousness (1971).
Political Writings (1972).
'Max Weber and German Sociology', *Economy and Society* (Nov. 1972).

K. Mannheim

Essays on the Sociology of Knowledge (1964).
Essays in Sociology and Social Psychology (1956).
Ideology and Utopia (1960).

T. Parsons

The Structure of Social Action (New York, 1961).
Toward a General Theory of Action (with E. Shils), (New York, 1951).
The Social System (1951).
Essays in Sociological Theory (New York, 1964).
Sociological Theory and Modern Society (New York, 1967).
Societies: Evolutionary and Comparative Perspectives (New York, 1966).
The System of Modern Societies (New York, 1971).

M. Weber

Economy and Society, 4 vols (New York, 1968).

From Max Weber: Essays in Sociology, ed. and trans. H. Gerth and C. W. Mills (New York, 1958).

The Theory of Social and Economic Organisation (New York, 1964).

The Methodology of the Social Sciences (Glencoe, 1949).

The Protestant Ethic and the Spirit of Capitalism (1965).

General Economic History (New York, 1961).

INDEX

247

DATE DUE		
MAY 2 4	JA 18 '85	
JUN 1 5 19	6	
	DE 8 86	
APR 2 8 1980	NOV.	7 1988
MAR 2 3 1981		
MAY 4 1981		
APR 2 1 1982		
OCT 1 1 1982		
APR 2 5 1983		
MAY 2 1983		
OC 17 '83		
MY 7 '84		